HOMEPRENUE

Build a Profitable Home Based Business in Few Steps

By

Vishen Smith

<u>**fab**</u>

Respective authors own all copyrights not held by the publisher.

The information herein is offered for informational purposes solely and is universal as such. The presentation of the information is without a contract or any guarantee assurance. The trademarks used are without any consent, and the publication of the trademark is without permission or backing by the trademark owner. All trademarks and brands within this book are for clarifying purposes only and are owned by the owners themselves, not affiliated with this document.

Table of Contents

The 9+1 Best Home-Based Business Model of 2021

Dropshipping Business Model on a Budget

Youtube, Tik-Tok and Instagram Made Easy

Short Stays Real Estate with No (or Low) Money Down

Bubble or Revolution? The Basics ofBitcoin and Blockchain.

The 9+1 Best Home-Based Business Model of 2021

Find Out how Millennials Have Built Millionaire Businesses from Home with Soap and Candle Making, Natural Cosmetics and much more

By

Vishen Smith

Table of Contents

Introduction

Karsanbhai Patel (Patel), the chemist at Mines and Geology Department of the Gujarat Government, produced synthetic powder of detergent phosphate-free in 1969 and began selling this locally. He priced the new yellow powder at 3.50rs per kg. It was at one time when Rs 15 was being charged for Hindustan Lever Limited (HLL) Surf. Soon, in Kishnapur (Gujarat), Patel's hometown, there was a big demand for Nirma. In 10x12 feet space in his home, he began preparing the formula. He had named powder after his daughter's name-Nirupama. On the way to the office by bicycle, about 15 kilometers away, Patel was able to sell around 15-20 packets a day. Thus, the new journey began. Hindustan Lever Limited (HLL) responded in a manner characteristic of many global corporations in the early 1970s, when washing powder Nirma was launched into the market of low-income. "That isn't our business," senior executives said of the new offering. "We don't have to be worried." However very soon, Hindustan Lever Limited (HLL) was persuaded by Nirma's performance in the detergent sector that this wanted to take a closer gaze at the less income market. Low-cost detergents & toilet soaps are almost synonymous with the brand name. Nirma, on the other hand, found that it would've to launch goods targeted at the higher end of the market to maintain the middle-class buyers as they moved up the market. For the luxury market, the firm introduced bathroom soaps. Analysts, on the other hand, claimed Nirma wouldn't be capable of duplicate its performance in the premium market. In the year 2000, the Nirma had a 15 percent share of the toilet soap market and a 30% share of the detergent market. Nirma's revenue for the year ended in March 2000 grew by 17 percent over the previous fiscal year, to 17.17rs. bn, backed by volume development and commissioning of backward integration projects. By 1985, in many areas of the world, washing powder Nirmabecame one of the most common detergent brands. Nirma was a global consumer company by 1999, with a wide variety of soaps, detergents, & personal care items. Nirmahas brought in the latest technologies for the manufacturing facilities in six locations across India, in line with its ideology of delivering premium goods at the best possible costs. The success of Nirma in the intensely competitive market for soaps & detergents was due to its efforts to support the brand, which had been complemented by the sales scope & market penetration. The network of Nirmaspread across the country, with over two million outlets of retail and 400 distributors. Nirma was able to reach out to even the smallest villages due to its vast network. Nirma spread to the markets overseas in 1999 after establishing itself in India. Viaa joint venture called Commerces Overseas Limited, it made its first foray into Bangladesh. Within a year, the company had risen to the top of Bangladesh's detergent market. Other areas such as Middle East, Russia, China, Africa &additional Asian countries were also intended for the entry of the organization. Nirma became a 17 billion Rs company in 3 decades, beginning as a single-product single-man article of clothing in 1969. Under the umbrella name Nirma, the company had several production plants and a large product range. The mission of the organization to have "Better Product, Better Values and Better Living" added much to its growth. Nirma was able to outshine Hindustan Levers Limited (thenHLL) and carve out a niche for oneself in the lower-ends of detergent &market toilet soap. HLL's Surf was the first to be used as a detergent powder in India in 1959. But by the 1970s, merely by making the product available at a reasonable price, Nirma led the demand for detergent powder. Nirma launched its Nirma Beauty soaps to the Indian toilet soap industry in 1990. Nirma had gained a 15% share of 530,000 tons per annum toilet soap industry by 1999, making it India's second-largest producer. Although it was way behind HLL's 65 percent share, the success of Nirma was impressive compared to Godrej, which had an 8 percent share. By 1999-2000, Nirma had already acquired a 38 percent share of India's detergent market of 2.4 million tonnes. For the same period, HLL's market share was 31%. In this book, we will study and analyze the case of Nirma and its rise to the top detergent companies of India. Besides, we will also give profitable ideas and options for starting a lucrative detergent soap,candle making, and natural cosmetics business.

CHAPTER 1: The Nirma Washing Powder's Success Story

The success story of the famous Nirma washing powder began in a small Gujarati farmer's house. We'll tell you about a billionaire father who lost his daughter in a car crash and later discovered a way to get her back to life. When she was alive, only a few people knew of her daughter, but it was the sheer persistence and willpower of this man that made his daughter famous in the world, even though she was no more. This is the story of a man who was born into a poor farming family and turned his daughter's nickname into India's leading detergent, soda ash, and education brand. A man of valor and passion who showed that nothing will hinder you if you have the willpower. Here is the story of **"Sabki Pasand Nirma, Washing Powder Nirma."**

1.1 Invention ofNirma detergent?

Karsanbhai was born in Ruppur, Gujarat, to a farmer's family in 1945. He had earned a bachelor's degree in chemistry by the age of 21. He attempted to do a normal job like his colleagues at first. He served as a lab technician for the Lalbhai Group's New Cotton Mills, which is credited with launching the Indian jeans movement. He also took up a position at the Geology and Mining Department of the Gujarat government after this short stint. The year 1969 marked the start of a turning point in the career trajectory of Karsanbhai. It was at this time that Hindustan Lever Ltd (now Hindustan Unilever) formed a full monopoly on the Indian detergent market under the brand name "Surf." A Surf Pack was sold somewhere from Rs 10-15 back then. The USP was that, unlike normal washing soap bars, it eliminated stains from your clothes and didn't irritate your skin. However, for middle-class families, which had no other choice than to return to the old bar soap, this price point was not affordable. The tycoon in Karsanbhai noticed the issue and devised a plan. A young Karsanbhai will come home from work and dedicate all his time and energy to making a phosphate-free detergent in his yard. He wanted to bear in mind that he needed to produce a detergent with a low manufacturing cost so that everybody could afford it. Karsanbhaiutilized a recipe for a yellow-colored detergent powder that could be marketed for a mere Rs 3 after several trials and failures. He chose to name the invention after Nirupama, his daughter. He finally got the formula right one day, and as an after-work business, he began making detergents in his 100-square-foot backyard. He will cycle around the neighborhoods, selling door-to-door homemade detergent packages. Patel set the price of his detergent at Rs. 3, almost a third less than Hindustan Unilever's well-known brand "Surf." The product's high quality and low price made it a success, and it was well-received by many who saw great benefit in purchasing it. Because of the business's high promise, Karsanbhai quit his government job three years later to pursue it full-time. Karsanbhai was so fond of the commodity that he called it Nirma, after his daughter Nirupama's nickname. To make sure that everybody remembers her, he used her picture (the girl in the white frock) on the pack and in TV advertisements. Such was a father's love for his daughter. While Karsanbhai Patel himself was not an MBA graduate, the techniques he adopted to expand his company left marketers bewildered and amazed. 'Nirma' was not only a game-changer but also a trendsetter for several small companies. Here are a couple of 'Washing Powder Nirma's' management lessons.

1.2 Karsanbhai Patel's sale policy for Nirma detergent

Karsanbhai Patel agreed to start marketing it once the product had a strong formula. On his cycle, he used to go door-to-door and neighborhood-to-neighborhood every day for three years, pitching the detergent. As it was a brand new product, if they found the product poor, he gave his consumers a money-back guarantee. Nirma has been the cheapest detergent in Ahmedabad at the time. As a result, Karsanbhai's product was an immediate hit. He left his government job three years later and set up a store in Ahmedabad to carry out this full-time enterprise. In some areas of Gujarat, his brand was doing very well, but there was a need to expand its scope. At the time, the standard was to offer the product to retailers on credit. This was a huge gamble because if the product didn't sell, Karsanbhai would have had to close down the company. At that time, he chose to try something different. He planned to spend a little money on advertising. These commercials, with their catchy jingles, were directed at housewives. And this bet paid off well. Nirma became a famous household brand and it had to be purchased by people. He did, however, remove 90% of the stock from the market at this time. Potential buyers had asked for the detergent at their local retailers for about a full month but would have to return empty-handed. During this time, retail store owners flocked to Karsanbhai, demanding that the detergent supply be increased. After another month, he eventually decided. Nirma was able to take over the sales and even beat Surf at their own game due to this approach. It went on to become the country's highest-selling detergent. It remained India's largest-selling detergent even after a decade,

1.3 Invest In Research and Development

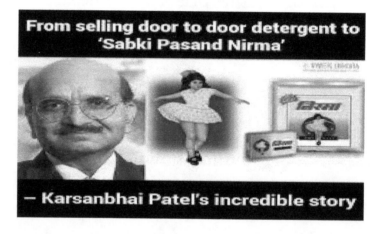

Karsanbhai Patel had little means and was not a man born with a silver spoon in his mouth. Karsanbhai loved experimenting with chemicals after completing a B.Sc. in Chemistry at the age of 21 and then working as a laboratory technician. He noticed that only MNCs in India were selling detergents and there was no economy brand detergent for the country. His excitement about bridging the distance grew, sensing a massive opening, and Karsanbhai began experimenting with chemicals. He quickly succeeded in manufacturing a detergent of high quality at a much cheaper price, which was an immediate success in the industry. Every good product needs a substantial expenditure in time, resources, and commitment in research and development.

1.4 No Higher Costs

Nirma had rewritten the rules of the game within a short time, by delivering high-quality goods at an unprecedentedly low price. Nirma's success was due to its cost-cutting policy. Patel had concentrated from the very beginning on delivering high-value goods at the lowest price possible. The corporation sought to keep improving efficiency while reducing prices. Nirma sought out captive processing plants for raw materials to keep production costs to a minimum. This led to the backward integration initiative, as part of which, at Baroda and Bhavnagar, which became operational in 2000, two state-of-the-art plants were established. This also led to a reduction in raw-material prices. Ahead of time and at a much smaller cost than anticipated, the two new plants were completed. The Baroda plant's second phase was finished 6 months ahead of schedule and at a cost of Rs.2.5 billion compared to the initial projected cost of Rs. 2.8 billion. Compared to the initial projected cost of Rs. 10.36 billion, the Bhavnagar plant was finished in a record period of 2 years at a cost of Rs.9.86 billion. This plant had a workforce of just 500 employees. ConcerningNirma's plant, Tata Chemical's plant, which had around twice the amount, employed ten times the number of workers. Almost 65000 tpa of N-Paraffin was produced by the Baroda plant for Linear Alkyl Benzene (LAB) and Synthetic detergents. Similarly, almost 4.20,000 tpa of soda ash could be produced by the Bhavnagar facility. Akzo Nobel Engineering in Holland produced the Akzo Dry Lime technology used in this factory. The plant had 108 kilometers of salt bunds, which would assist in the potential development of vacuum iodized salt. Patel said, "We have a processing potential of three lakh tons of pure salt. No one in the world had a related plant, but Tata Salt." Nirma had reduced its distribution costs by obviating the need for middlemen. The item went to the dealer straight from the manufacturer. Hiren K Patel (Hiren), CMD, explained to Nirma Customer Care Ltd., "An order is placed and the truck immediately leaves. It's similar to a bank account. We're sending stock, they're sending money." In states like Tamil Nadu, Andhra Pradesh, and southern Karnataka, the company-maintained depots, as it was often difficult to bring stocks to these regions. Stocks were shipped directly from the plants in states like Madhya Pradesh and Uttar Pradesh. In March 2000, Nirma opted for in-house packaging andprinting by obtaining Kisan Factories at Moriya, near Ahmedabad, in a further cost-cutting exercise. Nirma hoped that this would increase the packaging's quality.

1.5 Be Proactive in your approach as it is beneficial for the business

Karsanbhai Patel was the only person who started this business and starting selling Nirma. He was educated and had a government career, but he was never afraid of selling door-to-door detergent. He was diligent in doing something and knew that the company was tiny and bootstrapping, so he had to consider everything and anything about his business that could be fruitful. There is no such thing as a small or large undertaking. And if you are the CEO, you should embrace the obligations that are valuable to the company without guilt.

1.6 Provide Customers with 'Value for Money'

Customers noticed the advantages of purchasing Nirma, and it became an immediate success. They considered the standard to be at par with the giant Surf brand, but to take advantage of the same perks, they just had to pay one-third of the amount. Customers would only appreciate the product if you show them the advantages and give them decent value for their money.

1.7 Define Your Segment

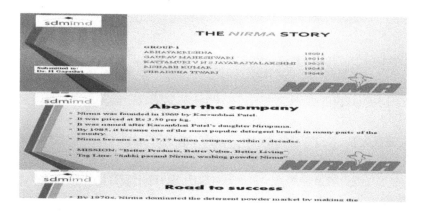

Karsanbhai Patel identified the target segment for his detergent almost as soon as he found the magical formula. He realized that a luxury brand sold in tier 1 cities was the alternative Surf brand, so he concentrated on marketing his brand in tier 2-3 cities. He priced his detergent low and made it a mass brand to get more consumer traction. People from the lower middle class and middle class quickly adopted the product, and it quickly rose in popularity. Where most firms adopted the conventional top-down strategy, i.e., spreading from metro towns to rural cities, Nirma did the reverse and changed the whole game. It is really important to evaluate the competitors for every company and define the most lucrative segment.

1.8 Focus on Building a Brand

It was failing to find vendors outside the city in the early 80s, although the commodity was approved on a small scale in Ahmedabad. Since clients were unaware of its presence, retailers were wary of keeping the detergent in their stores. It resulted in overdue payments, return on inventory, and large business losses. Karsanbhai Patel came up with a good publicity approach to handle the situation and launched a TV advertisement campaign. The popular "Washing powder Nirma, detergent tikiyaNirma" jingle became an anthem for the company and customers began to equate Nirma as a strong brand. The demand for Nirma soon peaked, and with his products, Patel flooded the retail stores. A good brand decreases a buyer's potential risk and increases the company's bargaining power.

1.9 Astutely Manage the Brand Wars

Nirma also had innovative marketing campaigns. Nirma successfully spread the name to other product segments in the mid-nineties, such as premium detergents (Nirma Mega Detergent Cake and Washing Powder), premium toilet soaps, and (Nirma Sandal, NimaPremium, Nirma Lime Fresh). In both the economy and luxury markets, it maintained its initial pricing andmarketing plans. In 2000, with Nirma Beauty Shampoo, NirmaShikakai, and Toothpaste, the firm entered the hair care market. Soaps, unlike detergents, were a private-care commodity. Many consumers had strong emotional attachments with their soap products. Furthermore, HLL segmented the market by price, fragrance appeal, and brand personality. So, against Lifebuoy, Nirma put Nirma Wash, Nirma Beauty Soap against Lux, Nima Rose against

Breeze7, and Nima Lime against Jai Lime. Explaining how Nirma hoped to win this match, playing by the rules of HLL, Hiren said"Worldwide, there are only four or five channels that account for most of the soaps sold: floral, fashion, fitness, freshness." With the relevant scents, Nirma manufactured high-fatty-matter soaps and priced them much lower than other brands. As a result, the 'sub-premium' section was born. The game of controlling the geographical variety of market desires was also perfected by Nirma. The North, for instance, favored pink soaps, and green ones were favored by the South. In the South, sandal soaps were more common. Initially, the company's promotional budget, relative to other FMCG firms, was very poor. In contrast to the usual 6-10 percent, Nirma spent just 1.25-2 percent of its sales on ads. The firm used starlets such as Sangeeta Bijlani, SonaliBendre, and Riya Sen, who were comparatively unknown at the time, to endorse soaps. The promotional messages were both transparent and centered on the product's benefits. Nirma still chose to first put the item on the shelf, get reviews, and then create a lasting ad campaign. Nirma used its tried-and-true tool, price, to introduce toilet soaps and detergents in the premium market. In these divisions, the company intended to rely on quantities as well. However, the margins granted to retailers had shifted. Unlike economic goods, where the cost advantages were passed on to customers, this advantage was passed on to retailers by Nirma. It provided them with massive profit margins. For instance, it offered 52 percent for Nirma premium soap and an incredible margin of 140 percent for Nirma shampoo. In the luxury segment of the soap industry, observers were pessimistic about Nirma's chances of success.

Unlike detergents, the demand for soaps and shampoos was incredibly fragmented. There were only 15-20 brands, and it was hard to get a considerable market share for any soap. This market was also less price sensitive. So, it was hard for any enterprise to support itself on price alone. Analysts thought that shifting the brand value of Nirma would take years. According to a survey conducted by Nirma's marketing agency, Samsika Marketing Consultancy, Nirma was viewed as a low-cost brand. Many people were almost afraid to say they used it. Nirma published corporate advertisements worth Rs 10 bn in India in the late nineties to shed this image. Analysts claim that the fast-growing shampoo market is a safer investment than luxury soaps. Just 30% of the population in India used shampoo, with more than 70% of this group living in urban areas. However, according to some researchers, while the rural market's presumed potential was very high, it was difficult to convince rural folk to use shampoos in actual practice. A further concern faced by Nirma was that of insufficient facilities. While it had a good presence in the smaller towns and villages, it lacked the requisite network for urban centers to penetrate. As a result, Nirma's foray into high-end soaps and shampoos proved to be a flop.

1.10 Diversify the Portfolio

For low-income groups, Nirma began with a low-cost detergent, but later introduced products for higher-income groups, such as Nirma Sandal soap, Nirma Beauty soap, etc.

Not just that, but in 2003, Karsanbhai Patel formed Nirma University to diversify the company's brand portfolio. The brand is currently exploring its options in the cement industry to grow its market. Diversifying the portfolio decreases the company's potential risk of loss while still allowing it to serve a broader variety of consumers.

1.11 Conclusion

While Nirma was best known as a manufacturer of goods for the low-cost economy, it was popular in the middle and upmarket segments. Yet rivalry was also growing at the same time. Although HLL continued to be a major threat, offensive initiatives were also introduced by P&G and Henkel SPIC. In the detergent and washing powder market, participants from the unorganized field were also introduced to the rivalry. Patel was confident of tackling the rivalry, though. "He added, "We keep the price line and the happy customer returns to us normally. Based on its growth strategy, the company has risen in demand and volume in the last three decades: "A buyer is not looking for one-time frills or feel-good variables. The landlord, on the other hand, is searching for a long-term solution to his or her issues." Karsanbhai Patel, who began with a vision of making his daughter famous through his brand and ended up being one of the greatest entrepreneurs of all time, exemplifies the relevance of this quotation. He began with an aim of creating his daughter famous through his brand and ended up becoming one of the greatest entrepreneurs of all time. His name not only gained tremendous respect but also became a trendsetter for many new firms. The brand has taught young entrepreneurs many useful lessons and has proven to be a valuable resource for the region. Karsanbhai Patel has shown that no goal is too lofty if you have the ambition and zeal to achieve it.

1.12 What Karsanbhai Patel and Nirma detergent did for the Indian Economy

Nirma's meteoric growth in prominence culminated in the introduction of a new economic market for detergent powder. It was of good quality and was inexpensive. Plus, contrary to the others, the fact that it was manufactured without phosphates made it the most environmentally-friendly detergent. In comparison, a labor-consuming process was the process of producing the detergent. And thus, Nirma went on to hire more than 14,000 workers and became the country's leading employer.

1.13 Karsanbhai Patel's ventures other than the Nirma detergent

Karsanbhai wanted to grow his FMCG business after Nirma dominated the detergent industry. Nirma launched its line of toilet soaps, beauty soaps, and even shampoos in the premium market. While the latter venture failed, one of their products, edible salt Shudh, is still available and doing well. Overall, Nirma has a 20 percent market share in soap cakes and a 35 percent market share in detergents. That isn't it, however. In 1995, Karsanbhai Patel founded the Nirma Institute of Technology in Ahmedabad. Later, it became one of Gujarat's most prestigious engineering schools. After that, the whole structure was merged under the Nirma University of Science and Technology, which is supervised by the Nirma Education and Research Foundation, and in 2003, the entire structure was unified under the Nirma University of Science and Technology. This is overseen by the Nirma Education and Research Foundation. Since 2004, Karsanbhai's CSR initiative,

Nirmalabs education, has aimed to train and incubate entrepreneurs. Karsanbhai Patel has now turned over the reins of his profitable company to his two sons. Pratibha Patil, the then-President of India, bestowed the Padma Shri on him in 2010. Nirma is now the world's biggest manufacturer of soda ash, and the company has been privately owned since 2012. Karsanbhai Patel invested his huge fortune on a six-seat chopper in 2013, which cost Rs 40 crore. After Gautam Adani (Adani Group) and Pankaj Patel (Zydus Group), he became the third Ahmedabad-based industrialist to purchase a helicopter. Nirma, on the other hand, is still one of India's most popular detergents. And the jingles will live on forever.

CHAPTER 2: Start a Profitable Soap Making Business

As a soap manufacturer, you'll create your recipes for soaps and probably other personal cleaning and beauty products. Ecommerce, farmers markets, arts events, wholesale positioning in spas and boutiques, and even door-to-door sales are all options for selling the goods. You'll test several solutions and see if you can find a steady stream of clients. Learn how to launch a soap-making company of your own.

Steps for starting a soap making business

You've uncovered the ideal market opportunity and are now prepared to take the next step. There's more to launching a company than simply filing papers with the government. We've put together a list of steps to help you get started with your soap-making business. These measures will ensure that the new company is well-planned, legally compliant, and properly registered.

Plan your business

As an entrepreneur, you must have a well-thought-out strategy. It will assist you in figuring out the additional data of your organization and uncovering any unknowns. Given below are some key points to consider:

What are the startup and recurring costs?

Who is the targeted audience?

What is the maximum price you will charge from the customers?

What would you name your company?

What are the costs involved in opening a soap-making business?

You've got a good start if you have a kitchen or workspace as well as a few simple kitchen utensils. Making soap isn't an expensive business to undertake, but you would need to invest in some basic equipment. Ingredients cost at least $200. Lye and fats or oils are used to make soap. That's a good start, but it'll be your special formula that sets you apart. For superior feel, fragrance, and lather, you can use coconut oil, olive oil, almond oil, and several fragrance oils, extracts, and natural additives. To keep materials costs down and simplify production, you could start with only one or two simple recipes. Equipment for producing soap will cost around $300. Your equipment specifications will be determined by the type of soap-making you do. Hot process, cold process, rebatching, and melt and pour are the four basic forms of processing, and each needs different equipment. But, regardless of the route you take, you'll almost definitely need soap molds, packing, and shipping items. You can get your basic ingredients, additives, equipment, and supplies from several online retailers. Marketing software will cost up to $750. A professional-looking website with enticing product images is key to the company's growth. Since your online consumers can't touch or smell your goods, they must be able to judge the good quality of what they see. That means recruiting a graphic designer and web developer to help you make the best out of your logo and online presence is a smart investment. To express your love and dedication to product quality, your visual imagery will be carried through in your labeling and branding. Skilled services will cost up to $200. Is it legal in your state and society for you to run this sort of business from home? Before you put up your shingle, meet with a lawyer for a quick consultation. The Handcrafted Soap & Cosmetics Guild charges a membership fee of $100 per year (HSCG). Small-batch soap makers will benefit from this organization's preparation, funding, and useful networking opportunities. Insurance for general liability and product liability would cost $265-$375 a year. This is also accessible via the HSCG.

What are the ongoing expenses for a soap-making business?

The consumable commodity materials you'll need for ongoing development would be your greatest ongoing expense. Your increasing variable expenses would be more than offset by a rise in revenue if you've priced your offering correctly.

Who is the target market?

While women make up the majority of the demand for homemade soaps, some firms have had success selling male-oriented soap scents. You may approach consumers who admire your product's consistency and luxury, or those who only purchase organic or vegan goods. Customers will note the difference in quality among your soaps and those sold on the shelves of a traditional supermarket.

How does a soap-making business make money?

In the majority of the cases, all of your revenueshall be derived from the products you make or sell.

How much can you charge customers?

Your goods could be sold for $5 or $6 a bar. This is more than your consumers are likely to spend for mass-produced retail soaps, but your product has a high perceived value. Other price points can be met by providing discounts on multiple orders, marketing multi-bar bundles, and extending the product range. Look at local rivals' websites to see what they're costing and how that would impact the pricing. Will you charge more to suggest a higher-end product range, or will you charge less to compensate for the lower per-unit sales margin with higher volume?

How much profit can a soap-making business make?

There are a few well-known soap makers who began their careers in the same way you did. Take, for example, Burt's Bees. Others in your business run it as a side venture, something between a crafts hobby and a modestly profitable business. You will go as far as your dedication, imagination, promotional skills, and hard work can take you, as with many home-based companies.

How can you make your business more profitable?

Many soap makers diversify their product range to include more exotic soaps (goat's milk soap is one example) or complementary goods. Making candles is a natural progression for soap makers who still use a hot process. Others are involved in home fragrances, lip balms, hair care, and even pet products. Focus on what else will cater to the consumer base when speaking about expanding your product mix. Many companies aim to maximize their net income by lowering the cost of goods produced. Growing the earnings by issuing bigger batches at a time is a cost-effective technique.

2.1 What will you name your business?

Choosing the correct name is vital and daunting. If you own a sole proprietorship, you should start using a separate company name from your own. We suggest reviewing the following references before filing a company name:

The state's business records

Federal and state trademark records

Social media sites

Web domain availability

It's important to have your domain name registered before anyone else does.

2.2 Form a legal entity

The sole proprietorship, partnership, limited liability company (LLC), and corporation are the most traditional corporate structures. If your soap manufacturing company is used, creating a legitimate business entity such as an LLC or corporation prevents you from being found legally accountable.

Register for taxes

Before you can start doing business, you'll need to apply for several state and federal taxes. You would need to apply for an EIN to pay for taxation. It's very basic and free.

2.3 Small Business Taxes

Depending on which business arrangement you select, you can have various taxation choices for your corporation. There could be state-specific taxes that apply to your business. In the state sales tax guides, you can read more about state sales taxes and franchise taxes.

2.4 Open a business bank account & credit card

Personal wealth security necessitates the use of dedicated company banking and credit accounts. If your personal and corporate accounts are combined, your personal properties (such as your house, vehicle, and other valuables) are put at risk if your company-issued. This is referred to as piercing the corporate veil in business law. Furthermore, learning how to create company credit will help you receive credit cards and other borrowings under your business's name (rather than your own), lower interest rates, and more credit lines, among other advantages.

2.5 Open a business bank account

This protects your assets from those of your business, which is essential for personal wealth security, as well as making accounting and tax reporting simpler.

2.6 Get a business credit card

It will help you achieve the following benefits:

It builds the company's credit background and will be beneficial for raising capital and profit later on.

It lets you differentiate personal and business expenditures by placing all of your business's costs under one account.

Set up business accounting

Understanding your business's financial results includes keeping track of your different costs and sources of revenue. Maintaining correct and comprehensive reports also makes annual tax filing even simpler.

2.7 Obtain necessary permits and licenses

Failure to obtain required permits and licenses will result in hefty fines or even the closure of your company. If you intend to market homemade soaps, you must first acquire a business license.

2.8 State & Local Business Licensing Requirements

Operating a handmade soap company can necessitate the procurement of some state permits and licenses. Furthermore, several states have varying laws governing the manufacturing of cosmetics and other body care goods. Visit the SBA's guide to state licenses and permits to read more about your state's licensing criteria.

2.9 Labor safety requirements

It is essential to comply with all Occupational Safety and Health Administration protocols.Pertinent requirements include:

Employee injury report

Safety signage

2.10 Certificate of Occupancy

A Certificate of Occupancy is normally required for businesses that operate out of a specific location (CO). All requirements concerning building codes, zoning rules, and local requirements have been followed, according to a CO.If you're thinking about renting a space, keep the following in mind:

Securing a CO is normally the landlord's duty.

Before signing a contract, make sure your landlord has or can get a legitimate CO for a soap-making operation.

A new CO is often needed after a significant renovation. If your company will be renovated before opening, add wording in your lease agreement that specifies that lease payments will not begin before a valid CO is issued.

If you intend to buy or build a place:

You would be responsible for securing a legal CO from a local government body.

Review all building codes and zoning standards for your soap-making business's place to ensure that you'll comply and eligible to get a CO.

2.11 Trademark & Copyright Protection

It is wise to protect your interests by applying for the required trademarks and copyrights if you are creating a new product, idea, brand, or design. The essence of legal standards in distance education is continually evolving, especially when it comes to copyright laws. This is a regularly revised database that can assist you with keeping on top of legal specifications.

2.12 Get business insurance

Insurance, including licenses and permits, are necessary for your company to run safely and legally. In the case of a covered loss, corporate insurance covers your company's financial well-being. There are several insurance schemes tailored for diverse types of companies with various risks. If you're not sure what kinds of risks your company might face, start with General Liability Insurance. This is the most popular form of coverage required by small companies, so it's a good place to start.

2.13 Learn more about General Liability Insurance

Workers' Compensation Insurance is another essential insurance scheme that many companies need. When your company hires staff, your state may mandate you to carry the Workers' Benefits Package.

2.14 Define your brand

Your company's brand is what it stands for, as well as how the general public perceives it. A good name would set the company apart from the market.

How to promote & market a soap making business

Look for areas where you can stand out. Try having a larger-than-usual bar of soap or one that is formulated to last longer. Perhaps you should market a six-pack of sampler soaps in smaller sizes so that your customers can check out your whole product range and pick their preferences. Consider an uncommon fragrance or texture additive for applying to your soaps to make them stand out. When you've found a winning design, publicize it on your website and social media. Also, if you're showing your soaps at an exhibition, bring some unwrapped samples of your entire product line so consumers can touch them, see what they're made of, feel their textures, and experience the various scents.

How to keep customers coming back

bear in mind that you're offering an aesthetic experience. Make sure your logo, labels and packages, and the name of your product line all cater to consumers looking for a low-cost luxury experience. One benefit is that the more your consumers like your stuff, the faster they can consume it and require more. Ensure that you retain contact with your clients and that they are aware of how to contact you. Request email addresses from all of your clients to obtain their approval to send out a monthly e-newsletter or catalog. It's important not to bother someone with so many promotional newsletters, but a monthly newsletter will keep consumers updated on all of the new items you have to sell. You might want to add a toll-free phone number for orders as your company expands.

Establish your web presence

Customers can learn more about your business and the goods or services you deliver by visiting your website. One of the most successful ways to build your web presence is through press releases and social media.

2.15 Soap Making Plan

If you live in the jungle and love your body odor, you would not need soap. It is a regular need and one of the common goods. As a result, soap has a huge demand. There are various varieties of soaps available due to the wide range of skin types. Soaps are manufactured in a multitude of ways to suit the needs of all. One of the most promising FMCGs is soap production. Perhaps this is why so many people are drawn to this sector year after year. Every day, in a country like India, there is a massive demand for soap. However, there are only a few competitors in the business. We have a few ideas for you if you want to launch your own soap company. Let's get this started.

Tips for soap making using the cold process method

Soap making is easy at the most fundamental level. The cold process approach is the most common way to produce soap. It's "cold" because the ingredients aren't heated before being combined. Using the "hot process" technique, you can make soap with heat. We will use the cold process. Soap is made by mixing fats and oils with a lye and water solution in the most basic form. Soap is made from a combination of water, lye, fats, and oils. The fun starts as you change the components and quantities of the various materials. But, to keep things simple, note that soap is essentially a solution of fats and oils, lye, and water. It's as plain as that.

Is making soap without lye possible?

Is it possible to produce soap without lye? Not at all. Soap bases that can be heated and poured into molds can be purchased. You didn't have to use lye to make the base as everyone else did. However, you have no idea what's in those bases. Sodium hydroxide is the lye used to produce bar soap. Soft soaps are made of potassium hydroxide. Leaching lye from wood ashes is an easy way to create it. This form of lye results in a smoother soap. Unless you have access to a chemical supply house, lye is typically difficult to come by locally. It is, however, simple to put an order. Lye is highly caustic, and it can sear the skin and strip color from whatever surface it comes into contact with. If it gets into your eyes, it will blind you. This is a toxic drug and can never be used in a place where children may reach it. Adults, on the other hand, would have no trouble with the lye if they take simple precautions. When dealing with lye, please wear safety goggles. Long sleeves and protective gloves are also recommended. Leave lye or lye mixtures unattended at all times. Uncured soap should be used similarly to lye.

Fats and oils required for making the cold process soap

Another fundamental to producing soap can be found here. To turn oils and fats into soap, different quantities of lye are needed. Every fat that is likely to be used in soap making has a known amount of time it takes to turn oil or fat into soap. Simply look up the amount of lye needed to produce soap from a certain oil in a table. The volume of lye used in each recipe is then determined based on the oils used. Using a little less lye than is needed to transform all of the oils into soap. This is achieved as a precautionary step to ensure that all of the lye is absorbed during the process. The lye discount is the volume of lye used that is reduced. It's normal to use around 5% less lye than is needed to completely transform the oils into soap. Coconut, palm, and olive oils are the most common oils used in soap making. If you just use those three oils to make soap, you will make amazing results. Each of these oils has its collection of characteristics that make it useful as a soaping oil. You can produce a soap with only one of the oils, but the results won't be as strong as if you used all three. This is why. If you want a lot of bubbles in your soap, coconut oil is the way to go. It's the root of a slew of big, light bubbles. However, soap made entirely of coconut oil cleans so well that it extracts much of the oil from the skin, leaving it dry. This is why it can only account for about 30% of the soap oils. Palm oil is important for hard, long-lasting bars, but it isn't as clean or bubbly as coconut oil.

This fat is often referred to as "vegetable tallow," but it is similar to beef tallow in any way. If you don't want to eat meat fats, use them instead of beef fat. Then you should ask about olive oil. Just olive oil is used to produce castile soap conventionally. If you've ever used this form of soap, you know how good it is as a skin conditioner. It's amazing. However, if olive oil is the only oil used in the soap, the effect is tiny little bubbles and bars that fade away quicker than you'd like. As a result, this type of oil is only used to make up about 40% of the oils in a recipe. Granted, soap can be made from almost any form of fat or oil, and there are several alternatives.

Adding ingredients for premium luxury results

If you choose to use other oils, just apply a small amount during the final stages of the soap-making process. you'll find that you can use almond oil in your example recipe. Simply raise the amount of olive oil in the formula and leave out the almond oil. It was chosen because it brings a little more to the bar's feel and quality. Soap can be used for a lot more than just producing pure soap. All of the additives are what make soap production so exciting. Clays, natural oils, medicinal products, colors, patterns, and a slew of other alternatives are available as additives. The first step to perfect soap is to get the fundamentals correctly, which can be achieved fast and effectively. After learning the fundamentals of soap manufacturing, the soap manufacturer progresses to using a range of exotic ingredients.

How to make soap?

We'll go into the fundamentals of how the soap is made. Bear in mind that this is just the first step. Following that, you may need additional materials and a special recipe to distinguish the product from competitors.

Ingredients

Given below are the following ingredients that would be required for preparing soap:

Take 2/3 cup of coconut oil (that will create lather) and the same amount of olive oil. Moreover, 2/3 cup almond, safflower oil,or grape seed will also be needed.

Then you'll need a quarter cup of lye, which is sodium hydroxide in its purest form. Finally, you'll require 3/4 cup of cool water that is distilled or pure.

You'll also need oatmeal, aloe vera gel, cornmeal, clay, salt, and any other items you choose to use.

Instructions

Listed below are the step-by-step directions that you must follow in the preparation of soap:

Put on your gloves and pour lye and water into a canning jar. Allow them to sit for a few minutes after they've been stirred gently and the water has begun to clear.

Now pour in the oil from the pint jar. Then Stir well, then put the jar in a warm pan of the water that is bubbling (and/or you maymicrowave it, when you do, place temperature to one hundred and twenty degrees F).

Remove the lye after that is finished. Allow the lye to cool. Remove pint jar & allow your oil to cool as well. Both can achieve a temperature of 95 to 105 degrees Fahrenheit. If the temperature drops below 95 degrees F, the soap will begin to crumble.

Pour them into a mixing bowl until they've hit the ideal temperature and whisk until fully combined. After stirring for five minutes, mix it with an immersion blender.

Then, to make the soap special, apply herbs, essential oils, & any other things that go with it. They can be thoroughly combined so they appear coarse. Place them in molds & cover with a towel.

After a day check the soap and let it stay for an additional 12 to 24 hours if it's either warm or soft.

When the soaps are fully cured, wrap them in the paper wax & lock them in an airtight jar for a week. Since this soap contains oil on its own, we'll need an airtight jar. As a consequence, interaction with air will cause it to pick up debris and dust.

Soap making machine and price

fiber covered mixing machine will cost you at least about US$ 1000. This price includes a fiber-covered mixing machine capable of producing 200 kilograms of detergent powder.

Where to get soap making machine?

Online, you can buy a soap-manufacturing machine. Soap manufacturing machines are available from several online retailers. These websites sell the requisite appliances, including the microwave, blender, wrapper, mold, and labeler, also the main device. A soap-making unit, for example, can be bought for the US

$ 5000. This item can be used to produce toilet soaps and detergent cakes. If you're searching for something less costly, say under the US $ 1500 apiece, you can easily find it on the market. It can be used to produce soap for bathing purposes. There are also other products of varying price points. However, the budget may start at one dollar an item. You'll get a good detergent maker for this amount.

Soap making raw material and price

The Soap-making ingredients may be bought for a very cheap price. It is much less costly if you buy them in bulk. If you may get the price correct upfront, the rest of the company will be a breeze later on. As a consequence, we prefer bulk raw materials. Alkali and fat are the two main raw materials used to produce soap. the raw material which is most commonly used in soap manufacture is sodium hydroxide. Potassium hydroxide, on the other hand, maybe used. The latter makes a soap that is more soluble in water. As a result, potassium hydroxide creates "warm soap." Locally, raw products are available at a reduced quality. You can discoverraw materials for manufacturing soaps online or in your neighborhood with a fast Google search. People typically buy this locally so it cuts the price even further. Rest assured that rates can differ depending on your needs. It depends solely on how much you're making & how much of the raw material you'll need. Caustic soda costs about US $ 150-250 permetric ton on the market. The price of 1000 grams of laundry soap ranges between US$1 and $1.25.

Soap making formulae

legitimate chemical formulae for the soap's $C_{17}H_{35}COONa$. Its chemical name is thus sodium stearate. However,it is important to note that it's for the common soapthat is used for personal purposes only. For the detergents, there arenormally long chains of carboxylic acid as well as sulfonate salts or ammonium salt.

2.16 Soap selling process

Let us now go through the packaging, distribution, marketing, and promotion processes.

Colorful wrappings

Choose a bright & eye-catching label that will guarantee that the product is noticed. To set it apart from the competition, style it & use the proper design.

Branding

Make the most of this opportunity to build your brand through packaging. Choose a design that you think best reflects your business.

Go simple

Today's entrepreneurs aim for simplicity. Examine the performance of POP displays as well. If they don't live up to your standards, it's time to make a change.

Soap marketing strategy

You can use the following strategies for marketing soap:

Email marketing

And the ones who also sign up for your offer are truly interested in the soaps, email marketing is the perfect way to market. It's also becoming highly customizable and cost-efficient these days.

Blogging

The next logical move is to start blogging. You'll need to hunt down some prominent bloggers who may help you spread the word about the business. You may even invite them to write a review on their blog about a sample of the product.

Social media

Due to availability of the social media, it is now easier to create a brand. Furthermore, guess what? It's the shortest and least expensive alternative. The secret is to make something go viral. this could be the merchandise, online presence, or your ads.

2.17 Soap making supplies

To make it function properly, you'll need some modernized tools equipment, as well as a lot of the space. You will need to find rental space to make the soap. Some of the typical things you'll need to get started include cyclone, mixing vessels, perfumers, blowers, reactors, furnaces, weighing scales, and blenders.

2.18 Marketing area for soap

The marketing region you select will be decided by the audience you're targeting. You would be able to segment your customers depending on age and demographic in social media marketing. Your marketing field can be decided by the type of soap you sell. If you're selling detergent cakes, for example, they're mainly aimed at homemakers of different ages. As a consequence, you will show the commercial depending on age & gender. Marketing is successful on a variety of measures. It simply depends upon whether you've online or a physical company. In any case, it's better to entrust this to a practitioner.

2.19 Total investment

The Investment isn't based on raw materials. Just As mentioned above, different raw materials are used for personal and detergent soaps. Therefore investment will be different for each category.

You must take into consideration the size and place of the business for starting the business. SoYou need minimum money of US $ 20,000to purchase the machinery along withprimary raw materials –if you decide to start with little.

Raw materials shall cost the US $ 2500 per month. Moreover, making unit rentalswouldcharge not less than the US $ 1000 per month. In addition to the above-mentioned costs, the salary of the plant manager is expected to be aroundthe US $ 500. Equipment shall cost around the US $ 10,000 or more.

In addition to the above prices, you need the US $ 500 for license & registration. Moreover, you will need another US $ 800 to cover the accidental coverage. the Marketing might cost you approximatelyUS $ 500 per month.

2.20 Selling price

Supply, materials, brand, packaging, and other factors impact soap pricing. When you're only starting, keep the rates comparable to those of your rivals.

Prices are determined by several factors. A lower-cost soap is generally assumed to be of lower quality. As a result, we won't keep prices very low about market prices.

Additionally, too high prices could decrease overall demand. As a consequence, we will arrive at the golden middle & retain it just marginally, so at all, below current levels.

2.21 Profit margin

Measure profit margins through factoring in your annual manufacturing expenses. You must also remember manpower, raw materials, utilities, and maintenance costs.

This business has a high-profit margin, but it also has a lot of competition from well-known brands. As a result, profit margins would be dictated by the price of the goods.

Know more about your rivals' prices and, as a result, determine which would give the greatest return – find the "golden value point" for the sales.

2.22 Precaution

It is important to obtain insurance. it is why, in addition to other necessities, insurance must still be part of the investment.

Another crucial step's to understand the company's legal framework. Obtain both the "consent to establish" and "consent to operate."

2.23 Risk

In the soap industry, the risk is not creating a large enough brand to compete with the rivals. There are a lot of competitors in the business, so making a name for your company can be challenging.

Another danger is that the company will collapse due to a lack of consumer awareness. To run a good soap company, you must first select the right market.

2.24 Conclusion

Soap production, as satisfying as this is, necessitates thorough study and measured risk-taking. Seeking your niche and launching a company are just simple activities. However, careful preparation and intervention are necessary to make this a success. Make sure you don't undersell yourself & that you also stand out.

2.25 Advantage of starting a soap making business at home

Soap making requires little investment to start with

The supplies needed to make soap can be easily acquired

Equipment required can also be easily acquired

It is comparatively much easier to learn the making of soap

There is already good demand for handmade soap and people are willing to purchase handmade soap,

You can easily specialize in your particular field

It's rather easier to make soap that is both distinctive and different from the existing ones

You can create other products that can gel in with your existing products

You can generate handsome profits by selling soap

It is very easy to locate a market for the soaps

2.26 How Much Money Can You Make Making Soap?

That's a tough question to answer because so much depends on you. And, just to be clear, producing soap is not lucrative. Of course, the money is in the soap sales. To make money selling a product, much as with any other business endeavor takes a lot of time and commitment.

CHAPTER 3: Start a Profitable Candle Making Business

Candlemakers are extremely professional artisans who pay particular attention to the sensory aesthetics of their products and experienced business people who know how to entice consumers with innovative marketing tactics. Learn how to launch a candle-making company of your own.

3.1 Steps for starting a candle making business

You've uncovered the ideal market opportunity and are now prepared to take the next step. There's more to launching a company than simply filing papers with the government. We've put together a list of steps to help you get started with your candle-making business. These measures will ensure that the new company is well-planned, legally compliant, and properly registered.

Plan your business

As an entrepreneur, you must have a well-thought-out strategy. It will assist you in figuring out the additional data of your organization and uncovering any unknowns. Given below are some key points to consider:

What are the startup and recurring costs?

Who is the targeted audience?

What is the maximum price you will charge from the customers?

What would you name your company?

What are the costs involved in opening a candle-making business?

You will be able to start your business at home, based on local zoning rules, making use of your kitchen heat source as well as utensils. Many online retailers, including Candle Science and CandleChem, offer a starter kit of items. To start, your candle materials shouldn't cost more than a few hundred dollars. This includes:

Paraffin, gel, soy, beeswax, or other wax

Wicks

Jars, tins, or other containers (though bear in mind that if you're just selling pillar candles, you won't need containers)

Fragrance oils

Coloring agents

Packaging materials

Transportation costs of raw goods in and finished products out

Web growth, which can cost anywhere from nothing to a few hundred dollars based on the expertise in the industry and at least properly contributes to some other start-up costs. A booth will cost $100 per day if you intend to showcase your goods at different exhibits and festivals, plus you'll have to pay for fuel and other travel expenses. You can also contact an insurance provider first. Since there is a chance of a fire accident, you can ensure that your company is fire-proofed and that you have a fire extinguisher onboard. You can also have an initial consultation with a lawyer to decide what licenses or permits are required in your region.

What are the ongoing expenses for a candle-making business?

The majority of the business revolves around different varieties of wax, your containers, and paint and scent additives. You can purchase these goods in bulk at lower per-unit prices once you've established your business model is viable. Wax, for example, can be ordered in 25-pound sizes for as little as a dollar per pound. Wicks are sold in 100-foot spools. Bulk amounts of containers, such as glass pots, mason jars, and tins, are also available.

Who is the target market?

Anyone who needs candles is your end customer. Some may have specific concerns, such as lights in the case of a power outage, and others are searching for a more sensory experience. Churches that use candles to decorate prayer offerings or stores that wish to bring a dramatic effect to their showrooms are often fantastic consumers. You may also approach resellers that can order the goods in vast quantities. Shop owners from the neighborhood and beyond will be among them. Customers like these are usually seen at arts and crafts shows. Try renting stalls at arts and crafts shows, flea markets, festivals and fairs, and other similar venues if you love seeing your customers face to face in an atmosphere where they can truly appreciate the aesthetics of your goods.

How does a candle-making business make money?

Candlemakers market candles to customers directly or indirectly through resellers such as boutiques, gift stores, and other arts and crafts shopping outlets. Since candle making is such a wide field, differentiate yourself by the types of candles you sell (pillar, floating, votive, tea, etc.) or the quality of your offering. Experiment with scents, textures, and molds to come up with something unique that is worth premium pricing. Furthermore, for optimum profit margins on your sales, you can still be on the lookout for low-cost raw material suppliers. To widen your target audience, think of related products or candle styles.

3.2 How much can you charge customers?

Your goods could sell for as little as a few bucks or as much as $20 or more per unit. Pricing will be dictated by the nature and reach of your product line, as well as your target market, marketing plan, and competitiveness. If you want to be the lowest vendor, make sure you're buying your raw materials at a discount and that you're still aware of what your rivals are charging. To save the most cost per unit, you'll want to buy wax, wicks, coloring agents, scents, and other products in bulk. If your goal is to market a higher-end product line, price is less important as long as your goods are visually pleasing. If you find a retail reseller that can move a lot of your product, you might want to consider giving deep discounts on prices.

How much profit can a candle-making business make?

Profit margins of 50% or more are not out of the question. While the cost of materials is not especially high, make sure you have the resources to devote to making your company profitable.

How can you make your business more profitable?

Consider expanding the product offerings once you've perfected the principles of candle-making. For example, learning how to mold or carve candles into any shape will improve the cost and revenue potential. Alternatively, you might start selling fancy oil lamps made from liquid candles. Find scented soaps and incense as well as other sensory items. You might be able to learn how to make these additions to your expanding product line, or you might be able to figure out where to purchase them for resale. Consider offering candle-making lessons if you have the requisite space in your workshop. You might contact the local community center or community college in this effort and see if they'd be involved in adding your class to their program. Finally, is the company prosperous enough that you might consider franchising it? You have to give this important factor a thorough consideration if you want to enhance your profits.

What will you name your business?

Choosing the correct name is vital and daunting. If you own a sole proprietorship, you should start using a separate company name from your own. We suggest reviewing the following references before filing a company name:

The state's business records

Federal and state trademark records

Social media sites

Web domain availability

It's important to get your domain name registered before anyone else. After registering a domain name, you should consider setting upa professional email account (@yourcompany.com).

Form a legal entity

The sole proprietorship, partnership, limited liability company (LLC), and corporation are the most traditional corporate structures. If your candle manufacturing company is used, creating a legitimate business entity such as an LLC or corporation prevents you from being found legally accountable.

Register for taxes

Before you can start doing business, you'll need to apply for several state and federal taxes. You would need to apply for an EIN to pay for taxation. It's very basic and free.

Small Business Taxes

Depending on which business arrangement you select, you can have various taxation choices for your corporation. There could be state-specific taxes that apply to your business. In the state sales tax guides, you can read more about state sales taxes and franchise taxes.

Open a business bank account & credit card

Personal wealth security necessitates the use of dedicated company banking and credit accounts. If your personal and corporate accounts are combined, your personal properties (such as your house, vehicle, and other valuables) are put at risk if your company-issued. This is referred to as piercing the corporate veil in business law. Furthermore, learning how to create company credit will help you receive credit cards and another borrowing under your business's name (rather than your own), lower interest rates, and more credit lines, among other advantages.

Open a business bank account

This protects your assets from those of your business, which is essential for personal wealth security, as well as making accounting and tax reporting simpler.

Get a business credit card

It will help you achieve the following benefits:

It builds the company's credit background and will be beneficial for raising capital and profit later on.

It lets you differentiate personal and business expenditures by placing all of your business's costs under one account.

Set up business accounting

Understanding your business's financial results includes keeping track of your different costs and sources of revenue. Maintaining correct and comprehensive reports also makes annual tax filing even simpler.

Labor safety requirements

It is essential to comply with all Occupational Safety and Health Administration protocols. Pertinent requirements include:

Employee injury report

Safety signage

Certificate of Occupancy

A Certificate of Occupancy is normally required for businesses that operate out of a specific location (CO). All requirements concerning building codes, zoning rules, and local requirements have been followed, according to a CO. If you're thinking about renting a space, keep the following in mind:

Securing a CO is normally the landlord's duty.

Before signing a contract, make sure your landlord has or can get a legitimate CO for a soap-making operation.

A new CO is often needed after a significant renovation. If your company will be renovated before opening, add wording in your lease agreement that specifies that lease payments will not begin before a valid CO is issued.

If you intend to buy or build a place:

You would be responsible for securing a legal CO from a local government body.

Review all building codes and zoning standards for your candle-making business's place to ensure that you'll comply and eligible to get a CO.

Trademark & Copyright Protection

It is wise to protect your interests by applying for the required trademarks and copyrights if you are creating a new product, idea, brand, or design. The essence of legal standards in distance education is continually evolving, especially when it comes to copyright laws. This is a regularly revised database that can assist you with keeping on top of legal specifications.

Get business insurance

Insurance, including licenses and permits, are necessary for your company to run safely and legally. In the case of a covered loss, corporate insurance covers your company's financial well-being. There are several insurance schemes tailored for diverse types of companies with various risks. If you're not sure what kinds of risks your company might face, start with General Liability Insurance.

This is the most popular form of coverage required by small companies, so it's a good place to start.

Define your brand

Your company's brand is what it stands for, as well as how the general public perceives it. A good name would set the company apart from the market.

How to promote & market a candle making business

The first and most crucial step is to decide who you intend to reach. Is your average customer a cost-conscious shopper, or is she more concerned with the sensory experience? If your target market is the former, you should be able to deliver fair prices. If it's the latter, make sure your product range is well-presented and that your color and scent options are pleasing. Try building an online presence on sites including eBay, Amazon, and Etsy. Since these platforms have a lot of competition, keep the costs as low as possible. There is a slew of other arts and crafts marketplaces, but they aren't as well-known as Etsy (and therefore potentially less populated with competitors). Among them are ArtFire, Big Cartel, and Craft Is Art, to name a few.

How to keep customers coming back

You aim to not only retain buyers but to keep them coming back. Since candles are consumable goods that must be replaced daily, the current consumer partnerships may become profitable over time. As a result, make sure you fulfill their needs so that they appreciate the quality of your goods and know-how to reach you if stocks run out. As a consequence, any order must provide easy-to-find contact information, such as your website, email address, or phone number (or all three). As part of the packaging, you could add a business card or sticker with this detail. Make sure shoppers and passers-by alike get your business card when approaching clients in people, such as at art shows or flea markets. Often, get their names and permission to connect them to an email list you give out, maybe before peak candle-buying seasons like the holidays or Mother's Day.

Establish your web presence

Customers can learn more about your business and the goods or services you deliver by visiting your website. One of the most successful ways to build your online presence is through press releases and social media.

Top of Form

Bottom of Form

Is this Business Right For You?

The perfect candle maker is passionate about the craft and has experience in sales and promotion. Candlemakers may start small, with a minimal budget and inventory, in the kitchen and storage room of their home or apartment. Since candles are always thought of as commodity products, you must continually search for ways to brand your line to set yourself apart from the competition. Excellent image photography, a solid web presence, and savvy sales expertise can help you highlight your product line attractively.

What are some skills and experiences that will help you build a successful candle-making business?

The bulk of people get into this business as hobby candle builders. You should appreciate the aesthetics of making candles and related products and have a clear understanding of how to mark your business. You should be familiar with the principles of eCommerce and how to build an online presence. If you sell from a booth at a fair, your display presentation skills are relevant both online (in the quality of your images and written product descriptions) and in physical displays. If you plan to market your product line in person, either to consumers personally or to resellers, personal sales skill is important. You must trust in the goods and be able to convince people to do so as well.

What is the growth potential for a candle-making business?

A good full-time candle maker could earn between $25,000 and $50,000 per year. However, if you sell to a big reseller, you might make more money. Consider franchising your organization once it has become popular enough for others to choose to follow in your footsteps. Candle making is an easy business to launch on your own. However, your ambition likely is to become so well-known that you'll need assistance with crafting, selling, and/or shipping your merchandise. Begin by enlisting the support of friends or family members if required, such as to match seasonal revenue spikes. Don't recruit permanent full-time support once you've been through ample revenue periods to realize that you'll be able to easily reach payroll over the year. Also, contact the accountant to hear about all the hidden expenses.

Candles Pricing

From a business standpoint, you'll need to find out how much you need/want to receive every hour and how many candles you can make in that time. Divide the hourly wage by the number of units (candles) generated to get a figure to add to the basic cost of the supplies used to manufacture each candle until you have these two numbers. Consider the following scenario: You pay $50 on ingredients (not equipment) and can make 20 candles from them. For the supplies, you paid $2.50 per candle. Making candles is a way for you to earn $20 per hour. Since the 20 candles you made took two hours to make, the overall cost is two times $20, or $40. Then you divide $40 by 20 to get a $2 per candle labor rate. When you apply the $2 labor cost to the $2.50 content cost, you get $4.50 per candle. This isn't a great example because you'll need to pay for other expenses like the additional utilities needed to produce the candles and the expense of importing supplies like boilers, pots, and jugs.

How much should you charge for candles?

This is based on the sort of brand you choose to be affiliated with. If you intend to sell bulk candles at a low price, you should expect your company to turn out a huge amount of low-cost candles with a slight but steady profit per candle. Votive candles are cheap and can be ordered for as little as $0.50 each. This approach can be very successful, particularly when several cheap candles are purchased in bulk, resulting in several sales for each customer. The drawback is that you would have to bring in a lot of money to make a big profit. You'll almost definitely need to expand, recruiting someone to help you achieve your broad production goals. Another choice is to create your brand. This means catering to a more discerning public able to pay a premium price for a candle. Some high-end artisanal candles will cost upwards of $200 each. For a brand, you'd have to worry about the packaging theme and what you're encouraging your clients to do with their candles.

3.3 Benefits of candle making business

If you've ever visited a big shopping center, you've probably seen a variety of candle shops. There are whole areas devoted to candles in several major department stores. To give you an example of how strong the candle business is, over 1 million pounds of wax are used to produce candles for the US market alone every year. The candle industry is worth around $2.3 billion a year without additional products such as candlesticks, ceramic pots, and so on. Who makes the most candle purchases? Seasonal holidays account for just 35% of overall sales, making them an outstanding all-year-round investment. Outside of these days, candles are purchased for 65 percent of the year. The most popular motives for buying a candle as a present include a seasonal gift, a housewarming gift, a dinner party gift, a thank you gift, and adult birthday presents. People nowadays believe fragrance to be the most important consideration when buying a candle. Make sure the candles you're thinking of selling have high-quality scents since this can be the difference between success and failure in the candle industry.

Conclusion

In 1969, in a period when India's domestic detergent industry had very few competitors, predominantly multi-national firms, which targeted the affluent of India, Karsanbhai launched Nirma. The detergents were not affordable for most middle-class and poor citizens. Karsanbhai began producing detergent powder in the backyard of his home in Khokra, near Ahmedabad and selling it door to door for Rs 3 per kg, while other brands were charging Rs 13 per kg. Business Standard reported how Karsanbhai came up with a genius idea during the early 1980s, when theNirma was still struggling with the sales, for drying out market of the goods collecting all the due credits. This was accompanied by a huge ad campaign featuring his daughter singing the iconic Nirma jingle in a white frock. Customers were flocking to markets, only to return empty-handed. Karsanbhai flooded the industry with his goods as the demand for Nirma peaked, leading to huge sales. Nirma's sales peaked that year, making it the most successful detergent, well outselling its closest competitor, Hindustan Unilever's Surf. As Karsanbhai purchased the cement firm LafargeHolcim for 1.4 billion dollars that year, he showed once again that thebusinessappetite is away from over. Mint reported how the deal in Rajasthan and the surrounding area would help Nirma achieve a stronger grip. While a media-shy guy, Karsanbhai, an entrepreneur in the truest sense, has a sharp eye for nation-building. In 1995, he founded the Nirma Institute of Technology, which was followed by the Nirma University of Science and Technology, which was founded in 2003 and is supervised by the Nirma Education and Research Foundation. He initiated the education project Nirmalabs in 2004, aimed at educating and incubating entrepreneurs in India. Karsanbhai Patel received the Padma Shri award in 2010. Just like Nirma, you can also transform your soap and candle-making business into large corporate businesses with the help of your ingenious marketing and creative skills, dedication, perseverance, and unfearfulness of new and challenging situations.

Dropshipping Business Model on a Budget

The Risk-Low E-Com Guide to Create Your Online Store and Generate Profits with less than 47$

By

Vishen Smith

Table of Contents

Introduction

With very little startup expenses, dropshipping is an innovative business model.

A dropshipping business is where an owner finds a collection of distributors to deliver and offer goods for their website. However, as in an e-commerce business, instead of owning the merchandise, a third party does much of the distribution and logistics for them. That third party is usually a wholesaler, who on behalf of the business "dropships" the consumer's goods.

When you start a retail shop, there are several factors to consider, but among the most significant aspects, you have to decide whether you'd like to store inventory or have a wholesale distributor. You must purchase goods in bulk, stock, unpack and send them to customers of your products if you want to store inventory. You may, therefore, contract the phase of storing, packaging and exporting to a drop-ship supplier by picking a wholesale distributor. As direct fulfillment, a drop-ship supplier is often described, but both definitions may be used to define the same service.

The wholesaler, who usually manufactures the product, delivers the product at the most basic, any time anyone buys a product, and you get a part of the sale for the product marketing.

Unless the client puts an order for it, you don't pay for the thing.

Dropshipping is an internet-based business model that draws novices and experts alike to choose a niche, create a brand, market and earn money, with probably the minimum entry barriers.

Chapter 1. What is Dropshipping?

Dropshipping is a retail model of e-commerce that enables retailers to offer goods without maintaining any physical inventory. The company sells the product to the buyer through dropshipping and sends the purchase order to a third-party seller, who then delivers the order directly on behalf of the retailer to the customer. Dropshipping sellers may not need to spend in any commodity stock, inventory or storage room and do not manage the phase of fulfillment.

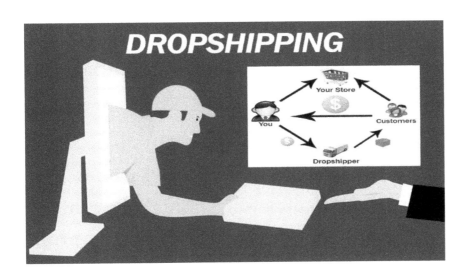

Dropshipping is a form of retail fulfillment, where the goods are ordered from a third-party retailer instead of a store stocks products. The goods are then delivered directly to the customer. This way, the vendor doesn't have to personally manage the product. A familiar sound? Maybe not, but dropshipping is a fulfillment model utilized by 35 percent of online stores.

This is mostly a hands-off process for the store. The retailer doesn't have to buy stock or, in any manner, meet the orders. The third-party retailer, instead, takes control of the product itself.

For startups, dropshipping is great since it does not take as much as the conventional sales model. You don't have to prepare, pay overhead, & stock merchandise in a brick-and-mortar store. Instead, you start an online shop to purchase bulk goods and warehouse space from vendors that already have products.

In dropshipping, the merchant is solely responsible for attracting clients and handling orders, ensuring you'll be a middleman effectively. Despite this, through pricing up the goods you offer, you can gain the lion's share of the profits. It's an easy model of business, so one that can be really successful.

Millions of entrepreneurs switch to dropshipping to get started because it takes less hassle and capital. That's why you're probably interested. And the best of all news? Through dropshipping, you can create a company right from your laptop that is profitable in the long term.

There are several pitfalls and benefits, of course, and it is essential that we check at them before you launch your own e-commerce dropshipping firm. However, once you realize the positives and negatives of dropshipping, it'll be a breeze to learn how to do so effectively.

1.1 Benefits of dropshipping

For aspiring entrepreneurs, dropshipping is a smart business move to start with, which is accessible. You can easily evaluate multiple business concepts with a small downside with dropshipping, which helps you to think a lot about how to pick and sell in-demand goods. Here are a couple more explanations why dropshipping is a popular business.

1. Little capital is required

Perhaps the greatest benefit to dropshipping is that an e-commerce website can be opened without needing to spend thousands of dollars in stock upfront. Typically, retailers have had to bundle up large quantities of inventory with capital investments.

For the dropshipping model, unless you have already made the transaction and have been charged by the consumer, you may not have to buy a product. It is possible to start sourcing goods without substantial up-front inventory investments and launch a profitable dropshipping company with very little capital. And since you are not committed to sales, as in a typical retail sector, there is less chance of launching a dropshipping shop through any inventory bought up front.

2. Easy to get started

It's also simpler to operate an e-commerce company because you don't have to interact with physical products. You don't have to take stress with dropshipping about:

- Paying for a warehouse or managing it

- Tracking inventory for any accounting reasons

- Packing & shipping your orders

- Continually ordering products & managing stock level

- Inbound shipments and handling returns

3. Low overhead

Your overhead expenses are very minimal, and you don't have to deal with buying inventory or maintaining a warehouse. In reality, several popular dropshipping stores are managed as home-based enterprises, needing nothing more to run than a laptop & a few operational expenses. These costs are likely to rise as you expand but are still low relative to standard brick-and-mortar stores.

4. Flexible location

From almost anywhere via an internet connection, a dropshipping company can be managed. You can operate and manage the business as long as you can effectively connect with vendors and consumers.

5. Wide selection of goods to sell

Because you don't really have to pre-purchase any items you market, you can offer your potential clients a variety of trending products. If an item is stored by vendors, you will mark it for sale at no added cost at your online store.

6. Easier for testing

Dropshipping is a valuable form of fulfillment for both the opening of a new store and also for company owners seeking to measure consumers' demand for additional types of items, such as shoes or whole new product ranges. Again, the primary advantage of dropshipping is the opportunity to list and likely sell goods before committing to purchasing a significant quantity of stock.

7. Easier to scale

For a traditional retail firm, you would typically need to perform three times as much work if you get three times the amount of orders. By using dropshipping vendors, suppliers would be liable for more of the work to handle extra orders, helping you to improve with fewer growth pains & little incremental work.

Sales growth can often bring extra work, especially customer service, however companies which use dropshipping scale especially well comparison to standard e-commerce businesses.

8. Dropshipping starts easily.

In order to get started, you need not be a business guru. You don't really require some past company knowledge, honestly. You will get started easily and learn the rest while you move along if you spend some time to learn its basics.

It is too easy to drop shipping, and it takes so little from you. To help you out, you don't need a warehouse to store goods or a staff. You don't need to think about packaging or storage either. You do not even have to devote a certain period of time in your shop every day. Surprisingly, it's hands-off, especially once you get underway.

All of this means that today you can begin your company. Within a matter of hours, you will begin getting it up and running.

You're going to need some practical skills and the right equipment and tools. You will be equipped with the skills you have to jumpstart your own dropshipping company by the time you've done it.

9. Dropshipping grow easily.

Your business model doesn't even have to alter that much at all when you scale up. As you expand, you'll have to bring more effort into sales and marketing, but your daily life will remain almost the same.

One of the advantages of dropshipping is that when you scale, the costs do not spike. It's convenient to keep rising at a fairly high pace because of this. If you choose to build a little team at any stage, you can manage about anything by yourself, too.

10. Dropshipping doesn't need a big capital.

Since you need very little to start a dropshipping business, you can get underway with minimal funds. Right from your desktop, you can create a whole corporation, and you do not need to make any heavy investment. Your costs would be reasonably low even as your company grows, particularly compared to normal business expenses.

11. Dropshipping is flexible.

This is one of the greatest advantages. You get to be a boss of your own and set your own regulations. It's one of the most versatile occupations anyone can try.

With just a laptop, you can operate from anywhere, and you can operate at the hours that are most comfortable for you. For founders that want a company that fits for them, this is perfect. To get stuff done, you won't have to lean over backward. You choose your own pace instead.

Dropshipping is indeed flexible in that it allows you plenty of space to create choices that fit for you. Whenever you choose, you can quickly list new items, and you can change your plans on the move. You should automate it to work when you're gone, whether you're going on holiday. You get the concept prospects are limitless.

12. Dropshipping manages easily.

Because it doesn't need you to make several commitments, with no hassle, you can manage everything. When you have found and set up suppliers, you are often exclusively liable for your e-commerce store.

Chapter 2. How Dropshipping Works

Dropshipping functions by third-party suppliers, which deliver goods for each order on a just-in-time basis. When a sales order is received by the retailer, they transfer the requirements to the supplier — who manufactures the product.

While dropshipping is used by many e-commerce retailers as the base of their business processes, dropshipping can be used successfully to complement traditional retail inventory-stocking models. Because dropshipping does not create any unused surplus inventory, it may be used for analysis purposes before committing to sale on a marketplace, such as testing the waters.

Dropshipping works because, with the aid of a third party such as a wholesaler or an e-commerce shop, a dropshipper fulfills orders to deliver the goods for an even cheaper price. The majority of dropshippers offer goods directly from Chinese suppliers because the prices of most products in China are very poor. If the wholesaler's price is 5 dollars for a product. A dropshipper sells it for $8 and retains $3 for himself. The bulk of dropshippers target nations with higher purchasing power.

2.1 Awareness about the Supply Chain

You'll see the word "supply chain" a lot in here. It seems like a fancy lingo for the business, but it actually applies to how a product transfers from seller to consumer. We'll use this to explain the method of dropshipping.

2.2 The Supply Chain Process

You, the merchant, are only one puzzle piece. An effective dropshipping mechanism depends on several parties all acting in sync together. The supply chain is just that: producer, supplier, and retailer coordination.

You should split down the supply chain into three simple steps:

- The producer manufactures the goods and supplies them to wholesalers & retailers.

Let's say maker A is manufacturing bottles of water. They are marketed in bulk to manufacturers and wholesalers after the bottles come off the assembly line, who switch around & resell the bottles to dealers.

- Suppliers and wholesalers market the products to dealers.

For a particular type of product, a retailer like yourself is searching for a supplier. An arrangement to operate together is then reached between the retailer and the supplier.

A little point here: Although you may order directly from product producers, purchasing from retailers is always much cheaper instead. There are minimum purchasing criteria for most suppliers that can be very high, and you will still have to purchase stock & ship the goods.

So, purchasing directly from the producer might seem quicker, but you would profit more from buying from distributors (dealing with the little profit).

Suppliers are often convenient since all of them are skilled in a specific niche, so the type of items you need can be quickly identified. This also implies that you'll get started to sell super quick.

- Retailers sell goods to buyers.

Suppliers & wholesalers should not market to the public directly; that's the task of the retailer. The last move between the product & the consumer is the supplier.

Online stores from which customers buy goods are provided by retailers. The merchant marks it up again to reach at the final price after the wholesaler rates up the items. By "markup," we apply to fixing a premium that covers the product's cost price and gives you a benefit.

It's that! From start to end, it is the whole supply chain. In business, it's a simple but crucial concept.

You may have noted that no other group has been alluded to as a dropshipper. That is because there is no particular function for "dropshipper." Dropshipping is actually the activity of somebody else delivering goods. Technically, producers, retailers, and merchants will all be dropshippers.

Later on, we'll discuss how to start a retail dropshipping company in this guide. In other terms, you can learn how to become a trader who buys commodities from wholesalers to market to the public. This may indicate that through an online storefront, you sell through eBay or even your own website.

Remember what it's like for the consumer now that you realize what the supply chain is like.

2.3 What is Fulfillment?

Order fulfillment that's all the steps a corporation requires in having a fresh order and bringing the order into the hands of the customer. The procedure includes storing, picking & packaging the products, distributing them and sending the consumer an automatic email to let them know that the product is in transit.

2.4 The Steps to make Order Fulfillment

There are some steps involved in order fulfillment, which are as under:-

1. Receiving inventory.

Essentially, there are two approaches for an eCommerce company to manage inventory. It can decide to receive & stock the in-house inventory, or it can employ an outsourcer for eCommerce order fulfillment to take control of the inventory and other associated activities. The organization would be liable for taking stock, inspecting the product, marking, and maintaining the inventory method if it opts for the first alternative. If the business wishes to outsource or dropships, the order fulfillment agent or supplier can perform certain duties.

2. Storing inventory.

If you plan to stock the inventory yourself, after the receiving portion is finished, there'll be another list of assignments waiting for you. Shelving the inventory and holding a careful watch on what goods come in and what goods are going out would be the key activities on the list so that you can deliver the orders without any complications.

3. Processing the order.

Businesses who outsource order fulfillment do not have to get through the nitty-gritty of order delivery since they actually move on to their partner's order request and let them manage the rest. This is the phase where the order is taken off the shelves, shipped to a packaging station, examined for any damage, packed and transferred to the shipping station for businesses who handle their own product.

4. Shipping the order.

The best delivery strategy is calculated based on the scale, weight and precise specifications of the order. A third-party contractor is typically contracted to complete this phase.

Returns Handling. For online shoppers, the opportunity to refund unwanted goods quickly is a big factor in the purchase phase. You ought to design a crystal straightforward return policy that is readily available to all the customers and workers to ensure the receipt, repair and redemption of the returned goods are as successful as practicable. It will help you prevent needless confusion and errors by making this step automated.

Chapter 3. Whydropshipping is one of the best way to make money in 2021.

According to Forrester (analyst) Reports, the magnitude of online retail revenues would be $370 billion by the end of 2017. In comparison, 23 percent, which amounts to $85.1 billion, would come from dropshipping firms. To many businesses, like startups, this sheer scale alone is attractive.

An online retailer following this concept appears similar to its traditional e-commerce competitors by appearance. Dropshipping may be a well-kept mystery in the e-commerce world as consumers just think about the goods, price and credibility of the shop rather than how the goods are sourced and who delivers the shipments.

In summary,' dropshipping' is a business strategy in which the supplier does not directly hold the inventory or process the orders in his or her control. Both orders are delivered directly from a wholesaler and delivered. This encourages the supplier to concentrate on the business's selling aspect.

Many major e-commerce names, such as Zappos, began with dropshipping. For those that seek motivation, billion-dollar dropshipping internet store Wayfair or the milliondollarBlinds.com are top examples today.

Five explanations of how the dropshipping business strategy appeals to both startups and experienced entrepreneurs are offered below. These issues in traditional e-commerce have been nagging challenges, which can be addressed with the dropshipping model immediately.

3.1 Dropshipping Is The E-Commerce Future

It seem that dropshipping will be the future of e-commerce. Here are some main reasons which explain this concept.

Sourcing of Product:

Conventional e-commerce stores must directly import supplies from wholesalers, frequently based in various countries. They often need goods to be bought in bulk and are then shipped prior to being promoted and distributed to the local warehouse. A lot of time, money & resources are required for the whole phase. The presence of expensive intermediaries, such as banks, freight shipments and export-import brokers, also involves it.

The dropshipping model, however, enables manufacturers to market goods for large quantities of each product without needing to think about sourcing. The entire method is substantially simplified with just a turn-key e-commerce storefront such as Shopify and a dropshipping software like Oberlo. The retailer may choose to notify the distributors via e-mail to tell them that their supplies are now being shipped to the store. The most of the procedure can be quickly handled from the dashboard, such as uploading product images, updating pricing and order monitoring.

Storage

A traditional e-commerce store, particularly as it carries multiple or large products, requires large storage spaces. It might be imaginable to store ten to 100 items, but storing 1,000 or 1,000,000 items will cost a real fortune that is not within the reach of a start-up. This high warehouse rent issue is addressed by the dropshipping model since the goods remain with the distributor or wholesale retailer until they are bought.

Order fulfillment

Many pioneers of e-commerce do not foresee investing most of their time picking, packaging and delivering orders. They should, of course, outsource the order fulfillment for ease to a boutique e-commerce fulfillment, such as ShipMonk. The dropshipping model, however, facilitates hands-free shipment, since the whole packaging and shipping process is in the possession of the wholesaler or distributor.

Cataloging & photography

A conventional e-commerce shop owner has to take professional-quality images of items that may be very pricey, like a decent digital camera, a light panel, lighting and some more. For a dropshipping control software, this issue is fixed, as the "product importing" function allows for instant picture import.

Scalability

Wayfair.com is a major online dropshipping store that holds 10,000 vendors of more than eight million items. Yes, $8 million. By this business model, such huge scalability is made possible.

Because the retailer just has to work on the publicity and customer care aspect, they don't have to think about the warehouse's rent and other operating expenses skyrocketing.

In conclusion, the dropshipping paradigm offers the ability for tiny startups with minimal capital to contend with large and medium online stores comfortably, rendering the field of e-commerce an equal environment for everyone. That being said, plan in the future to see more e-commerce shops adopting this model.

Chapter 4. Niche And Product Selection

You want a business to start, but the thing that holds you down is the market niche that you feel you need to pick. And, honestly, it can be tricky: you might mention all your interests & passions and yet feel like you haven't hit the singular thing that you were expected to do.

Yet, it can trigger paralysis to place some sort of burden on yourself to choose the very right niche.

Certainly, in choosing a suitable niche business, you like to do your careful research, but it's easier to get up and run than to wait around. You will try ideas that way, enter the market earlier, and benefit from the victories and losses. That way, too, you can still take what you have gained from previous attempts, so step on with fresh concepts if the first company does not take off.

4.1 Steps how to search your right niche

Using the following five methods to find your niche, whether you're unable to determine or you need more information to work with.

1. Identify your interests & passions.

This could be something that you have achieved before. But, if you haven't, quickly make a compilation of 10 topical passions and areas of passion.

Business isn't easy, and it can challenge you at any stage. If you work in an area you don't care for, the likelihood of leaving will increase significantly — especially like a first sole proprietor.

This doesn't mean that a better match has to be found. You can stay with it if you are excited about any part of running the business. If you don't care about the issue, you might not be able to easily find the drive to persevere within.

2. Identify problems that you can solve.

You're able to get to narrow down your choices with your list of ten topics in hand. You first need to identify challenges that your target clients are facing to build a viable enterprise, then decide if you can potentially fix them. Here are a few items you should do to find issues in different niches.

3. Research your competition.

There is not always a bad thing in the presence of competition. It can actually show you that you've discovered a market that's lucrative. Although you do have to do an in-depth analysis of competing pages. Build a fresh spreadsheet and start tracking all the competing websites that you can find.

And find out whether there's already an opening in the crowd to stick out. Are you still willing to rate the keywords? Is there really a way to distinguish and build a unique offer for yourself? Here are some indications that you will enter a niche and flourish, even though it is already covered by other sites:

- Content of poor quality. In a niche where several company owners are not delivering high-quality, informative content that suits the viewer, it's easy to outrank the competitors.

- Lack of transparency. By establishing an authentic and accessible identity in a niche where most platforms are faceless and unnecessarily corporate, many internet marketers have disrupted whole industries.

- The lack of paid competitiveness. If you have noticed a keyword with a relatively high search rate but little competition with paying ads, there is undoubtedly a potential for you to upset the business.

4. Determine the profitability of the niche.

You need to have a fairly decent understanding now about what niche you're about to get into. You might not have limited your selection down to a particular region of the topic, but you've certainly noticed a few suggestions that you feel pretty good about. It's important to have an idea at this stage about how much money you have the opportunity to make in your niche. A fine way to go to continue your search is ClickBank.

So, browse the category's best brands. That is not a positive indication if you can't locate any offers. It could mean that the niche could not be monetized by someone.

You're in luck if the quest throws up a good amount of products — just not an excessive amount of products. Take notice of pricing points such that your own goods can be marketed in a fair way.

Bear in mind, though, that you may not have to launch your organization with your own product offering. You should collaborate in your niche with product makers, marketers and site owners to start earning commissions when working on your innovative solution.

5. Test your idea.

You are now prepared with all the knowledge you need to pick a niche, and checking your proposal is the only thing needed to do. Setting up a landing page for pre-sales of a product you're producing is one easy way to do this. Through paying ads, you will then push traffic to this page.

That doesn't actually mean that you are not in a viable niche, even though you don't get pre-sales. Your message may not be quite correct, or you haven't found the right deal yet. You will maximize conversions by using A/B split testing to figure out whether there is something preventing the target group from taking action or not.

You will sell to two fundamental markets: customer and corporation. Such divisions are reasonably clear. "For example, if you sell women's clothes from a department shop, shoppers are your target market; if you sell office supplies, companies are your target market (this is referred to as "B2B" sales). In certain instances, for example, you could be selling to both corporations and people if you operate a printing company.

No company, especially a small one, can be everything to all individuals. The more you can describe your target group broadly, the stronger. For even the larger corporations, this method is recognized as building a market and is crucial to growth. Walmart and Tiffany are also stores, but they have somewhat different niches: Walmart caters to bargain-minded customers, while Tiffany tends to luxury jewelry buyers.

"Some entrepreneurs make the error of slipping into the "all over the map" pit instead of building a niche, believing they can do many things and be successful at all of them. Falkenstein warns that these individuals soon learn a difficult lesson: "Smaller is larger in market, and smaller is not across the map; it is extremely focused."

4.2 Creating a good niche

Keep in mind these important to create a good niche:

1. Make a wish list.

Who do you like to do business with? Be as descriptive as you are capable of. Identify the regional spectrum and the kinds of firms or clients that you want your organization to target. You can't make contact if you do not really know whom you are going to do business with. Falkenstein cautions, "You must recognize that you can't do business with everyone." Otherwise, you risk leaving yourself exhausted and confusing your buyers.

The trend is toward small niches these days. It's not precise enough to target teens; targeting adult, African American teenagers with the family incomes of $40,000 or more is. It is too large to target corporations that market apps; it is a better aim to target Northern California-based firms that offer internet software distribution and training that have sales of $15 million or more.

2. Focus.

Clarify what you intend to sell, knowing that a) to all customers, you can't be all items and b) smaller is better. Your specialty isn't the same as that of sector you are employed in. A retail apparel corporation, for example, is not a niche but a sector. Maternity clothes for corporate mothers" may be a more specific niche."

Using these strategies to assist you in starting this focus process:

- Create a compilation of the greatest activities you do and the talents that are inherent in many of them.

- List your accomplishments.

- Identify the important things of life that you've experienced.

- Look for trends that reflect your personality or approach to addressing issues.

Your niche should emerge from your desires and expertise in a normal way. For instance, if you spent 10 years of working in such a consulting firm and also ten years working for such a small, family-owned company, you may actually have to start a consulting company that specializes in limited, family-owned businesses.

3. Describe the customer's worldview.

A good corporation utilizes what Falkenstein called the Platinum Rule: "Do to the others as they're doing to themselves." You will define their desires or desires as you look at the situation from the viewpoint of your prospective clients. Talking to new clients and recognizing their biggest issues is the perfect approach to achieve this.

4. Synthesize.

Your niche can begin to take shape at this point when the opinions and the desires of the consumer and desire to coalesce to create something different. There are five attributes of a Strong Niche:

- In other terms, it relates to your long-term view and carries you where you like to go.
- Somebody else needs it, consumers in particular.
- It is closely arranged.
- It's one-of-a-kind, "the only city game."
- It evolves, enabling you to build multiple profit centers and yet maintain the core market, thus guaranteeing long-term success.

5. Evaluate.

It is now time to test the product or service proposed against the five requirements in Phase 4. Perhaps you'll notice that more business travel than that you're ready for is needed for niche you had in mind. That indicates that one of the above conditions is not met-it will not carry you where you like to go. Scrap it, and pass on to the next proposal.

6. Test.

Test-market it until you have a balance between the niche and the product. "Give individuals an opportunity to purchase your product or service, not just theoretically, but actually put it out there." By giving samples, such as a complimentary mini-seminar or a preview copy of the newsletter, this can be accomplished. "If you spend enormous sums of cash on the initial trial run, you're possibly doing it wrong," she says. The research shouldn't cost you a bunch of money:

7. Go for it!

It is time for your idea to be implemented. This is the most challenging step for many entrepreneurs. But worry not: if you have done your research, it would be a measured risk to reach the business, not simply a chance.

Chapter 5. How to start dropshipping business in 2021

It's not easy to learn the way to start a dropshipping company, as with any type of business. Nevertheless, it's a perfect first move in the world of business. Without keeping any inventory, you may sell to customers. You do not have to pay upfront for goods. And if you are passionate about your new venture, in the long term, you will create a sustainable source of revenue.

In this complete dropshipping guide, suggest taking the following market and financial moves if you are considering dropshipping.

Others are mandatory from the start, and others are only a smart idea, so it will save you time and stress down the line by coping with them up front.

Dropshipping is a method of order fulfillment that helps shop owners to deliver without stocking any stock directly to buyers. If a consumer orders a commodity from a dropshipping shop, it is delivered directly to them by a third-party retailer. The client pays the selling price that you set, you pay the market price of the vendors, and the rest is benefit. You never need to maintain goods or spend in inventory.

You are responsible for designing a website and your own label, as well as selecting and promoting the items you choose to offer in the dropshipping business strategy. Your corporation is therefore liable for the expense of shipping and for setting rates that result in a reasonable profit margin.

Steps For Starting A Dropshipping Profitable Business

Learn to find high-margin products, introduce them to your business, and easily begin selling them.

1. Commit yourself for starting a dropshipping business

Dropshipping, as in any other business, needs considerable effort and a long-term focus. You're going to be deeply surprised if you're looking for a six-figure benefit from 6 weeks of part-time employment. You would be far less likely to get frustrated and leave by entering the organization with reasonable assumptions regarding the commitment needed and the prospects for benefit.

You'll need to spend heavily when beginning a dropshipping venture, utilizing one of the two following currencies: time or funds.

Investing time in dropshipping business

Our recommended strategy, particularly for the first dropshipping developers, is bootstrapping & investing sweat equity to develop your company. For various factors, we prefer this method over spending a huge amount of money:

- You will understand how the organization works inside out, which, as the enterprise expands and scales, will be crucial for handling others.

- You would know your clients and business personally, helping you to make smarter choices.

- You would be less inclined to waste huge amounts on vanity ventures that are not vital to success.

- You will build some new talents that will enable you a stronger entrepreneur.

Realistically, most persons are not ready to leave their work in order to ramp up their own online shop for six months. It might be a little more complicated, but even though you're already doing a 9-to-5 job, it's surely feasible to get underway with dropshipping, assuming you set reasonable standards for your customers about customer support and delivery times. When you continue to expand, as much as working capital and profitability allow, you will move into working long hours on your company.

Both companies and entrepreneurs are specific, but it is feasible to produce a monthly income stream of $1,000-$2,000 within 12 months of working around 10 to 15 hours per week to develop the firm.

Excited regarding starting a new business but not knowing where to begin? This informative guide will show you how to identify great products with strong sales potential that are newly trendy.

If you have the choice of working long hours on your company, that's the best option to increase your profit prospects and the possibility of good dropshipping. It is particularly beneficial in the early days to concentrate all the energies on publicity when creating traction is essential. It would normally take approximately 12 months of full-time jobs based on our knowledge, with a heavy focus on publicity for a dropshipping firm to replace an annual full-time salary of $50,000.

For a very small payout, it might sound like a lot of work, but bear these two points in mind:

When the dropshipping company is up and going, it would actually require considerably less time than from a 40-hour-per-week work to maintain it. In terms of the reliability and scalability that the dropshipping paradigm offers, much of your expenditure pays off.

You establish more than just a revenue stream when you develop a company. You also build an asset that you will market in the future. Be sure that when looking at the true return, you remember the equity valuation you are accruing, and also the cash flow produced.

Investing money in dropshipping business

By spending a lot of capital, it is feasible to develop and grow a dropshipping company, but we suggest against it. We attempted all methods to growing an enterprise (bootstrapping it ourselves vs. outsourcing the procedure), and while we were in the trenches doing much of the work, we had the most progress.

In the early stages, it is vital to have someone who is profoundly involved in the company's future to construct it from the ground up. You would be at the hands of pricey engineers, developers, and advertisers who will easily eat away whatever money you produce without knowing how your organization operates at any stage. You don't have to do everything it yourself, but at the start of your company, we highly advocate becoming the primary motivating power.

To have your company started and operating, you would, though, require a modest cash reserve in the $1,000 range. For limited administrative costs (like web hosting and dropshipping providers), you may need this and to pay some incorporation fees, which we will cover below.

2. Dropshipping business idea to chose

The second phase in studying how to launch a dropshipping company is to do the market research required. You want to find a niche you are interested in and make choices based on how effective it can be, almost like though you were starting a grocery shop and checking at the numerous sites, rivals, and developments. But the fact is, it's tricky to come up with product concepts to offer.

Niche goods also have a more passionate client base, which, through increasing awareness about the items, will make marketing to unique audiences simpler. A good entry point to begin dropshipping without cash could be health, clothes, makeup goods, appliances, phone accessories, or yoga-related pieces.

Any instances of dropshipping stores in a niche may be:

- Dog bow and ties for dog lovers

- Exercise equipment for fitness

- iPhone cases and cables for iPhone owners

- Camping gear for campers

To try the dropshipping business ideas, you may also use the appropriate techniques:

Google Trends could really help you identify whether, as well as the seasons in which they tend to trend, a product is trending up or down. Notice the search volume is not indicated by Google Patterns. But if you're using it, be sure to use a keyword tool such as Keywords Everywhere to cross-check your data to determine the popularity of the product in search.

3. Do competitor research

You want to check about your competitors so that you know what you're trying to sell in your shop and appreciate the way they operate. Your competitors may have great success hints which can help you develop a better marketing strategy for your dropshipping firm.

Limit your study to only five other dropshipping firms, like one or two major players such as Walmart or Ebay, if your business has a number of competitors (that is a positive thing in dropshipping). It will help you remain centered and prepare your next phase.

4. Choose a dropshipping supplier

Choosing a supplier for dropshipping is a crucial move towards creating a profitable dropshipping business. A dropshipping company does not have any goods to ship to consumers without vendors and would thus cease to operate.

At this stage, you analyzed what goods you want to offer and realize that they can be profitable, and you want to know where to find a provider of dropshipping that provides you with the high-quality service that you need to grow. By linking Oberlo to the online store, eCommerce platforms such as Shopify provide a plug-and-play style alternative to find possible suppliers.

5. Build your ecommerce store

An eCommerce platform such as Shopify is the next what you need to launch a dropshipping business. This is the home where you deliver traffic, offer goods, and payments are processed.

These type of platforms makes the e-commerce website simple to create and launch. It is a complete commerce service that connects you to sell and receive payments in several ways, like online, sell in different currencies, and conveniently manage products.

To use e-commerce websites, you don't need to become a programmer or developer either. They have resources to assist with anything from domain name ideas to logo design, and with the store creator and Payment processing themes, you are quickly able to modify the feel and look of your store.

6. Market your dropshipping store

It's time to talk about promoting your new shop, now that you know to start a dropshipping firm. You may want to bring more work into your marketing and promotional activities while developing the dropshipping business strategy to stick out in your market.

You will invest time working on selling and supporting the company in the following ways, with too many stuff about dropshipping being processed:

- Paid ads (Facebook & Google).

 For a Facebook ad, the average cost is about 0.97 cents per click, that's not too bad if you're new to social media advertising. Facebook ads are extensible, goods can perform ok on them, and they click into the desire of people to purchase momentum. You can run Google Shopping Ads and target lengthy keywords that are more likely to be purchased by shoppers. Typically, with Google ads, there is more price competition, but it might be worthy of your time to check it out.

- Influencer marketing.

You may have a low funds for marketing your business as a new dropshipper. Influencer marketing is also an affordable way to target audience because individuals are more likely than traditional advertising to trust influencers. When you go this route, start negotiating an affiliate fee versus a flat rate with the influencer. It's a win-win situation, as every sale they're going to make money off, and the cost is going to be less for you.

- Mobile marketing.

Smartphone marketing is a broad term referring to a company that connects with clients on their mobile phones. You can start with a VIP text club, for example, and encourage website users to sign up for the exclusive promotions & deals. Or provide client support through Messenger in a live chat session with shoppers. You can create automated qualified leads, customer loyalty, and cart abandonment campaigns with a mobile marketing tool such as ManyChat to drive sales and profits for your dropshipping business.

Stay updated on what channels are operating and which are not, as with any profitable online business, especially if you invest money in them like paid ads. You can always adjust your marketing plan to lower costs as well as maximize revenue as you keep growing and improve your business.

7. Analyze your offering

You should start looking at the consequences of your diligent work after you've been promoting and operating your dropshipping company for some time. Any analytics will help you address some critical online shop queries, like:

- Sales

What are my channels with the highest performance? Where am I expected to put more ad dollars? What else are my favorite items for sale? What are my greatest clients?

- Behavior of shoppers

Do citizens buy more on their laptops or cell phones? For each unit, what's the conversion rate?

- Margins of profit

Why are the most profitable pieces and variant SKUs? What do my month-over-month revenue and gross income look like?

To track web traffic over time and optimize your search engine optimization activities, you can even use resources like Google Analytics & Search Console. Plus, you review the results monthly to guarantee that your overall plan succeeds with your business, whether you are utilizing third-party software for your social network or messenger marketing.

You want to build a data-informed analytics framework while building a dropshipping e-commerce store. Remain compatible with what you evaluate over time and calculate the consistency of your store against simple KPIs. This will encourage you to make better choices for your store, so move your small business over time to the next level.

Chapter 6. How To identify Best Suppliers For Your New Dropshipping Business

Dropshipping is a model for eCommerce that is increasingly attractive. That is because launching a dropshipping company is simpler (not to say less expensive) than managing inventory for a traditional digital storefront.

The whole model of drop shipment is focused on the retailer doing its job well and delivering orders timely and effectively. It goes without saying, therefore, that identifying the appropriate supplier is one, if not the most important, and a step towards creating a successful brand. If an order is messed up by your supplier/seller, you and your organization are liable, so the trick is to find someone who adheres to the schedule and is open to discuss any problems

The advantages and disadvantages of dropshipping are well known, but it has become far less obvious that the most significant part of beginning a dropshipping business is choosing the right vendors for your WooCommerce shop. Until now.

6.1 The Importance of Selecting The Right Suppliers

A special model for eCommerce is Dropshipping. To retain their own inventories, conventional online retailers compensate. Those expenses are all but offset by dropshipping, so dropshipping would not need substantial start-up investment.

In the other side, dropshipping suggests that you place the destiny of your eCommerce store in the possession of others.

With the dropshipping system, retailers focus on wholesalers, manufacturers, and dealers who meet the orders of the retailers.

The dropshipping puzzle has several parts, and for the greater image, each component is critical. Among those pieces, one of the most significant is dropshipping suppliers. In reality, the finest dropshippers know that a dropshipping eCommerce store can make or break the efficiency and overall reliability of dropshipping suppliers.

6.2 Finding Your Dropshipping Suppliers

It needs you to partner with manufacturers, wholesalers, & distributors to start a dropshipping business. You want to identify vendors who improve the dropshipping business rather than compromise it.

Research Your Products

You have to figure out what types of things you can sell before you can start finding and working with vendors.

You want to address queries in specific, such as:

- Where does the item come from?

- How long would manufacturing take?

- How is it done?

Are there factors of height or weight which might make fulfillment more complicated or more costly?

The purpose is not expertise; however, you want to get to know the goods so that you can help determine which ones are suitable for dropshipping.

Understand the supply chain and recognize the considerations

You need to get familiar with dropship supply chain after nailing down your goods. In other terms, you should to know how it works for dropshipping.

For dropshipping, the items never really go into the hands of the dealer. Instead, an order is issued by the retailer, and a supplier who manages packing and delivery initiates fulfillment. In this way, the dealer is like the director of a dropshipping company.

You can't sell goods if you don't have reputable vendors, which suggests that you don't have a dropshipping business.

You need to get familiar with dropship supply chain since nailing down your products. In other terms, you need to understand how it functions for dropshipping.

For dropshipping, the items never really go into the hands of the dealer. Instead, an order is issued by the retailer and a supplier who manages packing and delivery initiates fulfilment. In this manner, the retailer is just like the director of a dropshipping company.

You can't sell goods if you don't have reputable suppliers, which suggests that you don't have a dropshipping business.

Search for Dropshipping Wholesalers on Google

You will identify the major vendors for your preferred commodities or product types with a Google search.

When you build a preliminary list, by studying the next few queries, take notice of the various characteristics of dropshipping suppliers.

- What is supplier location?

- Will the retailer link with your WooCommerce shop so that fresh orders are immediately submitted for fulfillment?

- What (if any) is the sum of minimum order (MOQ)?

- What support (e.g., mobile, email, chat, etc.) does the provider offer?

- What kind of range of items does the retailer offer?

Subscribe to Dropshipping Suppliers Directories

And if lots of choices pop up in the Google searches, directories will bring even more options. For a broad selection of items, these repositories comprise of web lists of dropshipping vendors and wholesalers.

You should recognize that some of the finest are premium directories, such as Salehoo and Worldwide Labels, implying they need paying subscriptions. There are a lotof free directories accessible that you can access at no fee, like Wholesale Central. Free directories, though, are occasionally obsolete. Newer vendors do not exist, and suppliers are also listed who are no longer in operation.

Usually, premium directories vary in cost from $20 a month for lifetime access to a few hundred bucks. You can find the expense of a premium directory to be beneficial, with free directories often hit-

or-miss. There are also premium directories, like Doba, explicitly customized for dropshipping.

Figure Out Your Competitor's Suppliers

It follows that you must see what your competitors do if you want to be successful in the dropshipping field. Do any acknowledgment, in fact, to see which manufacturers are meeting their requirements.

There are a lot of methods to do this, but testing the markets that the competitors sell is the best.

If the supplier is not listed on the page, by making your own order, you will always show the supplier. Since the retailer is pleased, an invoice or packaging slip from them would possibly be included with the shipment. To ask about a partnership with your own dropshipping company, you can then contact the supplier directly.

Attend Trade Seminars

Trade shows have been considered to be an efficient place for manufacturers to set up and grow their companies. So, if you haven't been to a trade seminar yet, add it to the end of the list of to-do events.

You network with other participants within dropship supply chain, like distributors and dropshipping wholesalers, at trade shows. You get an insider's view on current and future products that you should introduce to your online store. For dropshipping businesses, you even get to "talk shop" face-to-face, which is also the most successful way to do business.

Join Industry Groups and Networks

Trade shows facilitate with locating vendors for dropshipping firms, yet another effective resource is business networks and groups.

The majority of retailers, like the identities of their dropshipping vendors, are not willing to share the secrets of their performance. The individuals who enter business groups, however, want to share, learn, & develop. Through being part of the dropshipping network, you will get valuable insight from industry professionals. Your colleagues, for instance, might recommend better suppliers or alert you about suppliers in order to avoid.

Connect with the Manufacturers

Not all manufacturers supply to consumers directly, although there are those who do. Until picking vendors for your eCommerce dropshipping shop, suggest reaching out to the producers of the goods that you will market.

You have far higher margins when a producer chooses to be the distributor than with a traditional retailer or wholesaler. Manufacturers, on the other hand, frequently impose minimum order amounts that could need bigger orders. You might find yourself with considerable inventory to deal in this situation, which is intended to circumvent dropshipping.

Ask the vendor to recommend vendors for you if a manufacturer won't work with you. A recommendation, after all, indicates that the agreements and commitments between a manufacturer and a supplier is successful. For that cause, it is definitely worth putting suggested vendors on your list of possibilities.

Order Samples

There's no substitution for firsthand knowledge, no matter how many feedback or testimonials you find. This is why ordering samples is the next phase in finding the correct dropshipping suppliers for the business.

Ordering samples teaches you a few key things about a supplier. First one is that you get to know the product's consistency yourself.

The second is that you will see how delivery is done by the retailer, and what shipment packaging seems to if a different vendor is involved, and how long it takes to ship and distribute. Suppliers will execute the requests, so buying samples provides you with an idea of what your clients will feel.

Confirm Contract Terms & Fees

You compiled several options, removed any but the most suitable possibilities, ordered tests to assess certain vendors, and decided on your dropshipping company with the right supplier (or suppliers). Negotiating deal conditions and payments is the last option left to do.

New businesses with unproven consumer bases have fewer bargaining leverage relative to mature companies with established customer bases. When it comes to communicating the margins, this is especially true.

Since dropshipping means that you don't have to hold your inventory, there would be low margins. The bulk of inventory costs and expenditures involved with meeting your orders is borne by your supplier(s). With dropshipping, because prices are smaller, gross margins are often lower than if you stored and delivered orders personally.

With margins generally poor, the fees concerned may be the biggest distinction between vendors. Such suppliers, for instance, charge flat per-order rates that are applied to the overall cost of the goods. Per-order payments typically vary from $2 and $5 to cover delivery and shipping costs (although big or unwieldy goods can require higher fees).

In the end, you want to select the supplier(s) that satisfies your specifications and give contracts of appropriate terms.

Chapter 7. Setting Up Your Dropshipping business On A Budget

The establishment of a dropshipping company as an eCommerce business is a perfect way to earn money. Managing a business without the hassle of product and shipping logistics is the most convincing aspect of a dropshipping store

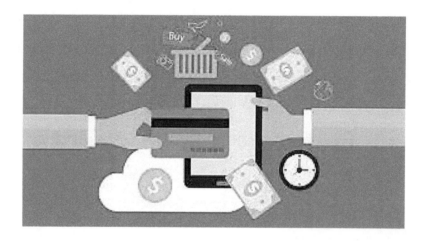

You have already heard stories from businessmen about how costly it is to start a business. This involve accounts of hopelessly pursuing buyers or firms failing because of bleak financials to remain afloat. Do not let this scare you from launching a dropshipping store, as this model enables you to offer low-risk products.

What you need to do is get the orders and call the supplier-the rest is up to them.

There are very few financial barriers associated with the establishment of a dropshipping store when it comes to financing the company. In fact, with around zero initial investment, you can get underway with an online store.

Here's a 7-step feasible plan for launching a dropshipping shop on a budget shoestring.

1. Research Your Options

You'll need to do some research before beginning some form of business.

It requires getting online and finding out the competitors that offer related goods. To see just what each has to suggest, you'll also want to spend a little time investigating the future vendors and distributors.

Each shipping group will have a specific way of doing stuff and pricing models, therefore pay careful attention to those specifics so that you can ensure that you team up with your dropshipping store with the right party.

2. Create a Plan to Stick

You'll need to get a solid plan in progress before you can launch your business activities. A budget is used with this. It's important to decide what your budget is, whether you have $100 or $500 to get underway and ensure that you adhere to it. The easiest way to achieve so is to maintain good track of all your spending to guarantee that as you start up your store, you do not go over the budget.

3. Find Your Niche

In reality, many believe that it is an impossible task. It may be really challenging to appeal to all. Instead, rather than attempting to market could product under the sun, choose the goods focused on a particular niche.

Select a particular area of the business, such as organic pet food or dog clothes, if you decide that you want to market animal-related items.

When you can refine your attention down, you can have a much higher sales rate, and you are more likely to be noticed when customers are looking for a particular form of a product. Your small shop can get lost in the noise of competitors if your focus is too big.

4. Set Up Your eCommerce website

This is the phase through which you finally launch and set up your site with a dropshipping store.

Three of the most successful eCommerce sites accessible to sellers today are Shopify and Wix. It's quick to get started, as well as its user-friendly interface, also for sellers who are not especially tech-savvy, makes configuration and maintenance easy.

With monthly prices of less than $40, Shopify and Wix are both inexpensive alternatives, making it a perfect way to get off on a budget in the digital marketplace. You may also open a Modalyst store to boost the delivery and streamline the distribution process.

You're able to move on to the next stage after you have set up a simple online storefront that has your products selected.

5. Make Meetings With Your Suppliers

When it comes to choosing which provider to use it for your dropshipping shop, there are lots of decisions out there. Because you've done your homework in phase one already, now is the moment where your decision is formalized. Through entering into a contract with the commodity distributor(s) of your choosing, you will do so. Any of the most successful shipping partners makes it simple to get started, and in no time, unlike having to pay such upfront costs, you will be on your way.

The most relevant issues you are asking your prospective suppliers are:

- Do you keep all products in stock?

- How do you care the returns?

- What is your normal or average processing time?

- In which areas do you ship to? Do international shipping available?

- What kind of support did you offer?

- Is there any limit for orders?

You would have a solid understanding about how your suppliers conduct their company until you meet a supplier who addresses certain questions to your satisfaction. In addition, as a seller dealing for them, you'll realize what you need to do. You're on the path to a successful working partnership at this point.

6. Start Selling

Oh, congratulations. In launching your online store, this is one of most exciting steps. It's time to add your product details to your website and start selling until you have all your arrangements and agreements in order.

If customers are not aware of the products, you will not have enough sales, to begin with. You'll want to waste more time and money on ads if this is the case. By beginning with low-cost advertisements on Instagram and Facebook, or advertising on blogs as well as other websites which have a common audience, you will keep advertising costs reasonably small.

7. Optimize Your Site

You should take some time to customize the website until you have some revenue and knowledge under your belt. You can do all this earlier in the process, but waiting to see what is really working before you start to make changes is often a good idea.

There are a broad variety of customization choices for sites such as Shopify and Modalyst, including templates that change the way your website looks and plugins to can customize how your website works. The primary aim here is to tweak the site in ways that make it smoother for your clients and more organized.

As you've seen, all it takes to set up an online store is a few steps, and most of them don't need any money. You're not lonely if you're excited about being an owner of an eCommerce company just don't have a ton of money to launch with. This is why so many platforms are accessible that make it easier to get started without investing a million in the process.

Making sure that it works and prepare a strategy that you will use to guide you when keeping under your budget by setting up your dropshipping business, no matter how small it might be.

Chapter 8. Mistakes To Avoid When Developing Your Dropshipping Business

In an environment that jumps at the chance to make a business deal quick and convenient, Dropshipping tends to have a no for retailers. It might seem like, now, acquiring the goods and marketing with a bit of savvy are your only worries. Yet, if you wish to hold the company afloat, you should not forget about the client's perspective. True, the boring duties of inventory, order filling, and then ensuring shipping can be passed on.

The dropshipping company, however, does not waste any time thinking about the feelings of your client. How do you assume if your client is going to be satisfied? The buyers are the ones who put the money back. Anything falls out the window if they're not satisfied. You would need to consider the duties and what failures typically trigger it all to backfire in order to completely enjoy the advantages of utilizing dropshipping.

Here are a common mistake that leads to the failure end of your dropshipping business, so you should hold these mistakes in mind all the time.

1. Worrying About Shipping Costs.

While shipping costs might be a doozy, it's never productive to stress. In this area, you will need to decide under which your priorities lie. Shipping prices can vary all over the board, depending on where orders come from. This stress can be relieved by setting a flat rate and generally evens out with time. Not only does this make things easier for you, but it's also simple and easy for customers.

2. Relying Much on Vendors.

By putting much trust in such a vendor, a good number of crises can arise. For example, they may go out of business or increase their rates on you if you only use one vendor. They might run out of the items that you expect them to supply. Where would you be then? This is why there should always be a backup for you. It is smart to write up the contract with your vendors for your own insurance to remain aware of your requirements. This will ensure that everyone involved has agreed to uphold what you demand.

3. Expecting Easy Money.

Dropshipping, as we've already established, offers a degree of ease that can seem to make your work easier. Yet, you can't ignore how critical your product is in marketing and all the competition you're going to face. This involves analysis and the creation of a unique approach that will allow the product more attractive than that of anyone else.

4. Making Order Difficult to Access.

When you assure your consumers a simple and quick procedure, they'll want to see the proofs. Set approximate location-based ship dates and require suppliers to keep you posted on the status of the order so that you can keep the consumer aware. This way, you can track shipments whenever you anticipate them to come longer than expected and easily fix issues.

5. Not Enough Brand Display.

Through dropshipping, it may be hard to guarantee the brand remains to be seen in the customer's overall experience. You may not want people to forget regarding you, so it's important to insert as many locations as possible into your brand. You should have customized packing slips, stickers and custom exterior packaging to hold the name included after delivery. Sending a follow-up thank you message or a survey to remind about of you and prove them you think for their feedback at the same time is also not a bad idea.

6. Return Complications.

If you do not have a system for returns set up, things can get messy very quickly. You and your vendor will have to establish a refund policy to avoid this. Customers are going to wait for their refund expectantly, and being disorganized on that front and will not make them feel good. They may also need guidelines explaining how or where to return the product. Organizing a structure for this will save a good amount of confusion and irritation for both you and the client.

7. Selling Trademarked Products

When most people learn about dropshipping and realize that it is not that complicated to do the process, they picture all the things they might sell and make a quick buck.

Many of these goods are items which have been trademarked by a manufacturer. Selling these goods without the manufacturer's specific consent to be a retail agent will lead you to legal issues. This can not only lead to the end of your online shop, but you can also be held personally responsible.

You should, consequently, look at generic items which you can add to your variety of products for sale. Best still, you should swap in goods with white marks. They are plain goods that are available to those who rebrand them through the manufacturer. You will order and get these items customized to suit the brand and display them.

8. Picking the Wrong Field

Once you have abandoned thoughts of selling any product you come across, by concentrating on one field, you can develop your dropshipping business.

You might, however, select the wrong niche in which to operate. Maybe you should pick a niche that isn't lucrative. This may be that it's out of vogue or it's simply not meant for shopping online.

Therefore, to see what will earn you money, you have to do proper market analysis. "Market research" might sound like a complex process in which only major brands participate.

Simple Google searches will, therefore, show you what individuals are interested in and where they purchase them.

9. Poor Relationship With Suppliers

Your vendors are part of your business; they promise that you have the best goods and that they supply your consumers with them. You can be inclined, though, to consider them as workers and handle them as though they are in the hierarchy on a lower rung.

They're not. They are your friends, without whom it would be effectively dead for your dropshipping business. Therefore, you can establish a better relationship with them.

This will have its benefits. When negotiating costs for commodity stock, a strong partnership will work in your favor.

10. Lowering Price To Extreme Levels

Reducing your prices to knock out your competition is also one of the dropshipping failures to avoid.

This is a logical way for you to rise your dropshipping business, you might think. You could have been no farther from the facts. Very low prices indicate to potential customers that your product may be of poor quality.

11. Poor Website Structure

The progress of your dropshipping company depends on the shopping experience your clients have when they browse your online store.

Thus, you have to make sure everything is convenient for them. However, you could rush through the process of establishing your website due to low barrier for entrance into dropshipping. Many beginners do not have the coding skills required to construct an online store.

In conclusion, the primary interest is the customer's experience. Although inventory management and shipping are not your responsibility, you can also ensure that all is well handled. All of these dropshipping failures can be prevented with adequate preparation and careful management, and the business can better manage.

Chapter 9. Smooth Running tips for Your Dropshipping Business

Well, you've done your research, decided to agree on the right dropship goods and roped in the right possible supplier. All of you are planned to begin dropshipping goods and make the mullah! Setting up the company, though, is typically one thing, but a totally different ball game is to manage it on a day-to-day basis. Even if it's a dropshipping company, there are various facets of running a business that you have to remember as a retailer: marketing, refunds, refunds, repairs, inventory, distribution, customer service, and far more. So dive into all these different aspects of managing a dropshipping business.

So far, when covered a lot of details, it involves everything from the fundamentals of dropshipping to the nuances of finding a niche and managing the business. You should have much of a base by now to begin investigating and establishing your own dropshipping company comfortably.

It's possible to get confused and lose track about what's really necessary, with too much to consider. That's why we've built this list of key elements for success. This are the main "must-do" acts that can make the new company or ruin it. If you can perform these effectively, you would be able to get a bunch of other stuff wrong and yet have a decent probability of success.

1.Add Value

The most important performance element is making a good roadmap on how you will bring value to your clients. In the field of dropshipping, where you can contend with legions of other "me too" stores carrying related items, this is critical for both corporations, but even more so.

With dropshipping, it's reasonable to think you're marketing a product to consumers. Yet good small merchants realize that they are offering insights, ideas and solutions, not just the commodity they deliver. You assume you're an e-commerce seller, but you're in the information industry as well.

If you can't create value by quality data and advice, price is the only thing you're left to contend on. While this has been an effective technique for Walmart, it will not help you grow a successful company for dropshipping.

2.Focus on SEO and marketing

The opportunity to push traffic to the new platform is a near second to providing value as a main key factor. A shortage of traffic to their sites is the #1 concern and annoyance faced by modern e-commerce retailers. So many retailers have been slaving away on the ideal platform for months just to unleash it into a community that has no clue it exists.

For the success of your company, advertising and driving traffic is completely necessary and challenging to outsource well, particularly if you have a limited budget and bootstrap your business. In order to build your own SEO, publicity, outreach and guest posting abilities, you have to consider taking the personal initiative.

Within the first 6 - 12 months, where no one know who you are, this is particularly crucial. You need to devote at least 75 percent of your time on publicity, SEO and traffic development for at least 4 to 6 months after your website launch, which is right, 4 to 6 months. You can start reducing and coast a little on the job you put in until you've built a strong marketing base. But it's difficult, early on, to bring so much emphasis on advertising.

3.Marketing Your Dropshipping Business

Marketing is indeed a subjective field, and that there are a billion strategies which can be used to position your brand successfully whilst driving awareness and sales of your brand. It will even help you root out the remainder of the market if the approach is well planned.

4.Social Media Source

Social networking is one of the most efficient ways to promote, advertise, attract clients and share content, so when social networks are now used for digital marketing, it comes as no surprise. For example, Facebook has more than 1.7 billion active members from diverse walks of life, and it is this diversity that makes it so appealing to online marketers.

One thing to note is that it's important to content. No matter how perfect a platform is or how good the product you are offering is, without high quality content backing it up, it means nothing.

5.Customer Ratings & Reviews

A few bad customer ratings will actually ruin a business in dropshipping business model. Think about it: As you order online from websites like ebay and aliexpress, the quality ranking and what other consumers had to tell about it will be one of the determining purchase variables, too, with decrease delivery. A few positive feedback will also give you an advantage over the competition because that is what will help you convert traffic to your website successfully.

6.Email Marketing

In a digital marketer's pack, this one of the most neglected tools. To keep your clients in the loop for any major changes within company, email marketing may be used: Price increases, promotions, coupons, content related to the commodity, and content unique to the industry are only some of the forms email marketing may be utilized.

7.Growth Hacking

Growth hacking is a cheap but highly productive way to get online creative marketing campaigns. A few definitions of growth hacking involve retargeting old campaigns and featuring in your own niche as a guest writer for a popular website. Any of this commonly involves content marketing.

Chapter 10. How To Maximize Your Chances Of Success?

There are only a couple more tips you should adopt to maximize the chances of long-term growth if you are willing to take the plunge and attempt dropshipping. Second, that doesn't mean you can approach a dropshipping business because it's risk-free simply because there are no setup costs involved with purchasing and managing goods. You're also spending a lot of time choosing the right dropshippers while designing your website, so consider it as an investment and do careful preliminary research.

1. Things To Remember

What do you want to sell? How profitable is the surroundings? How can you gain clients and distinguish yourself? Inside the same room, is there a smaller niche that is less competitive? When they find a particular market and curate their goods like a pro, most individuals who operate a purely dropshipping model have seen the most growth, ensuring that any last item they offer is a successful match for their niche audience with their brand.

After you develop your list of possible dropshippers, carry out test orders and then watch for the items to arrive, thinking like a consumer. How long can any order take? What is the feeling of unboxing like? What is the commodity standard itself? This will help you distinguish between possible dropshippers or confirm that positive consumer service is offered by the one you want.

Note that the goods themselves may not be the differentiator for your business.

After you have chosen your dropshippers and products, note that the products themselves may not be the differentiator for your business. So ask what else you should count on to make the deal. This is another explanation why test orders are a wonderful idea since they encourage you to obtain the item and explain its functionality and advantages as a client might. In a way which really shows it off, you can even take high-quality, professional pictures of the product. Armed with exclusive explanations of the goods and images that are separate from all the other product photos, you would be able to start standing out.

Your bread and butter is definitely going to be a well-executed campaign strategy, so devote time and money on each section of it, from finding your potential audience to interacting with influencers on social media in your niche. Targeted commercials can be a perfect way to kick start your site to bring your name on the mind of your client base.

When it relates to your return policies, delivery contact and customer support, ensure your ducks are in a line. You'll need to do what you could to serve as the buffer between a dropshipper and your client if something goes wrong somewhere in the process. Understand the typical cost of return for each item so that you will notice whether it is large enough to denote a quality issue. If you suspect a consistency problem, talk to your dropshipper or try a different supplier to your issues.

Eventually, note that dropshipping is not a model of "all or nothing." Many of the more profitable corporations follow a hybrid model, making or shipping in-house some goods and employing dropshippers to fill the gaps. The dropshippers are not the key profit-drivers for these firms but are instead a simple, inexpensive way to provide clients with the "extras" they can enjoy. Before you put it in-house, you can even use dropshipped products for upsells, impulse sales, or to try a new model.

As long as you consider the above tips to ensuring that the one you chose is suitable for your business needs, there is definitely a lot to learn from the streamlining and flexibility of using a dropshipper. You will make your dropshipping store run for you in no time with a little of research, negotiation, and setup!

Conclusion

So that concludes our definitive dropshipping guide. You now learn how to set up to kick start your new dropshipping business if you've made it here. Starting up your own business often involves a certain degree of dedication, effort, and ambition to make things work, much as in every other undertaking in life. It's not only about building the business but also about pushing through and knowing how to manage it on a daily basis.

The greatest feature of dropshipping is that you will practice in real-time by checking your goods and concepts, and all you have to do is drop it from your shop if anything doesn't work. This business concept is indeed a perfect opportunity for conventional business models to try out product concepts. Dropshipping creates a secure place to innovate to see what happens without incurring any substantial damages that will surely give business owners the courage to state that they have a working idea of how the market works. The dropshipping business model is an interesting business model to move into with little initial expense and relatively little risk.

A perfect choice to drop shipping if you are only starting to sell online and would like to test the waters first. It's a great way to start your business, even if the margins are low.

As dropshipping can still get started with little investment, before they build their market image, businessmen can start with that too.

Ecommerce sites such as Ebay, Shopify, Alibaba and social networking, such as Instagram, Twitter, Reddit, provide vast expertise in user base and content marketing. It also helps newbies to know about establishing an online store, optimizing conversions, generating traffic and other basics of e-commerce.

That's what you need to learn about beginning a dropshipping. Just note, it's not the hard part to launch your dropshipping store, the real challenge is when you get trapped, and your stuff is not being sold. Do not panic, and keep checking as it happens. You're going to get a product soon that sells well.

Youtube, Tik-Tok and Instagram Made Easy

A Collection of Filters, Entertaining Topics and Viral Trends to Gain 10k Followers and Generate Passive Income

By

Vishen Smith

Table of Contents

Introduction

Don't think you can compete against millions of creators and influencers? Well, let's set one thing straight, not only can you do it but also how you can do it. Working smarter, not necessarily harder, makes all the difference.

This book is for those who wish to make a name of themselves by leaving behind a reputation, legacy on social media platforms. Or maybe, all you want is to be able to do what you love for a living and offer that to the world. Either way, you're in the right place.

If you haven't been able to make much of a passive income from these social platforms for a while now, you should know it's probably not you; it's the platform. This book aims toprovide an insight into these social platforms by teaching you how to increase your audience by changing some basic habits and teach you a few new tips, tricks, and tactics you can use by first understanding their working. 10,000 is perhaps the right number of followers to be considered literally as an influencer/brand, get paying offers, and raise your account's value.

It may be sluggish as you try to win the starting few followers, but it does get a little easier after that. Understanding the algorithm plays a crucial role in enlarging your audience. YouTube, Tik Tok, and Instagram use algorithms to recommend various creators. Once you understand how their algorithms work, you can easily reach a larger variety of users. By gaining an active audience of about 10K, YouTube, Tik Tok, and Instagram may consider paying attention to your content, and you could even gain more than 10,000 depending on your consistency.

Now, you are probably thinking "easier said than done", right? Well, don't worry, this book is solely there to make these things easier. To provide a how-to gain 10K followers quickly, An easy-to-use reference to aid your growth on social media platforms (i.e., YouTube, Tik Tok, and Instagram.)

Try not to read this book as a novel; rather, truly study it and apply it in your daily practices to notice change and improvement in your channel/account/profile growth.

First, this book will teach you why earning a passive income through YouTube, Tik Tok, and Instagram is the way to go, especially in this day and age, next, how each platform has its own way of working and different method to win over the platform to your side. And then, if you're having a tough time generating content for these platforms, the last part will teach you how you can remove your creativity block and let yourmuse come to you.Last but not least, Afterthoughts will give you that push you need to get cracking, radiating motivation and energy to really get you started.

CHAPTER I: Why it's One of the Best Ways to Earn

In current times, the Internet is available in almost every part of the world. People interact, learn, and enjoy through platforms. More specifically, YouTube, Tik Tok, and Instagram. Since 2020, most people have spent their time at home, and so usage of these social media platforms has grown excessively. People discovered hidden talents, curiosity, and inspiration so much more than before.

Even if people hadn't spent half their time on their phones or other electronic devices, there are so many advantages of working on YouTube, Tik Tok, and Instagram for a passive income.

1.1: Freedom of Speech

YouTube, Tik Tok, and Instagram are the kind of social media platforms that allow an individual to really do anything and everything they want, needless to say, as long as they follow community guidelines.

"I do not agree with what you have to say, but I'll defend to the death your right to say it." ~ Voltaire

From a thriller,a short film to kids toy reviews, from gameplays to reactions, whatever.These are platforms where even the smallest of people have a voice, and they can make it known. Your creativity can literally pay the bills and put food on the table. And there can always be an endless supply of creativity, that is if you know where to look.

What could you possibly want more than being able to do what you love for a living? It's the ideal dream.And there are so many advantages of being able to do what you enjoy for a living.

High Efficiency

You become more useful and productive with your work as you can be excited for the next day. Your work won't even feel like a job,and so you would find yourself more relaxed as it wouldn't feel like a burden, finding other things to do in your spare time would be exciting too.

Inspiration

When you're having a tough time, doing what you love can spark inspiration and motivation in you. Once you feel inspired, your ideas run like a high-qualitycar engine, and it can sometimes even get difficult to do all these amazing things you have in mind.

New Perspectives

When you are following a boring schedule every single day and spend most of your time thinking about what you would do once the weekends here, you should realize you're doing it wrong. When working on a social media platform, you don't have a boss; in fact, you are your own boss, much like running a business. You set timings that are best suited for your work, and as being a public figure is constantly exciting, you won't find yourself in the same routine each day. Sure, you would probably have some ups and downs, but at the end of the day, you work for your own satisfaction and so view life from a different point of view than those who work solely because they feel they have no choice.

Better Wellbeing

Working on your chosen niche on these social platforms sounds fun and enjoyable, and it is. What you probably didn't know that being happy is great for your health. In fact, it's a lot cheaper than being miserable and stressed for everyday of your life. It even relieves all that stress, mental and physical tension.

1.2: Fame

An Audience

Working on being a public figure or influencer gives you an audience that cares for you; they show an interest in your content. It could make you a role model for them, or they see your content to put a smile on their faces, it could help them in some basic struggles they didn't know they had until they saw your work.

Your followers/subscribers may value your opinions on certain topics and appreciates you and your content in the respective niche. And being validated for your effort would make anyone happy.

They even help you grow by giving honest feedback and so you can easily tell what it is they like about your content.

Opportunities

Fame grants you several chances to work with well-known brands or companies. Whether that be in sponsored advertisements or partnerships for products(i.e., perfume, apparel, electronic gadgets, games, etc.)

For example,maybe you're a sports-focused content creator, you could get offers from sportswear companies to model with their products!

Not only brands but also popular public figures would notice you, and you'd be given numerous opportunities to work with them, especially if you're in the same niche as them. When an already successful creator acknowledges and validates your content, they bring in their fans to your work, ultimately broadening your audience.

Forinstance, YouTuber Lilly Singh, also known as superwoman, grew so big on YouTube that she now hosts a late-night show called "A Little Late with Lilly Singh" on NBC. She not onlyreleased a film that entailed her world tour but also a book named "How to Be aBawse: A Guide to Conquering Life," which made it to New York Times best-seller list. She also won a substantial number of rewards on multiple award shows over the years and made her own music videos, and so much more.Her Niche? Entertainment.And it's an understatement to say she entertained.

@lilly with @malala Via Instagram

Of course, it didn't come easy to her, but with time, her channel grew and not only on YouTube but also across other platforms like Instagram.

Like her, once you obtain that loyal audience, you could try new things whenever you want, but not too much, or you may drive your audience away. You'd be able to work on creative projects. (i.e., Liza Koshy acted in a tv show and other showbiz related content, PewDiePe who made not one but two games with another company as well as a YouTube original show called "Scare PewDiePie", Joey Graceffa who made his own YouTube original show called "Escape the Night".)

1.3: Money

The obvious reason for earning through YouTube, Tik Tok, and Instagram? The Money.Succeeding on any social platform often promises good fortune. Influencers often buy new cars, houses, editors to help them with their work, maybe even a new oven!

You'd finally be able to finish that bucket list. Get something for the people you care about! And most importantly, once you get that money you've been waiting for, be grateful and don't take it for granted.

YouTubers like Lilly Singh made use of their money by making her profile a little more professional by hiring a team and basically becoming a CEO of her team. A lot of influencers do live charity streams, raise money, or donate for the poor and needy in several ways as well.Well, that's not all she did with her money she spent it for fun too as I'm sure you can as well do whatever you want with it.

Merchandising

You would be able to sell your own products, which would be your signature merch (people would recognize it as yours). Often influencers get sweatshirts, T-shirts, caps, posters, phone covers, etc. This increases your profits as well as advertising yourself. You get something to represent yourself with and receive more recognition.

CHAPTER II: YouTube

2.1: How it Works

To know how to easily get 10,000 subscribers on YouTube, you first need to be able to understand the YouTube software's working and how you can use it to your advantage.

Video

YouTube is a free space where creators can store videos, pictures, and posts. But their main focus is the videos that various people of all types upload. Google owns it, and its search engine is the second largest around the globe. YouTube videos can be embedded into other websites as well.

Moreover, YouTube recommends videos that are viewed by a similar audience to the one a user is currently watching.

Being successful through YouTube won't happen in a week. You have to be prepared to go through the rough patches as well as the smooth ones.

Analytics

There is a reporting, and self-service analytics tool on YouTube which provides intel regarding every video you upload so YouTube can help you easily keep track of how many views each video receives, what type of people are watching your content (age group, where they are from, and such).

It can provide data about:

1. The age groups and genders it is commonly seen by.

2. The statistics: comments, ratings, and views.

3. The countries your content is mostly seen in.

4. The first time your video was recommended to a user, either when they are watching something similar or when your video was recommended when they search a keyword.

5. In the first instance, your video was embedded in a website by a third party.

Advertising

YouTube embeds features that allow various businesses to promote their content to users who may have an interest in it, aiming at clients by subject and demographics.

The advertisers pay you each time someone in your audience views their Ad. They can decide the areas in which the Ad will show, the amount of payment, and the format.

Channels

Create your own niche, don't constantly jump from one genre to another, or your audience will never remain consistent.

2.2: The Content

Watch Time

Videos that consist of a higher watch time get recommended frequently on the main YouTube homepage. So how do you increase it? Pattern Interrupts.

These result in making your videos more vibrant, which prolongs the viewers' attention span.

A pattern interrupt can be jump cuts, graphics, different camera angles, and cheesy humor. It can put a smile on the watcher's face or catch them off guard, which keeps them watching.

Trends

Keeping up with the current times is vital for small channels to grow. Trends are one of the catalysts of increasing your audience.

PewDiePie Via YouTube

As of February 2021,most YouTubers stream live, do how-to tutorials, DIY's, etc.

Things like the chubby bunny challenge, Reddit reactions (cross-platform), spicy foods challenge, etc., gives more room for the creator and audience to get to know one another. The goal is to make them feel like your friend, so they feel comfortable enough to come back.

Create longer videos.

Making long videos (10+ minutes) actually gives your video a higher rank in YouTube's search results in most cases. Of course, if you make the video longer with not much to add, then it will still be lowly ranked as users will prefer not to waste their time.

And definitely avoid making videos longer than an hour because it's likely the viewers' attention gets diverted.

Like, Share, and Subscribe

At any point of the video, remind your viewers to subscribe, but make sure you don't keep mentioning that along with 'Like, Share, and hit the notification bell' as this tends to irritate the viewers due to the fact that they just want to watch the video. Keep the message short and maybe even humorous to attract the viewers.

Link more videos at the end.

If the users watch more of *your* content, they will probably subscribe. So, promoting your videos will definitely increase the chances of them watching it as it would be convenient for them to just click on that instead of going to your channel and surfing through there.

Quality over Quantity

Viewers can never be fooled by the number of videos you upload every week, they value the effort and time put into each piece of content, and they are well aware that you are as human as they are.

Do try maintaining a schedule just to let your viewers know when they can expect a video, but don't force it, or it will not be valued.

Thumbnail and Video Title

Your thumbnails should be eye-catching and interesting, as it is the first thing they see when they are introduced to your channel. It's your first impression. Make sure it's a high-quality image.

If it's a professional website, a simple and sleek thumbnail will do. If it's a vlog or an entertainment purpose video, an exciting title with an image of the most important part of the video in place of the thumbnail would fit nicely.

For example, if you want to give your review on a certain product, give a strong statement as a title that would be intriguing for people to watch (i.e., 'Why I think the new Tesla cars are amazing', 'Why Harry Potter actually makes no sense', 'Public Speaker Reacts to PewDiePie')

More Content

At the end of your videos, hint at what you'll be doing next so your viewers can come back for more.

Keep track of your subscriber magnet. In analytics, creators can see what type of videos made by you have the most views. So, start by focusing on those. Obviously, don't make a hundred parts on the same topic, but keeping track of your subscriber magnet can help a lot.

2.3: Channel Profile

Keep an attractive and creative Channel with intriguing art styles, so it shows the work put in your banner. It welcomes the viewers. Here are some examples:

Jaclyn Lovey Via YouTube: here,Jaclyn made a minimalistic banner with her video update schedule and her genre of videos mentioned, so newcomers do not have to search for it; convenience.

jacksepticeye Via YouTube: Jack, a successful YouTuber with over 20 Million views, categorized all his videos in playlists so users can access any genre of his videos anytime. Also, notice a signature logo, and he mentioned all his handles, brand links too.

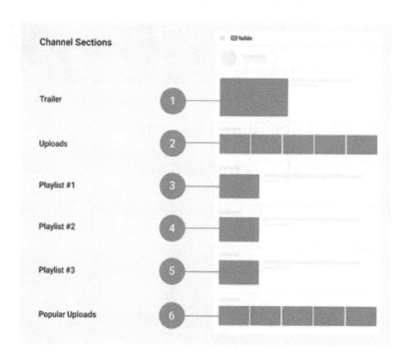

Make an exciting and persuading channel trailer. Preferably short and catchy, show the best you can here because these viewers came specifically to your channel, and you want to keep them there.

Organize the Channel page in a way that's convenient to the viewers.

Check out this basic layout:

Mention other platforms you use so they keep up with you if they don't rely on YouTube.

In 'About', make sure you provide at least 300 words about yourself, what kind of content you put out into the world, and why you think they'd be interested. If you have an upload schedule (please do), then mention that as well.

Persuade the viewers to subscribe by the end of it. Keeping a polite tone in your descriptions, whether it be a channel description or video description, gives the viewer a positive and kind tone. They wouldn't particularly enjoy watching someone who talks in a manner of giving orders rather than guiding or entertaining (depending on your content subject).

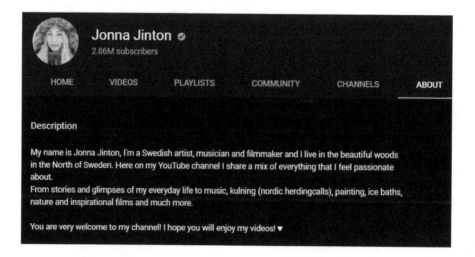

Make sure you use well-known keywords that describe your content. (i.e., Crash courses, funny, motivational, etc.) so the YouTube algorithm can detect these things.

Here's an easy comparison:

A:

Via YouTube

B: Via YouTube

Which is a better Description of the YouTuber? I hope you say B, because it is, in fact, B.

Categorize your videos into playlists. For example, if you are running a gaming channel, make sure long gameplays are divided into separate videos but put together in one playlist after you upload them. Not many people watch 4-hour gameplays all at once, especially when you are starting as a small channel. But suppose you divide your gameplays into videos and edit them to cut out the boring bits. In that case, they may enjoy watching multiple short videos, which would be around 15-20 minutes each-depending on your preferences.

2.4: Interactivity

Replying to comments is the best and simplest way to gain more subscribers. The more you interact with your viewers and give importance to their feedback, the longer they stay.

"When creators take the time to interact with their local community, it can encourage audience participation and ultimately result in a larger fanbase." ~ YouTube.

Creator Hearts- you can heart your favorite comments to recognize comments from your public. By doing this, the viewer gets a notification, and this keeps interactivity high by leading them back to your channel. These notifications receive 300% additional clicks than normal.

Once you get a handful of people that are consistent in watching your content, you can even ask for their opinion on anything related to the video or even an idea for the next video. To engage yourcommunity is perhaps the most important thing, especially when you are a growing channel. Doing Q&A videos every once in a while acknowledges the audience and engages them more.

Recently, YouTube updated, and now Creators can interact with their audience with polls and posts as well as comments. Using these frequently to keep your audience there is vital.

Shine Theory

Needless to say, they'd be more excited by a famous YouTuber replying to their comments, but you could be famous soon enough too! So, building a community that promotes each other does help. This concept comes from the Shine Theory.

Shine Theory is a long-term investment, where two individuals, creators, or consumers, help each other by means of advertising or engagement depending on the platform it is being used.

CHAPTERIII:Tik Tok

3.1: Down the Rabbit Hole

Over 2 billion people have downloaded Tik Tok all around the globe. Especially during the global pandemic, literally, everyone seems to have this app on their phone- and even if they don't have the app, it is taking over the apps they *do* have.

Tik Tok is super addicting, and the main reason for this is that each video is no longer than one minute, which gives viewers quick entertainment / tips / motivation.

Tik Tok famous is a word the vast majority seems to be throwing around as if it is a solid career, but the problem is, they all act as though it's a comfortable ride without even putting their back into it! Though it's a little more complicated than that, and you'd know that. But don't worry, here's a step-by-step guide to how you can be Tik Tok famous in no time.

This is the kind of platform that anyone can get into, from a 7-year-old to a 70-year-old *anyone*. Most people follow overnight after one of your Tik Tok's go mega-viral. Without further ado, let's start with all the things you need to remember to get 10 000 followers on Tik Tok.

3.2: The Algorithm

The Tik Tok algorithm was updated recently at the start of 2021, due to which a number of views on Tik Toks have started to go down. They did this because Tik Tok realized Tik Toks could go viral for almost anyone and a lot of creators' content was against community guidelines, so the early adopter advantage is lost. A way to tackle this is- keep pumping out more content. These algorithms will keep updating throughout the years, but the best you can do is give the viewers a reason to watch.

3.3: Your Profile

Username

Choose a simple yet unique username. One that is familiar to your niche would be most preferred as it would make users find you conveniently. (i.e., if your Tik Toks are travel-focused, you can call yourself JourneysInLife)

Bio

Think of an intriguing Profile Bio. Something welcoming, relatable, original, fun, and interesting your followers would enjoy. And definitely mention your niche to clarify your target audience. Often really good bios consist of a call to action (i.e., follow for a cookie).

Upload a Photo (high-quality image not to look cheap). Link your other social media handles like Instagram, YouTube, etc.

3.4: The Content

Target Audience

Before blindly making videos, you need to consider what kind of audience you're aiming for. Firstly, they use Tik Tok. If you think editing videos the same way you'd edit a YouTube or IGTV video will work, you're wrong. Every platform is unique in its own significant way,so you need to pay attention to how Tik Tok is entertaining and focuses on that.

Is it family-friendly content for youngsters? Short tutorials for artists? Perhaps it's professional cooking for beginners. You need to think about your audience's geolocation, age group, gender, so on and so forth.

This is an approximate age breakdown:

- Age 55+: 5%

- Age 44-53: 2%

- Age 34-43: 7%

- Age 24-33: 15%

- Age 17-23: 41%

- Age 13-16: 26%

What's your Niche?

Delivering high-quality videos (in both quality of the video and content) is the most basic important thing. Don't steal content from other underrated creators, or it will have dire consequences like getting banned.

Make it unique, edit your videos with your ability if you can because people get tired of seeing the same editing design used by the Tik Tok app. There are various editing apps like ViaMaker, Zoomerang, Quik, InShot, Funimate, etc.

Quality

You need a really powerful hook in the first 3 seconds the keep the viewers wanting to watch more. Your job is to do everything and anything to keep the viewers from clicking away then make them interested enough to follow!

To do this, you need a significant number of pattern interrupts-graphics, different camera angles, etc. It could be as easy as starting with a greeting or as concrete as taking the time to explore or finishing your wish list. A trend disrupts you to exciting new locations, both visually and psychologically. It jolts you away from your comfortable perceptions and rituals and then into broad freedom of possibilities.

Better quality videos are pleasing to the eye, and they will likely continue watching until it ends. Sometimes Tik Tok degrades your videos' quality, and the reason this happens is thatthe data saved on your app has been turned on often than naught. This feature is on means the Tik Tok application downloads your mobile data while you watch videos. This decreases the resolution of your clips too. So, to tackle this, you can turn off the data saver feature.

Collabs

Collaborating with some people you have good chemistry with really improves shares as it would be increasing both your and the other Tik Tokers views/follows another branch of Shine Theory.

Not just that, but Tik Tok allows you to reply to other influencers Tik Tok with your own, right? Use that! Make your reply unique and interesting to get them and other viewers to notice.

When it comes to collaborations with companies, sponsorships sound nice but try not to overdo it. While looking for new celebrities to partner with, be sure to review how many supported videos are posted. When a majority of their latest material is paying for updates, their commitment rate will not last. Alternatively, search for influencers with a decent amount of organic, non-sponsored material. As they probably have fans interested and involved.

Going Viral

When you post a video on Tik Tok, your creativity has the potential to ignite a chain reaction.

To get a decent amount of exposure, engage in trends, challenges, and duets. Put your own twists on patterns that captivate individuals. Paying attention to and bookmarking popular clips can prove useful to use it for inspiration. In Tik Tok, there are so many viral challenges. Engaging in various challenges will increase your visibility to the network and encourage you to get far more follows.

On the majority of your Tik Toks, for now, at least, use recommended and trending songs. Positive content almost always has more views, something quirky and enjoyable with a warm tone. Using a trending song is the next move (except when your music is original or a video idea in particular to a kind of sound.)

This is the reason why using trending songs is clever: basically, Tik Tok is a little wired in regard to trending songs to promote videos. It wasn't a random occurrence that Tik Tok also works with record companies; they work together to promote the artist's music in the app to improve the sales of the album and raise the likelihood that the song can hit the top rankings. Tik Tok practically dominates the music world. A mere peek at the week's Top 100 tunes. Most of those best hits on Tik Tok are those that are mega-famous. How do you know what tunes everyone's listening to? Simply choose one of the suggested tracks the platform recommends when you make your film.

Get on top of all those trends, except with a surprise. Do the idea of popular dances or rising clips, but add a twist on it and make it something of your own. You need to balance trending videos with fresh material when you're a small producer. A Tik Tok clip received millions of views, and that account got about 10,000 Tik Tok followers; it just happened overnight.

However, once you receive those views, you shouldn't anticipate the next day to be filled with that much fame, because you will probably be disappointed. Once you get over a million views, then you need to keep up the work or probably work even harder than before to keep everyone there.

Make sure you don't take part in really cringe trends, though!

Using Hashtags

Utilize hashtags as much as you can, especially hashtags that are trending. This actually matters because the Tik Tok algorithm detects these hashtags and recommends your content accordingly.

The cleverer and simpler your hashtags are, the higher your videos get ranked on Tik Tok, which in result increases your views and likes. Along with being in contact with record labels, Tik Tok often works with companies/brands, and their drives are almost always attached with a hashtag. This encourages your videos on people's For You Page during the duration of the campaigns.

1-2 hashtags are preferred. Go to the Discover tab and take 1-2 trending and 1-2 broad hashtags or tags related to your related to you exclusively and trendy.

Most Popular: #tiktokers #lfl #bhfyp #follow #explorepage #followforfollowback #explore #meme #tiktokdance #viral #memes #tiktokindia #photography #tiktokindonesia #k #cute #art #youtube #instagood #fashion #likes #bhfyp #likeforlikes #trending #music #funny#tiktok #instagram #love #like

Timing Matters!

What time you decide to post your content actually matters. When most people are online is when you'd want to put out videos and this depends on your geolocation heavily. If you're careful, you can get twice the followers you'd normally get.

Posting late at night (not too late), afternoon, and early morning tend to be the best times as most people would be looking through their phones then.

But that's just an average. To be more specific, go into your account analytics and content section, look at the past 7 days and what times your content was viewed most often, then make your posting times according to when your most interactive followers were active to make it as convenient for them as possible. Also, take into consideration the timings more well-known Tik Tokers in your niche are posting.

Repost and Share.

Sometimes, your video doesn't do as well the first time but reposting it several times a day and week can drastically change that because sometimes your followers just miss it. Saying things like 'Posting again till it goes viral' or 'Reposting since it didn't do too well last time' can really make a difference.

Sharing your videos on every other social media platform (i.e., Instagram, Twitter, Facebook, etc.)

Engagement

You need to turn your viewers, commenters, and likers into followers, especially at such an early stage. Basically, your early squad needs the spa treatment. To do this, perhaps the most important thing is engaging with your community. Interacting with them as much and as often as you can is vital to Tik Tok's growth.

Credits: wired

Reply to each and every comment.People love viewing comments seeing their opinion was acknowledged would be a satisfying feeling foreveryone. Follow everyone, and I mean everyone that has interacted with your account in anyway.

Go Live every single day, and it really boosts your page. Even if you're super busy, go live and work!

If you receive hate comments, reply back with a bit of humor! However, if it's constructive criticism, show interest, and try actually considering their opinion, this can really help your account develop.

Ask questions in your videos, so they feel the need to reply in the comments. This is a little trick most creators use.

Staying Consistent

Posting regularly is important. Post multiple times a day (considering the timings) and try avoiding uploading content right after each other, or it will not be pushed to the For You page.

Stockpile videos: If you have a day off, film as much content as you can so you can still upload videos if you're too busy another day. Posting 3-6 times a day is an ideal amount.

Duration

The duration of each video is preferred to be 11-17 sec long. The ideal time for something to be pushed out into the algorithm. And you'd get a good amount of watch time. Keep it shorter than you think it needs to be.

Tik Tok revolves around fun and concise videos, so if yours is too long than they would like, Tik Tok may decrease your rank on the For You page.

Ask them to follow, like, and comment.

The easiest method to improve the number of followers you have is by asking the viewers to 'double tap!' or 'let me know what you think in the comment section'; these things remind viewers to give you some sort of feedback on the content you create.

Asking for engagement in every video for a *very* brief period of time in the video and saying it in the description is important. Make sure it isn't mentioned for longer than 2-3 seconds, or the viewer will get bored and click away.

Keep all your content accessible.

Never delete any of your Tik Tok videos because it's likely your posts won't do well right away; you need to give it time. Your previous posts can go viral any time, so never keep them private or delete them.

There have been many times a Tik Toker posts a video, and it gets hardly 500 views in the first night, but about a few weeks later, it starts to become trending again, and you get a thousand more views.

Judge Yourself

Not to the point, you put yourself down, of course, but realistically judging yourself to keep track of your work is important.

How will this video contribute to your growth?

Is it interesting for people in my own niche?

Why would it be interesting?

What themes can I use to make this better?

If the most popular Tik Toker in my niche saw this, would they be impressed?

Take these things into consideration when you're done with certain Tik Toks.

Follow Guidelines

Especially with the recent 2021 update, you don't want to get on Tik Tok's bad side. Make sure you aren't copying someone else's work on your own profile, as that would really degrade your account.

Funded partnerships may not be as clear to Tik Tok as they are to other social networking sites, but that wouldn't imply that the very same FTC laws do not apply. Tik Tok celebrities are expected to report advertising with a transparent and obvious message that the material is funded or promoted.

Do not, under any circumstance, attempt to get free followers. This will never help you really grow. And it can have really adverse consequences later on if you are serious about Tik Tok as this is seen as a way to steal from Tik Tok. Trying to buy free followers will never get you the triumph you thrive for.

Stitch- The Tik Tok Feature

This adds yet another way for the user to interact with material that is created and posted every day by the creative Tik Tok users. Stitch is a feature the company called which enables a user to put in snippets of another Tik Tok video in yours.

How can you use it?

1. Search for the video you want to stitch and then click on 'Send to'.

2. Click on 'Stitch'

3. You can pull only 5 seconds out of the video, so choose wisely.

4. Make the rest of the video you want to put in with the stitched snippet.

5. Stitch them all together!

In the settings menu, you may select if you want to allow others to stitch your material. This is accessible on the Security and Confidentiality tab underneath "Settings and Privacy." You could allow or remove Stitch for any of your clips. Conversely, this feature can be customized for every clip you post.

Stay Stress-free

Don't try to push out more content forcefully, if your audience sees that you are, they would easily be able to get that your content came from a negative mindset. Keep it fun, enjoy making the clips, actually show your positivity.

Having a healthy mindset further nurtures your creativity and gets your ideas flowing, and you need as much of that as possible. Being authentic with your followers is key.

A few different tactics that have proved effective, such as constructive self-discuss and positive envisioning, can achieve encouraging thought.

Here are a few tactics that would prove beneficial for you to prepare your brain in thinking positively to get you started with generating content.

Concentrate on the good stuff. A part of our life is inconvenient situations and obstacles. Look at the constructive stuff once you're faced with one, regardless of how minor or relatively meaningless they are. You may still discover the ultimate positive aspect of any inconvenience if you search for it, even if it's not readily apparent.

Train with appreciation. Studying kindness has been shown to alleviate depression, boost self-esteem and promote endurance in some very trying situations. Image friends, experiences, or stuff that give you any type of warmth or delight, and struggle to convey your thanks at least once every day. This could be a thank you to a co-worker for assisting with a job, to a significant one for cleaning dishes, or to your cat for the affection they have provided.

Keep a diary of thanks. Research studies have reported that putting down stuff you're thankful for will boost your motivation and your state of wellness. You could do that by writing in a thankful diary daily or by setting down a range of items that you're happy for the days when you're going through a rough time. Using this to generate ideas even if it's really far-fetched should prove useful.

Find your motivation, whether that be intrinsic or extrinsic. You get to create the kind of content you like on Tik Tok, any kind! Use that as your passion and drive to work harder and do better.

Let's take a look at a few Tik Tokers

Daniel here has already made 10 parts of the same category and he still has millions of views. Why? Because he doesn't do the *same thing each* time of course, he changes it up, builds better for the next parts. His idea is original, unique, and entertaining!

But be careful not to overdo it, you can't go making 50 parts of the same theme as that would really just stretch it out too much and no one enjoys a guest who overstays their welcome.

daniel.labelle ✔ Daniel LaBelle

If people lagged. Part 10

♫ original sound - Daniel LaBelle

daniel.labelle Via TikTok

Zach shows a clip of the most absurd idea there is: fishing in your house, using these surprises and then a pattern interrupt which involves him falling into the water really is an odd sight to see though very entertaining and unique.

Because of this, a large number of people shared his video and commented in it to share their thoughts.

zachking Via TikTok

CHAPTER IV: Instagram

4.1: About You

Instagram is used by everyone in almost every part of the world. It's so popular because Instagram uses imagery rather than text, and people are extra quick to respond to that. It's easier to understand and process visual data rather than heaps of words. And so, visual marketing is blowing up.

The main focus on Instagram is are images. Captions are put out of the way and under the image for that exact reason.

Portrait photography is perhaps the most popular amongst the flock of imageries on Instagram. And most of these images are almost always edited by third-party applications (i.e., Snapseed, VSCO, Adobe Photoshop Express, Polarr).

Not just images, but also Boomerangs, IGTV videos, filters (of which most are created by users), stories, etc. These things push engagement to the front lines.

Naturally, every time Instagram's algorithm changes, it impacts every person who accesses it. You need to make sure youaren't going against the current of those waves. Becausethe fact is that their algorithm is constantly judging posts all over the globe and deciding which users can see each moment they open the app.

Instagram's algorithm works on machine learning, which makes the way your posts are ranked constantly changing. This book has the most recent details about how to deal with the algorithm to push you further in the marketing campaign and to keep developing engagement with your followers.

Ever since Instagram halted the inverted response in 2016, each specific feed on the site has been arranged as per the algorithm's guidelines.

As per the official @creators handle of Instagram, this concluded in a pleasant result for everybody. Basically, saying they won't be changing it back.

4.2: Ranking Factors

Genre/Niche

Design your account, configure it in a way people can know precisely what they can expect from you. After which, you post intriguing content that your audience will enjoy instantly. If people have liked those kinds of posts before, the system is much more likely to display them.

For example, Let's say Steven came in contact with a verified account. He will probably see more posts from that account, especially if he saw more content from there.

Simply put, users who communicatewith content similar to yours are probably going to come across your account as well.

Timing

Recent posts are always going to be recommended more than others. So,just like Tik Tok, posting in timing when your followers are normally active is vital.

People who spend over an hour scrolling on Instagram are obviously going to see numerous kinds of posts from top to bottom compared to someone who spends hardly a few minutes will only see only the top-ranked ones.

Instagram portrays the best at the top of users' feed every time the user activates the application. So, someone who follows hundreds of thousands of accounts will most likely miss a fair number of posts from people they are even really close to.

Engaging Your Audience

Just like every other social media platform, Instagram wishes for users to stay on the app as much and as long as possible as long as they are interested. As anend result, the software cranks up profiles in which the followersare already conversing. This guarantees that the stress on community participation is essential for advertisers and developers.

Credits: mavsocial.com

Sliding in DMs, tagging one

another in blogs, and consistently posting comments all are acts thatimply a strong bond among users as well as likes, shares, and views.

4.3: What You Need toDo

Pay Attention.

Seeing your Instagram stats is, perhaps shockingly, a few of the easiest ways to get insight into not only how your viewers think but also how the application looks at you.

Could you send everyone much of the same, or twists on the subject? Will they want better photos or videos? Just how many views come from hashtags? What kind of content is going to wow the audience?

Insights tell you did well, so it's up to you to work out where to run from that performance.

Keep It Coming

Some type of involvement, and figuring out where the intended crowd is. To have a grip on the Instagram algorithm, you have to create bonds with your followers first. And because the volume is simple to compute and accomplish than performance, the first item on the agenda is to create a social media posting schedule to stay on track.

What is consistency? Mean for Instagram? This is exclusive to your niche. As you just started, start with the way you want to progress. Think about what's affordable for the team to create.

If you draw viewers with a spark, three stories, two posts, and one IGTV video per day produced a certain amount of perception. Volume and layout selections would depend on the resources you currently have. And what's most critical, however, is to concentrate on publishing posts that you feel proud of regularly.

Reposting is Key.

Even after you have a nice schedule, you're following and knowing what your followers expect, pushing content out into the world isn't simple like butter on jam.Recycle, change-up your best work. Now, not only do you know Instagram wants it, but it also saves a lot of time.

You could transform the videos to gifs, similar pictures to a slideshow,and use pictures used in another photo shoot for multiple reasons, throwbacks, and repost on stories.

Just use the same thing but be extra creative with it.

Collaborating withOther Influencers& Brands

Keep an eye on what other public figures in your niche are up to, and if possible, try to do a collab with them.

Perhaps the easiest way to naturally broaden your scope to fresh eyes is to seek a suitable friend with a complimentary following while still attracting the viewers' interest with appropriate different perspectives.The outcome may very well provide an added strength from Instagram if the partnership is as enjoyable for your community as it would be for you.

Though you need to make surethat the person you choose to partner with is suitable and legitimate, as other influencers will judge you based on who you collab with, it is probably best if you do a detailed background check before setting a collab date with them.

As that influencer will be bringing in their audience, you need to see what kind of followers they have and their analytics. Making sure you don't bring in the wrong crowd who would go away as soon as they came. You could check this by looking at their engagement on posts. If the person you are intending to collab with is genuine and interactive with his/her audience, you should probably go for it.

As searching through every single person, you could collab with would take a significant amount of time, you could use means likeNinjaoutreach, Meltwater, GroupHigh, Newswire, Cision Communications Cloud, etc.This software allows you to make your listing in its database, making things a lot more convenient for you as time is, in fact, of the essence.

The kinds of sponsorships you could get fall into three basic categories: large accounts (120K followers) get at least $400 per sponsored post, middle-class (3K-100K followers) get at least $150, and small accounts (less than 3K)get around $100 or less.

After making a list of the sponsorships you'd like to go for, you need to send each one your pitch. But not in the first text, of course, that would be not polite. Tell them why you're interested in the subject they put out and communicate with them. Once you know what they want exactly, you could develop an amazing pitch.

Next, you need to plan your influencer publicizing campaign. Makesure you keep interacting with the influencers so you can get an insight into what they think. Consider other people's opinions to make a master plan using the influencers and your creativity.

As soon as you have initiated your campaign, please keep track of how it's doing and keep adjusting it accordingly.

An example:

@omayazein partnered up with a brand calledModanisa and gave her audience a discount code, which in turn gets a lot of shares, and she has about 1 Million followers!

@omayazein Via Instagram

Reward Them

As discussed before, Instagram values engagement A LOT, so give your audience what they want! When your audience shares your posts on story or DM, comments and likes push your posts to the top instantly.

The goal should be to create a kind of commitment and passion that motivates individuals to advocate and empower themselves. The service could do the job for you if you already have an outstanding Business-to-consumer service. Anything other than that, you would need to find means of subtly encouraging individuals.

Please stop posting everything sent to you from your community. Compile the latest and integrate material into the digital plan of your content whenever appropriate. And bear in mind that merely reposting the stories of other users has also been specifically noted as something that would not include your stories on the Explore List, so make sure you remain imaginative and on topic.

Like your followers' and viewers' comments, reply to each one, even the haters. Try getting into a conversation with them. Interact with them through stories, polls, use trending filters.

Ask questions on your stories and share them, be humorous, genuine, everything and anything interesting. It could be 'what's your opinion on....' Or 'what's your most embarrassing story!', etc.

If they reply to your stories, make sure you reply!! And not after days at a time, but as soon as you can. Enjoy your time with them. Really try and understand what they wish to see from you. Unless they're just there to hate on you, then you should probably ignore it or if you could do something creative with it (while following community guidelines), go for it.

Follow influencers that are familiar with your niche. This can link other people that are interested in your type of content to you. Not just follow, but also like and comment on their posts, share it! (Another way of utilizing the Shine theory). Showing interest in other people's content can help you too.

Use the Hashtag System

Just like Tik Tok, hashtags are an important part of Instagram. It is the middleman between you and the right audience. It's the lowest building block, especially when you're just starting out.

If you think using heaps of hashtags, including ones that do not correlate with your niche, will help, you might be wrong. It would be misusing the hashtag system, and that leads you to a direct road to the bad side of Instagram because they do, in fact, notice those who try abusing the algorithm. And not to mention, you are not gaining anything by trying to show it to people who have no interest in your niche.

The maximum quantity of hashtags you are allowed to use is 30 per post, and yes, use all those 30. Try writing those hashtags in the first comment rather than in the caption, so it looks a bit more well put together.

Perhaps not all hashtags that you assume are nice would be suitable for your own use. It is why every last one of you would want to verify to see whether the material is important to your subject.

When deciding whether a hashtag is right for your post, there are two key considerations to have a look at Niche and Dimension.

Never use only the most famous and vague hashtags, thinking you would be able to reach a larger crowd because you won't. You'll just be a hidden needle in a haystack. An invisible need at that. Why? Because they aren't specific enough, and a lot of popular influencers already use those so you wouldn't be too noticed yet.

Please make sure you have certain hashtags that you use in every post (with fewer follows) so that you can be noticed by at least one familiar audience (needless to say, they need to be your target audience too).

It would be best if you would be able to find a middle ground between hashtags that not one soul has ever heard of before and hashtags that everyone knows about. Both would reward you little. Try hashtags that have about 90,000-900,000 post range.

Sorry, But Buying Is NOT the Way to Go

You can purchase double-taps or follows in due to despair just to see whether a lift is what they needed to get moving all along. But while this may make you appear popular to random people; it couldn't be farther from the facts.

Finally, they consider giving up both as a waste of time on Instagram and stop bringing in any considerable effort to expand, since they just do not see what else there is to do. Don't purchase likes, fans, and also, don't try the old trick of interaction pods.

Yes, even Instagram notices it if you buy followers/likes/views. Not only Instagram but also your followers. Which makes things a lot worse. And so, you won't gain any kind of income from that.

Using Highlights

Utilize the highlights feature and make/or find suitable cover photos for each to maintain consistency.It is making a profile that's pleasing to the eye and fitting for your niche and target audience.

4.4: Seeing is Believing

You may think this is all talk and no action, so let's drive that notion away by looking at a few of the many influencers on Instagram.

Notice the overall layout of this account. The username and profile instantly tell the users what the account is about.

Just the username would do this for us too but @wedarkacademia further described what it was about as well as threw in a bit of personality to the description as well as handles for other social platforms.

Their posts are consistent and related to one another. See the Highlights categorized neatly too.

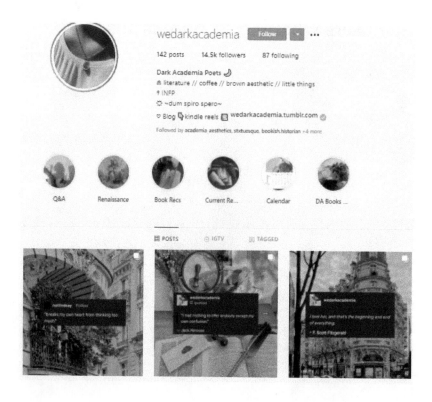

@wedarkacademia Via Instagram

Responses like these encourage so much growth and engagement amongst the target audience.

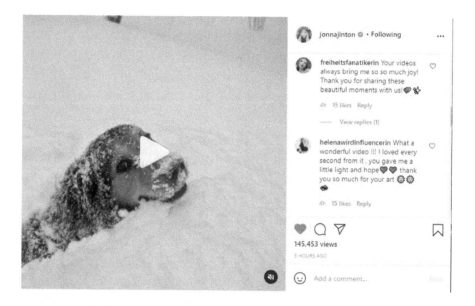

@jonnajinton Via Instagram

@madeyemoodswing interacting with their audience. Their username being humorous and instantly getting the attention of Harry Potter fans who understand the reference.

Drawing in users of various kinds though if @madeyemoodswing doesn't involve any kind of Harry Potter related content, those fans may lose interest.

@madeyemoodswing Via Instagram

Jonna Jinton, blogging her art, photography and life on Instagram whilst also mentioning that she works on another platform (YouTube). Her posts are coherent and in sync with nature and mostly winter in her home country.

Her description and highlights are simple and straight to the point which a lot of users would find convenient and contemporary.

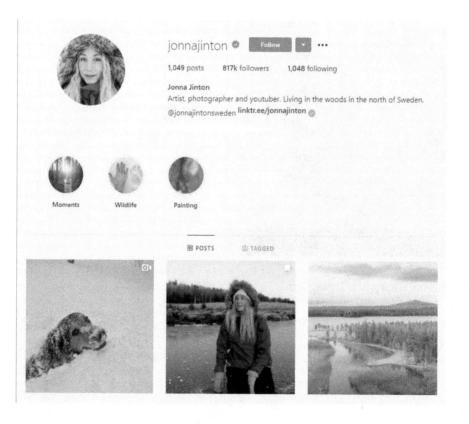

@jonnajinton Via Instagram

CHAPTER V: Ideas for Newbies

5.1: Idea Generation

There is not much to implement without ideas, and since the implementation is the secret to progress, creative ideas are required to enable some sort of change. It is clear that thoughts alone are not going to make creativity possible, since you need to be able to construct a structured mechanism to handle such innovations. The concept is not only about producing lots of it but also about bringing care to the nature of it.

It's not easy to create grade A content 24/7. Often people find it difficult to break out of their usual routine and habits when thinking about working on something new. In order to get out of the negative spiral, you need to glance at the development of creativity altogether and incorporate a few of the most key factors, strategies, and procedures that could be used more routinely to produce fresh concepts.

Perhaps you need original thoughts so a new possibility can be thoroughly explored?

Maybe you are trying to find a new way of solving a creativity barrier, or are you hoping for a decent answer to the dilemma?

Why does it matter?

Generating ideas is the outcome ofcreating complex, tangible, or conceptual theories. It's at the top of the funnelfor concept organization, which works on seeking potential alternatives to true or suspected challenges and possibilities.

Ideas are, as stated, the very first move into change. Fresh theories rely on you progressing as independent individuals. From the point of view of a person, whether you feel stuck with a job or otherwise unable to resolve that one dilemma, fresh solutions will motivate you to push ahead.

The aim of fresh concepts is to reinforce the manner in which you work, irrespective of your priorities or the kinds of things you're searching for.

To fuel productivity and improve nature on a broader scale, societies rely on creativity. Creativity improves emerging innovations and enterprises. They are providing creators with more opportunities.

How do you do it?

Chances are, you brainstorm. However, it's been found that brainstorming requires more time and tends to fewer ideas as ofplanning, logging, and managing the meeting would take a lot more time than it should. While there are certain approaches to boost the quality of brainstorming, it's preferred if brainstorming isn't your first thought.

Nevertheless, certain methods are worth taking a look at. As you're searching for various kinds of ideas, it is beneficial to have methods in mind that help in developing them. Several of these concept development approaches may be used for further productive brainstorming and another creativity type.

5.2: The Techniques

Challenging proposals

This concept is when you bring an issue or opportunity into view due to the possibility of innovatively solving it. It can let you make a certain doubt about your content and aim it at your audience to get more ideas and useful opinions after you have identified what you intend to gain from it.

These idea challenges come in handy, especially when you're looking to engage a large audience of up to 10000. When you plan an idea challenge, pre-define the outcomes you'd like, the niche, followers, subscribers, etc. Make sure you keep track of the time with this technique to make sure it's working.

Similarities

You can use data and statistics from previous posts or videos on social media platforms to improve on ideas for another piece of content; this is thinking simultaneously.It is the simplest way of generating fresh content as it's often experimented with and succeeded.

In Example, YouTuber's making reaction videos continually but of various kinds of content.

SCAMPER

This method applies critical thinking to alter creativity, which is already present — adjusting open-sourceideas to improve and agree on the best answer.

1. Substitution – Your old content being substituted with others to gain improvement.

2. Combining- Merging two or more ideas into one master idea for your content.

3. Adapting- Evaluates the options to make a method more versatile and works on the design, system, or principle alongside other related gradual changes.

4. Modification- From a broader context, changing not only the concept but also changing the concept looks at the challenge or potential and tries to change the outcomes.

5. Improvising by putting to another use- Searching for opportunities to use the concept or current content for some other reason and, if applicable to other areas of your profile or channel, analyzes the potential advantages.

6. Elimination- This technique studies all the possibilities, and if you find more than one fragment was removed.

7. Reversal- The emphasis of this procedure is to reverse the order of factors that can be swapped of your idea.

This technique was originatedfrom the idea of brainstorming, but it applies to your thinking technique too. If you make generating ideas a daily activity by a series of trivial things, you could have a decent chance of winning the main breakthrough. Occasionally all it takes is really to reflect on what you already have. Sometimes, creators want to worry about the next remarkable thing being discovered. It is easy to overlook that the endless gradual changes are the aspects that can have a difference in the medium haul while creating fresh concepts. As a baseline, utilizing your existing theories or methods will explain a lot in relation to your present content, and that is what the SCAMPER strategy is really about.

Reverse Psychology

This method will make you challenge your content-related perceptions. Reverse thinking comes in handy when you feel you are trapped in the traditional mentality, and it appears to be impossible to come up with such unique ideas. It helps in checking our routinely-habits as the answer to finding more content isn't always a straight-to-the-point road. You consider the possibilities of what the opposite would do for your profile or channel, even if you end up thinking of the most peculiar of solutions.

5.3: Once You've Got It

Organizing Ideas

Once you've got all those ideas down, planning and organizing them can be difficult if you don't know where to start. Creators need to collect this creativity as soon as it comes to them instead of using it as soon as it comes up.

Jotting down all your ideas in a notebook or on your phone can be helpful, and most people do this as it's only for personal use. But if you wish for other people's opinions on the matter to know their judgment, this could be a hassle. Not to worry though, there are things like idea management tools to aid you with that.

Management

A concept tool for effective functions as the foundation of the method of idea planning. This is how you can assemble the ideas, analyze them, debate, prioritize them, take account of their success, and the overall course of the operations of your idea generation.

Since concept planning is such a huge subject and famous influencers or public figures are likely to have loads of suggestions, it often makes perfect sense for most influencers or creators to use a designated idea management system.

It is just as productive to handle ideas with a designated method as the underlying mechanism at the back end. You could create a mechanism that makes it a lot easier to produce and refine fresh concepts and create ideas a persistent practice. The methods that are too confusing can infuriate people, so try not to make things too difficult.

5.4: Winning at Creativity

The Appropriate Crowd

It is necessary to include the right individuals in the equation for the content to be as efficient as possible. Start engaging all influencers who know about the content creation and are sincerely involved in you making a difference.

Ensure your community is the target audience and well educated on the topic if the aim is to involve a wider community of users to produce ideas.

Determine Your Objective

Aim to collect as much relevant data as possible about the content you wish to make before you begin to understand the source. Define what you understand about it by now and what data is still required.

Though it sounds simple, the further you can clearly explain your actual idea, the greater the odds of producing practical ideas are.

Limits to Keep an Eye Out For.

It can impede imagination to convey that every idea is a valid idea, so ensure the aims are ambitious and precise enough. One approach to get some of the viewers' genuinely innovative thoughts is to set limits.

If the ultimate aim is to cut prices, suggestions such as investing truly little on content would certainly come to mind when you want to save up. The thoughts you get, though, would vary greatly if you ask yourself: "How could I save 50% on expenses and create unique and engaging content?".

Deduction

The goal of creating original approaches is to improve what is already present as well as to produce something new.

From a different angle, coming up with entirely novel solutions will help you tackle your creativity block. It helps you to widen the spectrum of thoughts beyond the present style of learning, which inevitably leads to much more ideas.

Sometimes, creators, influencers, and public figures use current ideas or behavioral templates while attempting to get started on a social media platform instead of attempting to think of the latest ideas. The concern with this technique is that it does not encourage you to pursue multiple options and limits the number of possibilities.

5.5: About Yourself

Who are you?

Create a clip of yourself being introduced. Who are you, what are you doing? On your YouTube channel, Tik Tok, or Instagram profile, what should viewers hope to see? How frequently do you upload photos or videos? Create videos to let them know exactly what they should expect, inviting viewers to your channel or page. Aim to give a convincing argument for audiences to click on the subscribe button on YouTube and follow on Instagram or Tik Tok.

Vlogging

Making Vlogs can be informative, fun, intimate, anything you would like to create of it, much like traditional writing. Almost all influencers and public figures may use material from vlogs to involve fans and expand their communities.

A Day in Your Life

YouTubers love to walk through The Day in your Life videos from another's perspective. Once you wake up the next morning and lead audiences to a normal day in your schedule, start filming.

Matt D'Avella Via YouTube

Behind-the-curtainContent

Showcase to the viewers what's going on at the back end of your Instagram account, YouTube channel, or Tik Tok account. With this famous video style, let your audience see behind the curtains. You can display your room, your house, your workplace, your city, anywhere else you enjoy.

20 Questions

You could make short clips or long clips (depending on your preference or niche) playing a game of 20 questions. These questions can be personal or silly, and the best have a little bit of both. Letting your audience be closer to you is what this accomplishes.

'Draw My Life.'

These kinds of videos are often found on YouTube, where the creator essentially draws their life often on a whiteboard with stick figures and narrating their life so far. Of course, you decide how much or how little you wish to say about yourself. Majority 'Draw my life' videos include key events or milestones in their lives.

You can even introduce your family, background, and friends in these.

5.6: Trending Content Ideas

Teach them How to Cook (or how not to)

This kind of content is often made by entertainment-focused or cooking influencers. You can make it an A grade cooking tutorial, or you could completely twist it depending on your creativity and teach people how not to cook but let them have an enjoyable time watching creators do it wrong.

For example, YouTuber 'Simply Nailogical' made a video called 'Baking a cake with Nail Polish' on 18th September 2016, which got over 5 Million views. The cake was quite inedible but still entertaining to watch to over 5 Million people.

You can make this an Instagram post, a Tik-Tok video, or a YouTube video.

Workout Routine

As it's time to start working out, lots of folks look towards YouTube videos, quick Tik Tok hacks, or Instagram posts/IGTV videos for specific fitness routines, as well as how to do those workouts. Both common subjects are exercise, stretching, or shape footage.

Understanding the Complicated Mess

Informative and aurally captivating means of presenting data and figures that could otherwise be dull or difficult to grasp is infographics related content. Content that helps your audience's day a little easier. Every genre of content has specific things that not everyone understands, so try finding the most commonly found problem in yours and present content on that!

Reviewing other People's Products

One of the most common kinds of information on these social media platforms is product reviews. Before deciding to buy, thousands of viewers check out this insightful content. Tech gadgets and make-up items are common themes, but reviews can be sought for all types of goods.

For example, YouTuber Marques Brownlee's Niche is tech gadgets, and a majority, maybe even all, of his video's reviews on really expensive gadgets so often people who think about buying a new phone or the PS5 watch his videos to see his opinion on it. His video called 'PlayStation 5 Review: NextGen Gaming!' received almost 6 Million views!

You can make review videos on any and every genre of content! Games, movies, books, food, universities, perfumes, songs, shows, even countries! So, search for things you can review in your niche.

Comedy Videos

In the event that you need to turn into a web sensation, an entertaining video may very well assist you with getting there. A sizable number of the most mainstream recordings on YouTube, Instagram, and Tik Tok ended up in such a state since this sort of content made watchers chuckle or laugh.

Pranks

Viewers love watching tricks. Pull a trick on somebody (innocuous tricks, please) and share the outcomes on your social media platforms.

Tricks have not been altogether contemplated; however, scientists have discovered that individuals find being deceived an extremely aversive encounter. Trick based humor can be coldblooded or kind, cherished or detested; however, it's not straightforward.

Furry Creatures Content

Dogs, little cats, child elephants, the Internet loves charming/interesting creature recordings are considerably more popular than recordings of human children. So, if you have a pet, share it with the world! Everyone loves animals.

Music Videos

Singing a song cover, and original, or even lip-syncing is always a fun sight to see. Indeed, even late-night TV gets in on the good times. Pick a mainstream tune and give it a shot!

If you have a bad voice, don't worry; try making it hilarious by a funny parody where you impress the audience with clever and witty lyrics rather than your vocals.

Fact Check

What are some myths that are commonly believed by the vast majority regarding your niche? Compile all the misconceptions and make a post or video on the matter. Show emotion and teach your audience the stereotypes believed about your niche by the public.

As the internet is filled with so much information, a fair share of it is fake news, so spreading awareness about it would be intriguing for your audience (as long as you stay on topic).

Often people are found spreading rumors without even knowing they are rumors and not facts, so content that addresses the rumors is an interesting concept for anyone.

Needless to say, double-check whether the information you are giving your audience is proven with evidence to be right. Or else those mistakes can decrease your followers/subscribers quick.

Write a catchy caption or thumbnail with a question that quickly catches their interest. For example, '10 Myths you probably believed about professional cooks' or '6 reasons why you should not believe every thing you're told'.

Speed-run

Can you play games as fast as humanely possible?Finish your make-up in under 2 minutes? Or maybe you can make a 3-course meal in under an hour? Show off those skills on social media!

Speed-runs are commonly found on gaming channels so viewers can quickly experience a gameplay without having to play it themselves due to the cost of the game or less time of time.

Time-slip

@jonnajinton Via Instagram on April 17th , 2020

Time-lapse is a method where the casings of the video are caught at a far slower speed than expected. Traffic, mists, and the sunrise all will, in general, be well-known time-slip by subjects. The outcome is frequently hypnotizing.

Some creators make time-lapses of their artwork to show progress quickly as an art piece can take at least a few hours.

Shopping/Mail Hauls

This type of video is particularly well known with style vloggers and beauty. After an outing to the shopping center, flaunt your take piece by piece. From the freshest iPhone to an in-vogue membership box or the most trending toy, individuals love to watch others open boxes. So next time you do another package, don't simply tear into it; make sure you are recording first!

You could even give out your address and your audience would send you mail. Often YouTubers make mail opening videos reviewing all the heartfelt gifts their watchers send them.

Go Live

Why trust that the recap will show individuals what's happened? Take your watchers to the occasion with you by live-streaming to your Instagram Live, Tik Tok Live, or YouTube Live. Even after the session is over, the stream would still be accessible online.

You can schedule a certain day for every week in which you go live and make sure you let everyone know through all your social media platforms, so they are aware and wait for you to go live.

What Most Do

A substantial number of the top Instagrammersare singers, sports brands, actors, footballers, models, and ofcourse, Instagram themselves.The most famous YouTuber channels are often among the genre oftrailer channels, singers, gamers, kids show, hack tutorial channels, and so on.Tik Tokers are often found to be comedians, musicians, artists,etc.

The best content? Ones that are so good that people feel the need to see it on other platforms too, Tik Tok video compilations on YouTube, and Tik Tok videos on Instagram, Live videos on Instagram recorded and put-onYouTube. The type of content that is put across various platforms are the ones that have gone viral or loved enough that users wish to see it almost everywhere.

Conclusion

First things first, it would be beneficial if you ask yourself, what do you have to offer? Why would people want to watch your videos? What are they getting out of the time they spent on your video?

Is it educational? Hilarious? Scary? Relaxing? Silly?Helpful? Inspiring or motivational? Perhaps very random, either way, would your target audience enjoy or show any interest in it?

Maintain originality- the charm of social media is that you can express your thoughts and add a little more to *you*, so to speak. You can grow on YouTube, Tik Tok, and Instagram, only if you have something no one else has to give out. The basic rule to starting a business, 'what's so special about you?' or 'what do you have that no one else does?'. Write down all that comes to mind when answering these questions.

You can not copy peoples' ideas, only your own significant expression of those ideas into your videos, posts, stories, etc.However, if your content seems to be matching someone else's a little too much, change it up, brainstorm a little about what you could do to make it unique, and choose the best one. And be certain you aren't tuning out any other possibilities due to your fears.

Honesty- be honest about your opinions and where you stand. This can be a random video about car reviews or your opinion on white supremacy; it need not matter. Maybe you feel like changing your genre after a long time, but you're afraid of losing the number of followers/subscribers you've gotten so far. Your fear is valid, but you can't force yourself to put out content on something you have no more interest in anymore because you followers/subscriber will notice eventually, and they'll just fade out on their own. So, try being honest, raw, and authentic from the start.

However, being honest does not amount to being insensitive. You're trying to be the person people look up to or look forward to viewing when they're having a difficult day, so try to fill those expectations without disregarding your bad days, of course. Ending things on a positive note and be accepting of the honest truth your followers/subscribers/viewers offer in return.

Humility- Try not to overthink each comment they make because what seems like an hour of thought to you was probably not more than five minutes to them. When you start noticing your growth, don't become egotistic about it, or the people that put you where you are today will leave as fast as they came. Nobody likes a showoff.

Setting boundaries- deciding where you draw the line between your public and personal life is vital. You don't need to broadcast every minute detail about your personal life to the entire world, and you need to value the privacy of the people close to you if you wish for the same.

Motivation- find that mechanism that triggers, leads, and retains your aiming habits. Whether it be intrinsic or extrinsic motivation, keep a daily reminder for it, so you keep that drive and motivation to continue working hard. Grabbing a coffee, chocolate bar, reading, or some inspirational quote is what puts you in a nice mood and sparks wisdom, do it every day.

The physical, internal, cultural, and mental factors which trigger action are involved in motivation. Introjected motivation is when you are driven to work out of the guilt of procrastination or laziness. Identified motivation is when you know you have got work to do, yet you haven't determined anything in regard to it. Try to avoid introjected and identified motivation as it originates from a negative space.

Don't give up if you feel like you are not getting enough growth, stay consistent and keep at it no matter what. If you still feel like there has been no effect, try going over the points again and make sure you keep track of how you have been doing by statistically analyzing yourself.

Soon enough, you will catch yourself with 10,000 followers/subscribers on YouTube, Instagram, and Tik Tok. It is more or less a smooth ride from there. Good Luck!

Short Stays Real Estate with No (or Low) Money Down

The 7+1 Creative Strategies to Create Passive Income from Home Using the AirBnb Business Model in 2021

By

Vishen Smith

Table of Contents

Introduction

If you are a forward-focused person, you can dream of leaving the profession to enjoy a retirement life that is simpler, or you might even consider early retirement. But a dream is only a wish without a plan. You need to contemplate passive income to put a few wheels on the dream. There are also plenty of different options for passive income and rationales of how to build it. Passive income is the money you collect that doesn't cause you to do a lot of "active" work in order to continue to earn it. In essence, you may do much of the work in advance and do some extra effort to earn an income. For instance, to keep the money flowing, if you develop an online course, you only need to update the content. Likewise, passive income strategies like renting out property and/or building a blog can take some effort to get up and running, but while you sleep, they would eventually earn you cash. You've already heard the word, "make money when you're sleeping." This is the main attraction that allows individuals to generate passive income. Even when you're not working, you can develop something (a course, a blog, e-book, videos, and/or an online store) which generates income. Or you can own something that helps you to earn passive income (property or stocks).

So why do you need to build passive income?

In the presence of a full-time job, your salary is your biggest income tool, a tool that usually requires your active involvement. Even if you enjoy your career, you wouldn't mind making some additional money without the tears, blood, sweat, and time commitment of another job. If you lose your job or want to generate an extra source of income when you are no longer productive or if you outlive your retirement fund, developing a passive income will improve your wealth-building strategy, create the opportunity to retire early, and save you from a total loss of income.

And how much money can passive income generate?

Generally, passive income won't make you wealthy overnight, so ignore those get-rich-quick schemes you've read about. But, over the long term, consistent, profitable passive income strategies will produce some serious money. Depending on the income stream, we're talking about anything from two to three thousand dollars to thousands of dollars.

Some people like to think of investing when we mention "passive income" because, with the least amount of effort, it can yield the greatest returns. But you should think about your retirement plan & passive income as two distinct subjects. The entire premise behind the long-term investment is to produce retirement income. If your fund options are good and they offer a match, you want to make sure you invest in your company retirement plan, like that of a 401(k). These are great choices for establishing a powerful pension plan, but before a certain age, you will face taxes as well as penalties for every withdrawal. You need to let your money grow only for the long term with retirement planning and not touch it. However, a form of low-effort income which can be accessed at any time should be passive income. After you are debt-free and have some cash left, one way to build passive income is by buying real estate and leasing it out to tenants. Rental property may be a fantastic source of additional income, but it is not the most passive option because, unless you employ a property management company, you will have to put a lot of effort and time into maintaining the property. You need to be incharge of your property if you go on the rental property route. Pay off your own home first before you buy a rental property, and buy your investment property with cash. You must not go into debt in order to purchase property for rent. You could develop something like an informative blog and/or a YouTube tutorial series to be able to generate online traffic if you have a bright idea that appeals to a particular audience. You might sell commercial space on your blog or ad spots on your channel if your content is engaging and it sees ample regular traffic. You can sit back, relax, and reap sources of passive income after you put in the heavy lifting. The list of ideas for passive income could go on indefinitely. Never go for any passive income strategies that promise a fast return or require large sums of money upfront. Your other financial targets would be sabotaged by them. In this book, we will present ideas that are steady, profitable, and trustworthy.

CHAPTER 1: Understand Income and Importance of Passive Income

There are three main categories of income:

Active income

Portfolio income

Passive income

1.1 Active Income

Active income alludes to money made as a result of the provision of service. Examples of active income are wages, tips, salaries, fees, and income from companies in which there is material involvement. The owner must meet the criteria for "material participation," which is based on hours worked or other factors, in order for income from a company to be considered active rather than passive. The most popular example of active income is income earned in the form of a paycheck from an employer. "Money from business activities is deemed "active" for the self-employed or someone else with an ownership interest in a corporation if it meets the criteria of material participation by the Internal Revenue Service (IRS). That implies one of the following is valid, at least:

- The taxpayer works during the year in the corporation for 500 or more hours.
- The taxpayer performs the majority of the company's work.
- Over the year, the taxpayer works for more than 100 hours in the company and no other employee works more hours than the taxpayer.

However, income earned is treated as passive income if someone earns income from a company in which they do not actively participate. Meanwhile, portfolio income is income from investments, like dividends and capital gains. Depending on the legislation at the time, these various forms of income can be taxed differently. At present, for instance, portfolio income is taxed at lower rates than active income.

Example of active income from a business

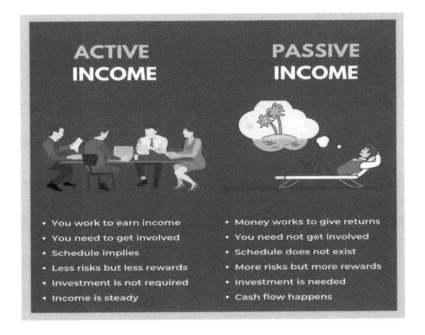

John and Laura are not married to each other. They have a 50% interest in an online business. John performs the majority of the day-to-day work in the business. Therefore, his income is considered active by the IRS.On the other, Laura helps with the marketing activities. She, however, works less than 100 hours a year in the business. It is for this very reason that her income from the business is considered passive income by the IRS. The material participation rule was established to prevent individuals that do not actively participate in a business from using it to generate tax losses which they, otherwise, could have written off against their active income.

1.2 Portfolio Income

Income from the portfolio is money received from investments, interest, dividends, and capital gains. Portfolio income streams are often known to be dividends received from investment properties. It is one of three main income groups. Active income and passive income are the others. Most income from the portfolio enjoys favorable tax treatment. Dividends and capital gains are charged at a much lower rate as compared to active income. Furthermore, portfolio income is not subject to Medicare or Social Security taxes. Income from the portfolio contains dividends, interest, and capital gains. Compared to active or passive income, portfolio income typically enjoys favorable tax treatment. Money from the portfolio is not subject to withholding from Social Security or Medicaid. One way to maximize portfolio income is to invest in an ETF that purchases dividend-paying stocks. Income from the portfolio does not come from passive investments. Moreover, portfolio income is not received from daily business activity. It is earned because of dividends, taxes, and capital gains or interest paid on loans. For tax purposes, the categories of income are important. Passive income losses can not necessarily be offset against portfolio or active income.

Ways to Increase Portfolio Income

Following ways can be employed for increasing portfolio income:

Purchase High-Paying Dividend Stocks

Investors can enhance their portfolio income by purchasing stocks that pay above-average dividends. Dividends can be paid directly to the shareholder. Moreover, dividends can also be used to buy additional shares in the company.

Purchase Dividend Exchange-Traded Funds

A cost-effective way to maximize portfolio income is to buy ETFs that explicitly track high-paying dividend stocks. For example, the FTSE High Dividend Yield Index is tracked by the Vanguard High Dividend Yield ETF. There are 396 stocks that have high dividend yields and are included in the index. For other dividend ETF options, the selection criteria concentrate on how many consecutive years the company has paid a dividend and/or on companies that have a history of raising their annual dividend payments.

Write Options

An investor can write call options against their stock holdings to enhance his portfolio income.

1.3 Passive Income

Passive income are earnings that come from a limited partnership, rental property, or another enterprise in which an entity is not actively engaged, such as a silent investor. Proponents of passive income tend to be boosters of the working lifestyle of a work-from-home and/or be-your-own-boss. Colloquially, it has been used on the part of the person receiving it to describe money being earned periodically with little or no effort. When used as a technical term, passive income is defined by the IRS as either "net rental income" or "income from an enterprise in which the taxpayer does not participate materially" and may include self-charged interest in some cases. Passive income is a source of income that may require some initial effort or investment but continues to generate payments in the future. Examples are music and book royalties and house rent payments. Passive income is the return on savings accounts. Passive income is created by a limited partnership in which a person owns a share of a company but does not engage in its functioning. Passive income consists of earnings generated from rental property, a limited partnership, or some other enterprise in which a person does not engage actively. Usually, taxes are charged on passive income. Portfolio income is perceived by a few analysts as passive income, and interest and dividends will also be considered as passive income. In order to earn and maintain, passive income needs little to no effort. When an earner puts in one of those little efforts to produce income, it is called progressive passive income. In many ways, a passive income investment can make an investor's life easier. This is true when a hands-off strategy is followed. Examples of passive income investment strategies include - Peer-to-Peer Lending, Real Estate, Dividend Stocks, and Index Funds. These four choices suggest different risk and diversification levels. As with any kind of financial investment, calculating the anticipated returns in relation to a passive income opportunity versus the loss potential is important. The main types of passive activities are explained below:

Cash flows from property income, including cash flows from a property or from any piece of real estate, capital gains, rent through resource ownership such as rental income, and in the form of interest from financial asset ownership.

Trade or business-related activities in which an individual does not engage in a company's operations other than investing during the year.

Royalties, that is, payments initiated by one corporation (the licensee) to another firm/person (the licensor) for the right to use the intellectual property of the latter (music, video, book).

Standards for Material Participation

The standards for material participation include:

- Five hundred plus more hours toward an activity or a business from which you are earning
- If the participation for that tax year has been "substantially all."
- Up to 100 hours of commitment and at least as much as every other person involved in the operation
- Material involvement in at least five of the past 10 tax years
- For personal services initiatives, material engagement at any point in three previous tax years

According to the IRS, there are two passive activity categories. Rentals, including equipment and real estate, are the first type; and businesses are the second type, where the individual does not engage materially on a daily, continuous and significant basis.

Examples of passive activities

The following are considered passive activities:

- Equipment leasing
- Limited partnerships

- Partnerships, S-Corporations, and LLCs where the individuals do not materially participate
- Rental real estate (some exceptions apply)
- Sole proprietorship or farm where the individual does not materially participate

1.4 Taxing of passive income

There are various forms of passive income, ranging from capital gains and dividends. Then the question arises whether the passive income is taxable or not. The brief response is, yes. Tax rates can differ depending on how long the assets are kept, the amount of benefit gained, and/or net income on each form of passive income.

Short-Term Passive Income Tax Rates

For assets retained for a year or less, short-term gains apply and are taxed as ordinary income. In other words, at the same rate as your income tax, short-term capital gains are taxed. The prevailing tax rates for short-term gains are as follows: 10 percent, 12 percent, 22 percent, 24 percent, 32 percent, 35, and 37 percent.

Long-Term Passive Income Tax Rates

Long-term capital gains (assets that are held for more than one year) are taxed at three rates: zero percent, fifteen percent, and twenty percent, based on your income bracket.

Taxing of real estate income

With lower tax rates, investing in real estate and high yield rental assets is now even more advantageous for individuals. The authorized business income deduction is now a twenty percent deduction on the taxable income while buying and holding real estate. This deduction of 20 percent now requires investors to subtract a portion of the real estate investment holdings, which may lead to a higher ROI.

1.5 Why Passive Income Beats Earned Income

income Earned is the income that you earn when you work the job full-time or run a business. Notice that, in most instances, "running business" doesn't require rent real estate corporate. Money gained from royalties,rents, & stakes in the limited partnerships is passive income. Income from the portfolio is the income from interest, dividends, and stock sales capital gains. Earned income would be subject to heavy taxation at all levels. Earned money should be utilized to rapidly create wealth, but your wealth must be transferred into the portfolio and passive income pools in order to reduce your tax position. Earned incomes are subject to FICA taxation and the full marginal income tax rate. There are undoubtedly ways of minimizing tax liability, such as operating an S-earned Corporation's revenue, investing in the firm and currently earning deductible expenditures, etc., but high marginal tax rates would also be subject to net income. The issue with earned money is that you still have to spend more cash in order to minimize tax liability. Passive incomes from the rental property aren't subject to the high operational tax rates. Rental property income is privileged by amortization and depreciation and contributes toa much lesser effective rate of tax.

Let's assume, for instance, you now own a rental property,which nets 10,000 dollars before the depreciation & amortization. Let's just say that $8,000 is the total amount of depreciation and amortization. It leaves with a taxable revenue of $2,000. You can paya tax equivalent to 740 dollars if you fall in the 37 percent tax bracket. Yet you see an effective rate tax of just 7.4 percent as we equate the $740 with the amount raised ($10,000). If you made the same 10,000 dollars in the earned income, inorder to minimize the amount available to tax, you would need to expend more. Otherwise, with $10,000 into taxable income, you'd pay $3,700, meaning you're in 37 percent tax brackets. With the rental real-estate, every year, you don't have to be paying for depreciation. It's a ghostly cost which you have to claim. That's why, from a tax standpoint, passive income knocksout earned income.

1.6 Reasons Why Passive Income Is So Important

It's no wonder passive income's, and for a good cause, one of the most thought about, sought after aspects of personal finance. Passive income will have an incredibly positive effect on only about any financial situation, from creating vast wealth to avoiding a paycheck-to-paycheck lifestyle. But that posesthe question: why does passive income matter so much? In short, passive income's essential because in financial life, it provides flexibility, prosperity, and independence. In addition, because your time & resources do not limit passive income, it may havea beneficial and important impact on the ability to build wealth. Passive income, in different words, is 1 ofthe easiest ways to upgrade the financial condition. But if that's not compelling enough, we've listed the top reasons whypassive income's important.

Improved financial stability

One ofthe most significant milestones you will hit on the road to prosperity is monitory stability. In different words, even if you really can see your financial position and realize, with certainty, that you're capable of coping with a powerful financial storm, so then you're on a very stable path. If you may count on the money rolling inside without having to fight for every cent of it, even more than that, so financial security is just a nearby corner. More money which comes in more you can be secure and comfortable in the finances. It helps you in relaxing, look atthe bigger picture, & make smarter financial decisions because you don't have to grind for every dollar you earn, which, in turn, increases your financial health. This is a magnificent little cycle & one of key reasons whypassive income is playing such a major role inpersonal finance.

Less reliance on a paycheck

The discomfort that comes with living paycheck to paycheck is not comparable by any means. And if it is your case, then one of the best moves you can take is to adda bit of the passive income in your life. There is no secret in that sometimes it may get a bit stressful as you trade time for dollars. And the more you will distance yourself froma focus on the next paycheck, the lighter it can be in your life. One ofthe greatest advantages of passive income is avoiding the paycheck-to-paycheck lifestyle.

It's easier to achieve your goals

Did you ever say to yourself, " only If I made extra money, then I could accomplish my monetary goals much more quickly..."? Well, that's just another explanation why the passive income's so awesome. It doesn't what financial targets you're trying to attain; you can accomplish your goals much quicker if you build certain passive income sources that enable you to make money allthe time of day.

More freedom to pursue your passions

You will unexpectedly find yourself with the opportunity to pursue your passions or, for that matter, your ideal job, along the same line as avoiding the paycheck to the paycheck lifestyle, while you get some ofthe passive income flowing through the bank account. Remember that it's easy to end up trapped in a position you can't bear when you focus on the active income to make ends meet. It is tough enough to leave a career. But it is particularly tough to leave a job if you don't have sufficient money to pay the rent that is due in two weeks. On theother hand, you have the opportunity to do the things you really want to do when you have a stable stream of passive income running into the finances of yours. Passive income, to put plainly, offers you choices. & with those choices, independence comes.

Location independence

Likewise, in many ways, passive income encourages you to live and working from anywhere you like. Since you don't have to work constantly to earn a passive income, so you don't have to be working from a particular position either. You could tour the world if you like, as far as you earn passive income sufficient to support your lifestyle. And plenty of people do.

Early retirement

Retirement is,to some degree, for many people, that may only be done later inlife. Although, if you're building any passive income sources, retirement may not be far away as you thought. Really, if you love the thought of retirement at a young age, so then your primary financial priority should be passive income. If it means creating a company that operates even without you needing to be present there, participatingin real estate, or a mix of few different sources of income, if you desire to stop working at a young age, passive income is necessary.

More financial margin

more financial margins you will build in life, better off you will be in personal finance. In different words, the more distance you've between the expenditures & your income, the better it will get for financial life. And when you produce a constant stream of the passive income per month, it becomes much simpler to build the financial margin. Let's say, for instance, that your monthly gross expenditures increase upto 3,000 dollars. Now, if you're earning $4,000 inactive household revenue, then the monthly margin is $1,000. Yeah, that's not bad. However, if you add an additional $2,000 in passive monthly income in to the mix, life just got a lot better.

Reduced stress

There's one unity between all, after everything we've spoken about so far. It's plain; passive revenue has a distinctive way to reduce the financial burden. A passive income life is considerably less difficult than a life deprived of it. Because your financial security, margin, independence, and too much more are improved by passive income, it's only logical that it will help alleviate your financial burden. So, if financial condition makes you feela little tightened around the collar, you may just want to give passive incomea little more priority.

It's exciting

Passive income is not constrained by the effort and time that you can put into it. In different words, at all the hours of night and day, passive income can be earned, including while you are sleeping. Yet, at the same time, making money is incredibly thrilling. There's nothing like waking up inthe morning thinking that you've won a few hundred bucks while you're sleeping. And the more you are enthusiastic about the financial condition, the more probable you are to continue to improve it.

CHAPTER 2: Passive income ideas to help you make money in 2021

Passive income may be a wonderful way of helping you produce more cash flow, & global upheaval created primarily by the pandemic isevidenceof the importance of having many income sources. Passive income lets you cross the gap whether you unexpectedly become jobless or even whether you willingly take the time from work away with the pandemic tossing the working condition of most people into disarray. You might get the cash rolling in from passive income even while you follow your primary career, or if maybe you can build up a good passive income pool, you may needa little to kickback. Anyway, you are granted additional protection from passive income. And if you are concerned about being capable of saving enough money to reach your retirement objectives, accumulating capital throughpassive income also is a tactic that could be appealing to you. Regular earnings from a party other thanthe employer or the contractor are counted as passive income.IRS (Internal Revenues Service) notes that passive revenue will come from 2 sources: a company or a rental property in whichone is not directly participating, such as paying book royalty or dividends on securities. Most individuals agree that passive income's about getting more for nothing. It's got get-wealthy-quick charm, but it also includes work inthe end. What you offer is work upfront. You may do any or all the job upfront in practice, but the passive income also requires some extra labor alongthe way too. To keep the passive dollars flowing, you might have to saveyour merchandise updated orwell-maintained rental property. But if you're dedicated to the approach, it could be a perfect way to make income, and by the way, you'll build some more financial stability for yourself.

2.1 How many streams of income should you have?

"When it comes to generating revenue sources, there is no "one size fits all" advice. How many revenue streams you have can depend on where you are financially and what your potential financial targets are? But it is a decent beginning to get at least a handful. "With multiple lines in the sea, you'll attract more fish. Rental assets, revenue-producing shares, and company ventures are a perfect way to diversify your income stream, in addition to the earned income produced by your human capital. You'll want to make sure, of course, that bringing work into a new passive income stream would not cause you to lose sight of the other sources. So, you want your efforts to be aligned and make sure you pick the right options for your time.

2.2 Passive income ideas for building wealth

So,if you're considering building a passive income source, look at these techniques and absorb what this takes to succeed with them, whereas still recognizing the dangers involved with each strategy.

2.3 Selling information products

One common passive income approach is to produce information products, such as e-books, orvideo or audio lessons, and then kick back while cash rolls inside from product sale. Via platforms such as Skillshare,Udemy, and Coursera, courses could be distributed & sold. Otherwise, you may think of a "freemium model"-making a free content follow-up and only charging for the more comprehensive details or for the ones who wish to learn more. Language teachers or / &stock-picking guidance, for instance, can use the model. Free material serves asa demonstration of talents and can draw those who want to be going tothe next stage. You may use advertising (or sponsor) to make your revenue as the third alternative for this concept while offering information or material ona free forum like YouTube to a growing audience. Take the love of music or video games, for instance, and transform it into the content.

Opportunity

The Information products will have an outstanding revenue stream, so after the initial time outlay, you quickly make money.

Risk

development of this product typically requires a huge amount of effort. And it needs to be good in order to make great money off it. There isn't space out there for trash. If you wish to be competitive, you must create a strong base, advertise your products & prepare for other products. Unless you get very lucky, one product isn't business. Generating more outstanding products is the easiest way to market an established good. You could create a strong income stream once you understand the business model.

2.4 Rental income

A successful way of earning passive income is to invest in rental properties. But more work is always needed than people expect. You could risk your money if you do not take the time to know how to create a profitable venture.

Opportunity

If you want to earn the passive incomes from the rental properties,then you must determine three things:

- Financial risk of owning property.

- Property's total expenses and costs.

- How much profit you need on investment.

For example, suppose your objective is to make $10,000 ina year in the rental income. At the same time, your property has monthly mortgages of 2,000 dollars and charges another 300 dollars in one month for the taxes & other expenses. In this scenario, you will have to cost 3,133 dollars in the monthly rent foraccomplishing your objective.

Risk

few questions should be considered: Is there a marketplace for a property? How if you have a homeowner who pays off the property late or harms it? Suppose you cannot rent the property out? The passive income could be significantly impacted by any of the variables. And pandemic also has raised new threats. You could suddenly have occupants who could no longer afford their rent because of the economic crisis, although you may already have a mortgage of your own to be paying. Or, if earnings fall, you couldn't be capableof rentingout homes for as far as you did before. So, to secure yourself, you'll want to consider these threats and have a contingency plan in place.

2.5 Affiliate marketing

However, with affiliate advertising, website owners, "influencers" on social media or blogs support the goods of third parties by including a link to the product on the forum or the social media network. The best-known associate partner maybe Amazon, but Awin, ShareASale and eBay, are all among the bigger brands. And for those watching to develop a following and sell goods, TikTok and Instagram have become major websites. To attract attention to the blog or else steer people to goods and services which they may like, you might also start growing an email list.

Opportunity

The site owner receives a fee if visitors click on the link and make a transaction from a third-party associate. The commission may vary from 3-7 %, so it would obviously need substantial traffic to the site to produce serious revenue. But you could be able to make some serious coin if you may expand the following or even have a more profitable niche (like tech, fitness, or financial services). Affiliate advertising is deemed passive, and, in principle, only by adding a link to your social media platform or website, you will gain money. In fact, if you cannot draw readers to the site to tap on the link and purchase anything, you won't earn anything.

Risk

You'll have to be taking time to develop content and generate traffic if you're just starting out. Building a following will take important time, and you'll need to discoverthe best formula to reach the crowd, a task that could take a while on its own. Worse, the audience might be likely to fly to the next famous influencer, topic, orsocial media site after you've expended all that energy.

2.6 Flip retail products

Make use of online sales sites like Amazon or eBay, and offer goods you find nowhere at prices of cut-rate. You will arbitragethe difference between the prices between your purchase & selling, and you will be able to create a following of the people who monitor your transactions.

Opportunity

The price disparities between what you'll find & what average customer will be capable of finding would encourage you to take advantage of them. If you've contact that may help you obtain affordable goods that some other individuals can locate, this might work extremely well. Or you might be capableof uncovering useful products which others have completely missed.

Risk

Although deals can happen online at any moment, you'll probably have to rush to find a reputable source of goods to help keep this strategy passive. And you're just going to have to knowthe competition so that you don't buy ata price that's too much. Otherwise, in order to market, you can finish up with goods that nobody needs. Moreover, you may be forced to slash the price drastically inorder to make the product worthwhile for the buyers.

2.7 Peer-to-peer lending

Peer-to-peer (or P2P) loan's personal loan supports bythe intermediary of third-party like LendingClub or Prosper between you &borrower. Funding Circle that targets firms & has greater borrowing caps, and Payout, which targets better collateral losses, are other players.

Opportunity

You generate income as a lender from interest payments made on loans. Yet, you face the possibility of default because the loan is insecure, implying you might end up with nothing. You must do two things to cut the risk:

By paying smaller sums on different loans, diversify the lending portfolio. Minimum investment for each credit is $25 at Prosper.com and LendingClub.

To make educated choices, evaluate old data on the prospective borrowers.

Risk

It takes time to learnthe lending metrics of P2P because it's not completely passive, and you'll want to vet your prospective borrowers closely because you ought to pay particular attention to payments earned when you're engaging in several loans. If you intend to create profits, whatever you make for interest can be reinvested. Economic recessions may also make the high-yielding personal loans more likely to default candidates because if the COVID-19 manages to harm the economy at higher than historical rates, these loans will go bad.

2.8 Dividend stocks

The Shareholders in companies with dividend-yielding securities receive a payout fromthe company atregular intervals. The Companies pay the cash dividend out of the earnings on a quarterly basis, and what you need to be doing is to own stock. Per-share of stock, dividends are funded, meaning the more shares that you hold, the larger your compensation.

Opportunity

Since stock income is not linked to any operation other than the actual financial investment, it may be one ofthe most passive ways of money-making to own dividend-yielding securities. In your bank account, the money will simply be deposited.

Risk

Choosing the correct stocks is a tricky aspect. Without carefully researching company issuing stock, too many novices leap into the market. You have to study the website of each organization and be acquainted with their financial statements. 2 to 3 weeks you can spend researching each venture. That said, without wasting a massive amount of time analyzing firms, there are some ways to participate in the stocks dividend-yielding. ETFs, or Exchange-traded fund, are strongly recommended for income generation. ETFs are hedge vehicles containing collateral such as equity, commodities & bonds but trading like stocks. The ETFs arean excellent alternative for novices because, due to much lower prices than mutual funds, they are easier to understand, affordable,highly liquid, and offer much higher potential returns. Another key risk's that the stocks or the ETFs will decrease dramatically over short periods of time, particularly in times of volatility, such as when the financial markets were shocked by the Coronavirus crisis in 2020. Economic uncertainty may also cause certain firms to fully cut the dividends, while the diversified funds can experience less of a pinch.

2.9 Create an app

Creating an app may be a method to invest time in advance and then enjoy rewards over time. Your software may bea game or one that allows smartphone users to execute any feature that is difficult to do. Users download it once the application is public, &you can generate revenue.

Opportunity

There's a big upside to an app if you can create something that captures your audience's fancy. You'll think about how it's best to generate revenue. You could run in-application advertisements, for example, or else make users paya small fee to use the app. You'll definitely add incremental improvements to keepthe product current and popular as the app gains attention or you get feedback.

Risk

Perhaps the greatest risk here's that you spend your time unprofitably. You have no financial drawback here if you contribute little to no money to the project (and/or money which you'd have spent otherwise, for instance, on hardware). It's a competitive market, though, and genuinely popular applications must give consumers a persuasive benefit of experience. If your app gathers some data, you would also want to ensure that it is in accordance with privacy rules, which vary across the globe.

2.10 REITs

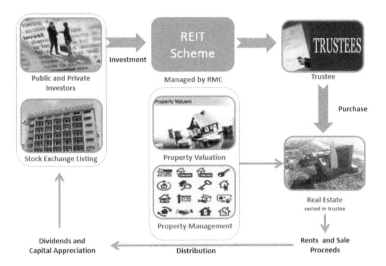

For a corporation that owns and manages real assets, REIT is a real estate investment trust, which is a fancy word. REITs have a special legal arrangement such that although they pass over any of their income to owners, they pay no or little corporate income tax.

Opportunity

In the stock exchange, you can purchase REITs much as every other business or dividend stock. You're going to earn whatever the REITs payout as a payout, and the strongest REITs have an annual record of growing their dividend, meaning over time, you might have an increasing supply of dividends. Specific REITs could be more expensive, like dividend stocks, than buying an ETF composed of hundreds of REIT stocks.Fund offers instant diversification, which is inherently much better than owning specific stocks & you can always earn a good return.

Risk

You'll have to be capable of selecting good REITs, much like dividend stocks, that means you'll have to evaluate any of the firms you might purchase, which indeed isa time-taking process. Also, while it isa passive activity, if you do not know what you're doing, you might lose a lotof money. And neither are REIT dividends safe from difficult economic times. If REIT does not produce enough income, this would possibly have to slash or totally remove its dividend. So just when you want it, most of the passive income could get hit.

2.11 A bond ladder

 bond ladder's sequence of bonds maturing over a number of years at various periods. The phased maturities help you to reduce the risk of reinvestment, which isa risk of locking up your cash as bonds offer interest rates that are too low.

Opportunity

bond ladder's a traditional passive investmentthat for decades has attractednear-retirees and retirees. You will sit back to collect the interest payments, and you "extendthe ladder," transferring the principle into different package of bonds as the bond matures. For starters, you could start off with one year, three years, five years, and seven years of bonds. In the year that 1st bond matures, you have two years, four years, and six years of bonds left. You may use proceeds from the newly aged bond to purchase another one year or roll out an eight-year bond with a longer-term, for example.

Risk

Bond ladder reduces one ofthe big dangers of purchasing bonds, the possibility that you may have to purchasea new bond as the bond develops when the interest rates will not be attractive. Bonds, too, come with the other risks. Althoughthe federal government backs Treasury bonds, corporate bonds aren't, meaning you could risk your principal. And to diversify the exposure& eliminatethe risk of someone bond harming your total portfolio, you'll want to buy multiple bonds. Many investors move to bond the ETFs because of these issues, which include a diversified fund of bonds that you may put up on a ladder, removing the possibility that a single bond will harm your returns.

2.12 Invest in a high-yield CD or savings account

Investing in an online bank's high-yield deposit certificate (CD) or savings account will help you to produce passive income and get one ofthe country best interest rates as well. In order to make money, you won't even have to leave home.

Opportunity

You'll want to do a fast check of the nation's great CD rates or the top savings accounts to make the most of your CD. Going to the online bank instead ofthe local bank is typically far more advantageous since you will be able to pick the highest rate available inthe region. And if the financial firm is backed by the FDIC, you will also receive a fixed return of principal of up to 250,000 dollars.

Risk

Your principal is secure as far as the bank is backed by FDIC and under limits. So, it is just as secure a return as you'll find to invest in a CD or savings account. Nevertheless, though the accounts are secure, these days, they return even less than before. And with Federal Reserve aiming at 2% inflation, the least in the short run, you're going to miss out on inflation. A savings account or CD can, though, yield less than keeping your cash in cash or in a non-interest paying checking account where you will earn about zero.

2.13 Buy Property

Real estate can be a decent way to make a passive income, depending on where you invest and when. There has been a rapid growth in the value of property in common cities such as Toronto-44 percent in Canada alone in the last five years. You will find some lower-cost properties by purchasing pre-construction condos, which will rise in value by the time it is eventually completed, enabling you to sell the property once it is complete for a profit. Like for all investments, it can be dangerous, so if you're new to the market, it's better to talk to a real estate agent to help you purchase the correct investment property.

2.14 Rent out your home short-term through Airbnb

This simple approach takes advantage of space that you don't need anyway, and converts it into an opportunity to make some money. Whether you're leaving for summer and/or have to be outside of the town for sometime, or maybe even you want to fly, try renting your present space out while you're gone.

Opportunity

On a variety of websites, including Airbnb, you may list space and set rental conditions yourself. With limited additional work, you'll receive a check for efforts, particularly if you rent to a tenant who might be in place for a couple of months.

Risk

You do not have a lot of financial downsides here, but it's a gamble that's atypical of the most passive investors to let strangers stay in your house. Tenants can, for instance, even deface or ruin your property or steal valuables even.

2.15 Air BnB Business as a Passive income Strategy

Airbnb is an online website for selling and renting urban homes. It ties hosts and travellers and promotes the rental process without owning any rooms on its own. Moreover, it cultivates a cooperative economy by allowing private flats to be leased by property owners. Airbnb is an internet platform which links individuals that wish to rent the homes to an individual in that area who are searching for a room. It currently surrounds more than 100 thousand cities in the world and 220 countries. The name of the business derives from the "air mattress B and B." Engaging in Airbnb is a way for hosts to gain some money from their home, but with the possibility that it may be damaged by the visitor. The benefit could be comparatively cheap lodging for visitors, but with the possibility that property wouldn't be as advisable as the listing has made itlook. For less than the cost of a hotel bed, travellers may also book an Airbnb. The traveler's biggest concern is that the property could not live up to its listing. The primary concern for hosts is that their property may be badly damaged by guests.

Airbnb

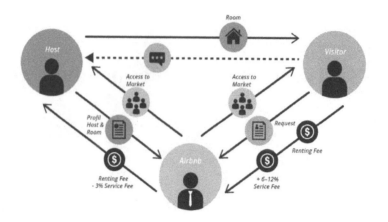

The Advantages of Airbnb

It offers the following advantages:

Wide Selection

Airbnb hosts list several different categories of properties on theAirbnb website, like single rooms,a suite ofrooms, moored yachts, , whole homes, studios, houseboats, even castles.

Free Listings

In order to list the assets, hosts don't have to be paying. Listings may contain written descriptions, captioned photographs, and user profiles so prospective visitors canhave the knowledge about hostsa little better.

Hosts Can Set Their Own Price

It is the host's prerogative to decide how much to charge per night, per week, or /and per month.

Customizable Searches

The Guests can filterthe Airbnb database and not only through date & location, however also by price, property type, amenities, and the host's language. To further limit their search, they may also add keywords (such asclose to the Louvre').

Additional Services

Airbnb has increased its services to include events and restaurants in recent years. In addition to a list of available hotels for the dates they expect to visit, individuals searching by the venue can see a list of opportunities provided by nearby Airbnb hosts, like classes and sightseeing. Restaurant listings also contain Airbnb hosts' reviews.

Protections for Guests and Hosts

As a protection for customers, before transferring the funds to the host, Airbnb keeps the guest's payment for 24 hours following check-in. For guests, Airbnb's Host Guarantee program "provides security for up to $1,000,000 in damage to covered property in eligible countries in the rare incident of guest damage."

The disadvantages of Airbnb

It has the following demerits:

What You See May Not Be What You Get

Booking Airbnb accommodation is not like booking a space with a big hotel chain, where you have a fair promise that the property will be as described. Individual hosts, though some may be more truthful than others, create their own listings. Previous visitors, however, often post updates about their experiences, which may offer a more critical perspective. To make sure the listing is correct, review the reports of other guests who have stayed at the Airbnb house.

Potential Damage

The greater concern for hosts is potential that their property will be damaged. Although most stays go without incident, when the Airbnb hosts assumed they were renting to a peaceful household, there are reports of entire houses being trashed by thousands of partygoers. Some insurance is offered by Airbnb's Host Guarantee program, mentioned above, but it does not cover anything, like cash, rare artwork, jewellery, and pets. Also, hosts whose homes are destroyed can experience significant inconvenience.

Added Fees

A number of extra charges are imposed by Airbnb (just like, of course, hotels and other lodging providers). To cover Airbnb's customer care and other programs, travelers pay a guest management fee of 0 percent to 20 percent on top of the reservation fee. Prices are shown in the currency that the customer chooses, provided it is sponsored by Airbnb. Banks or issuers of credit cards can, where applicable, add fees. And though listings are free, to cover the cost of handling the transaction, Airbnb charges a service fee of at least 3 percent for each reservation.

It Isn't Legal Everywhere

Would-be hosts need to review their municipal zoning codes before listing their properties on Airbnb to make sure it is legal to rent their properties. To receive special permits or licenses, hosts may also be required.

2.16 Advertise on your car

By merely driving your car across town, you can be able to raise some additional income. Contact a specialized advertisement firm to determine your commuting patterns, like when and how many miles you drive. The firm will "wrap" your car with the ads at no cost to you if you're a match with one of their advertisers. Newer vehicles are being searched by agencies, and drivers should have a clear driving record.

Opportunity

If you're still putting in the miles anyway, though you may have to get out and drive, then this is a perfect way to earn hundreds every month at little to no added expense. It is reasonable to pay drivers by the mile.

Risk

Be extra cautious about locating a reputable operation to work with if this idea seems good. In this space, many fraudsters set up schemes to try to bilk you out of thousands.

2.17 Invest in Stocks

When you look at the wealthiest people in the world, it's pretty fair to conclude that their deep, endless savings accounts are a result of their major investment in stocks. Warren Buffett reads 500 pages a day, but he doesn't read your usual mystery novel. He reviews the annual corporate reports. He better knows whether or not a company is doing well by reviewing annual reports each day, which helps him improve his decision to invest in stocks. While the act of investing in stocks is very passive, the analysis that goes into it is active. Nevertheless, investing in shares will help you gain passive income that goes well beyond what your value is worth at your 9 to 5 work. So, if you enjoy reading about the success of different firms, consider this passive income approach.

2.18 Make Your Car Work for You

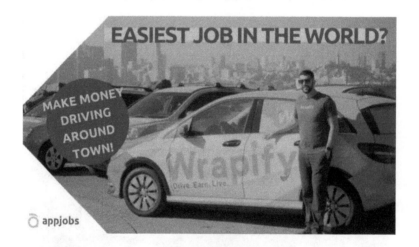

Driving is another everyday practice that you can translate into passive income. When you're just walking around, why not pick up a commuter or two to run errands? Uber can help you make money by taking people to their designated destination by driving your vehicle. You may also put ads on your vehicle to collect cash as you drive around. When your car is not used while you're on holiday, driving, or just during a normal workday, it will still make money. You will make thousands of dollars with an app like Getaround by renting out your car if you're not using it. Plus, drivers of Getaround vehicles get the best parking spaces in town, a $50 monthly rental credit on any vehicle they want, and one million U.S. dollars in primary insurance coverage.

2.19 Sell your Videos

We live in a day and age where video content fascinates hundreds and thousands of humans. You would want to take out your phone and hit the record if you still find yourself in the middle of drama and excitement. To allow you to make some passive income, you can sell stored content. Why? It is because the video can be sold to a news site. And you can make some recurring income for weeks, months, and maybe even years if the video takes off. Of course, being at cultural gatherings such as marches, rallies, and festivals is the best way to get in on the action. You'll find ways for your material to be sold anywhere there's controversy. And corporations will pay you to make viral videos along with providing a share of total earnings if you are successful at creating engaging content.

2.20 Create YouTube Videos

The passive income source that just keeps on giving is YouTube. You'll find that you can make a regular income from your YouTube channel, from funded videos to ad sales. Creating videos on a regular basis for a long time is the key to creating a profitable YouTube channel. If you stick with it in the long run, you will finally start reaping the benefits of passive income.

2.21 Write an eBook

In 2009 and 2010, e-books came onto the scene and are now a hugely successful content medium. While they first became popular a few years ago, to this day, there is still a very decent chunk of individuals who make passive income from writing e-books. It's an insanely dynamic business, of course. Yet, you might find yourself with a nice slice of the profits if your writing chops are stellar. You could build a fanbase of loyal readers by designing how-to e-books on famous niches and marketing them.

2.22 Sell Digital Products

You can make digital goods if you're trying to create your own products rather than selling someone else's. You can sell your digital goods online using Shopify. From e-books, educational classes, PDFs, custom graphic templates, stock images, or some other digital goods, digital products will contain anything. Selling these items is the epitome of passive income, and with immediate updates, the whole operation can be streamlined on Shopify.

Car Wash

Car wash is a perfect way to earn a semi-passive income. Although a car wash will need daily cleaning, it is something you can either contract out or do once a week. We are talking about the very simple car wash that is cinderblocks, a pressure washer, and the powered coin, as a side note. It's certainly a corporation vs. a passive income stream if you're trying to run a drive-through car wash.

2.23 CPC Ads (Cost Per Click)

You get really paid whenever anyone clicks on your link and signs up for something or orders something through affiliate ads. On the other hand, show advertisements charges depend on the volume of traffic and eyeballs that you receive on their ads. On the other hand, for CPC advertisements, also known as "cost per click" ads, anytime someone clicks on an ad, you get paid no matter what they do after that. You don't have to hope or pray that they're buying anything or signed up for something. Any single click takes money into your account with the bank. Does that mean that all day long you can go to your own website and click on ads? It is not realistic since the corporation will inevitably find out what you are doing and cut you off. With all that in mind, it should not be a part of your plan here to click on your own ads. Instead, aim to build up traffic so that more and more viewers every day see the ads.

2.24 Minimize your taxes on passive income

A passive income may be a wonderful side-income generation strategy, but you can still create a tax burden for your effort. But by setting yourself up as a business and building a savings portfolio, you can reduce the tax bite and plan for your future, too. However, this solution will not work with all these passive strategies because to qualify. You will have to be a legal organization.

Register with the IRS to make your company receive a tax identification number.

Then call a broker, such as Charles Schwab or Fidelity, who will open a self-employed retirement account.

Determine the type of savings account that will fit well for your needs.

CHAPTER 3: Airbnb Offers The Best Passive Income Generation Strategy

rental vacation industry is rising quickly. It is real quick indeed asa matter of fact. The sector is currently generating 57,669 million dollarsin sales, according to recent analysis reports from Statista.com. The revenue is awaited to grow to a market value of 74,005 million dollars by 2023 and is projected to see an average growth rate of 6.4 percent. This data illustrates just how broad & robust the holiday rental management industry is. And you should expect demand for Airbnb property management to pursue to grow overthe coming years with the growth of Airbnb rental properties in recent years. Therefore, if one day you are aiming to become amanager of Airbnb property, now is a great time to be entering the business. But how are you able to get started? We will supply you with what you have to know regarding how to be an Airbnb vacation rental property manager. We're going to teach you what this takes to handle rental Airbnb properties, particular instruments you're going to be needing before you start, andstop points for the beginners for achieving successful property management. So, without further ado, over here are all six steps to beginning an Airbnb property management career inreal estate.

3.1 Understand the Vacation Rental Industry

Just like some other business, without learning at leastthe fundamentals of this area, you can't succeed. However, no formal qualification is necessary to become an Airbnb property manager,and many find success with the onlydiploma of high school in this profession.Thorough knowledge of howthe holiday rental industry & Airbnb run is what you need to have.So, if you don't already have it, having this information now is the 1st step to being the manager of the Airbnb properties. Ideally, as Airbnb hosts yourself, you should have some experience. If you've already hosted your rental property on Airbnb, run it yourself, you can show to potential buyers which you know exactly what you are doing. Furthermore, this will allow you to be prepared better to predict challenges, recognize potentially troublesome travelers, and cope with common issues. But if you don't have the experience, through online guides and classes, you can empower yourself about the rental vacation industry &how Airbnb works. There are plenty of those out there that can help you create a good base on which you have to learn. For instance, you may take marketing coursework to know how to extend your scope and get bookings more and business courses to know how to manage a company, keep records, &file tax. As an Airbnb property manager, it'll help you improve your creditability. Before you start, another significant point to learn is where the Airbnb hosts invest in rentals for the short-term. You'll know the place to find customers looking for management support with this detail.

3.2 Create a Maintenance Management System

Managing rental of short-term rentals ensures that you'll get visitors checking in & out repeatedly. One of many duties of the property managers, of course, is to review property before visitors visit &after they depart. Every now & then, operators of holiday rentals must also conduct repairs to ensure that the properties are in perfect shape. This is vital to ensure the happiness of both your customer and guests. For instance, imagine having visitors who had parties and had rental property trashed before leaving. Nobody with such a situation is going to be happy to step intoa rental. As a consequence, before addressing the issue, themanager of Airbnb property can never leave the maintenance as an afterthought or even wait forthe property owner to receive several inquiries. In addition, to offer high-quality care on their behalf, great short-term property rental operators often work alongside a dependable maintenance team. Your staff should include, among others, plumbers, house cleaners, and electricians. For any check-in, these entities will ensure that Airbnb assets you handle are tip to top.

3.3 Put Together a Vacation Rental Marketing Strategy

The most significant tasks of property managers are promoting and selling holiday rentals to attract prospective visitors. Today, there are millions of listings on Airbnb & morerental sites for the short-term, which is creating rivalry among the Airbnb hosts. It is why one of the first things potential users would like to know is how you're going to get reservations and increase their occupancy rates for Airbnb. As a consequence, you must havea basic comprehension of tactics and methods for property marketing. Therefore, having a marketing campaign that will draw Airbnb visitors to the holiday rentals you run isthe next step towardsbeing Airbnb properties manager. Start by writing an enticing listing that will maximize the probability of retaining a high rate of occupancy

&a positive flow of cash. To make rental properties under your management stand out, think about investing in advanced photography & videography facilities, also branding services. Moreover, selling holiday rentals suggests that you have to go outside the listing platform. It is why active rental managers of Airbnb use social media and also SEO to meet the target tenant audience. If you don't know how it works, before you begin handling rentals inthe short term, we strongly suggest that you begin to read about real estate marketing.

3.4 Invest in Property Management Tools

You can handle them with hard work and a few spreadsheets as you becomemanager of Airbnb property for the first time when you have only some rental properties underneath your belt. This becomes difficult, though, as you continue to add more assets to manage. How are thirty check-ins & cleanings going to be done in 1 day? At an early point, it is best to begin thinking about it so thatyou're planning yourself & your company for success and expansion. Using real estate management ofproperty software that allows to automate & remain structured is the best approach for this.

In order to operate their businesses more effectively, modern holiday rental property supervisors rely a lot on technology. There are several high-tech solutions that make it easy to handle Airbnb rental, from the smart lock to invoicing, pricing, and the guest screening software systems. You will even find holiday rental apps which will synchronize schedules and handle multiple Airbnb profiles for free from different platforms. Not only does the use of such instruments make your life more effective asa manager of real estate properties, but they can also give youthe strategic edge to keep rising. Mashboard, for instance, is a software that lets managers of Airbnb property connect with their customers and findthe right properties for those to expand their business.

3.5 Outline Your Guest Management Strategy

Amazing client care is one of the abilities that any manager of real estate property wants to provide when handling both conventional and holiday rentals. It is how effective operators of Airbnb assets set themselves away from the audience. A good selling point, particularly for Airbnb travelers, is customer service that goes beyond and beyond. Getting a guest engagement plan ensures that during their visit, the services can be open to visitors and their demands at whatever time. Expect the short-term visitors to have to inquire or inquire over something. You must be capable of responding in a timely way to such unannounced requests. How can you treat a case, for instance, where the visitor has misplaced keys toa holiday rental and can't get in? There will be a contingency in it and other cases for a successful Airbnb property manager. In addition, to manage communication with visitors, managers of top-performing properties also have automation tech systems in place. Airbnb guests really enjoy great customer service & show this by posting favorable feedback. This, in essence, helps to get more bookings & boost cash flow, that will surely make the customers happier. As you could see, oneof the most critical skills for good management of Airbnb property is definitely customer service, so don't consider it asan afterthought.

3.6 Set a Reasonable (But Competitive) Price

To becomea manager of Airbnb property, the only thing you need is a pricing plan. Usually, the holiday rental manager takesa percentage cut from the real host's secured rental fee. A selection of online outlets recommends anywhere from ten to twenty-five percent. At the same time, others believe that more consumers would be drawn by charging the lowest price; that isn't the case. Customers base their options on the quality o facilities rendered by property managers-not dependent on costs. Thus, providingthe lowest price means that you don't have top-tier facilities for owners of Airbnb property. You need to take several factors into account in order to fix the correct price. First of all, as stated, is what kind of services you are providing. Naturally, for something that you don't sell, you do not charge. Look at experience instead, what distinctive points of selling you may give, and set rate accordingly. The local economy and what the other rental property (short-term)managers in the area charge, the seasonal demands, also current events, you will need to remember. Ultimately, you need to seta fair price which you are sure will be getting you back that your serviceis worth.

3.7 How an Airbnb Business Works

Nearly everyone has listenedto Airbnb or has used it. It is the platform for online home rentals that helps hostsrenting vacant private short-term accommodation from asingle room to whole homes. Airbnb launched in 2007 &has expanded exponentially to have listings in further than 65 thousand cities in the world with more than three million available properties. Here is how tostart a sustainable Airbnb company if you have sufficient rental space and are searching for additional revenue. Through uploading photographs and details of the room for rent, the first move is to bea host on Airbnb and register the home. When an Airbnb property's listed, travelers searching for a room inthe host area will access it. Guests may use a number of requirements to check for Airbnb listings, like:

- Availability dates
- Destination

- No. Of rooms, such as bedrooms and washrooms

- Price

- Host language

- Amenities such as hot tub, breakfast, pets allowed, and etc.

- Facilities like air conditioning, parking,etc.

Prior to booking the chosen space through the Airbnb guest may establish a contact withhosts directly for gathering additional information through the Airbnb service of messaging.

Access

Along with browser access, Airbnb offers mobile applications for Android and Apple IOS devices.

Security

For security purposes, the hosts are expected to provide Airbnb with appropriate identification. Travelers should post the reviews of hotels to create a trustworthy group (and the hosts may review the guests). The Reviews aren't anonymous.

Guest Services

Airbnb offers a stable payment platform for the guest's calmness of mind, and fees to the hosts are deferred until 24 hr after the arrival of the guest. In the event that any difficulties are faced during the renting time, Airbnb hasa 24-hour hotline forthe guest.

Fees

Host sets the price for lodging. Moreover, Airbnb chargesunder-mentioned fees:

Host: Three% transaction payment fee

Guest: six to twelve% booking fee

The Hosts can also ask fora security deposit&couldwell charge a cleaning fee.

Taxes

Airbnb could apply provincial, state, or city taxes for guest bookings depending on the jurisdiction.

Travelers Prefer Airbnb Rentals

One ofthe best things about operating an Airbnb company is that, for several reasons, travelers choose Airbnb over motels, hotels, or hostels:

Cost: Usually, Airbnb rent is much inexpensive thana similar hotel room. In certain instances, an entire house may be rented through Airbnb forthe cost of a single suite of the hotel, depending on the location.

Living locally: Living the life of a local person is the key advantage ofthe Airbnb service. Most guests of Airbnb choose to stay inside the community and explore the destination way the locals do, instead of renting a generic hotel room.

Privacy: customers of Airbnb are not continuously surrounded by visitors and workers at the hotel.

Peace & quiet: the Airbnb rents are usually more secure and do not suffer from loud hotel events, such as guest exits early in the morning, young children, maid service, and traffic.

Witness what you get already: Unlikea hotel where you can see a snapshot of similar rooms on their Airbnb page at best, you get full images and explanations of the real premises.

Diversity: From yachts and boathouses to castles and lighthouses, Airbnb has an immense variety of available accommodations.

Home comforts: Airbnb hasa homey atmosphere of a real living space instead of generic hotel spaces (few haveresident pets even). Kitchens allow the guests to cook their own food if they desire to save money on outside dining or have dietary issues.

Friends or Family: Through Airbnb, you may savea lot of money by renting a whole apartment/ house/condo rather than the multiple rooms of a hotel for family and friends.

Is Renting Your Space Permissible or Advisable?

Ensure you're legally permitted to bean Airbnb host into jurisdiction before you plan to start an Airbnb business, & you're prepared to respect local laws &regulations. Depending on the state/ cityor regional rules, municipal laws governing the hosting of paid visitors will vary greatly; they are absolutely banned in some areas whilst they're subject to occupancy tax in others if space is condominium or apartment,check to view if it is allowed to sub-let the premises. There are also regulations in place for apartment landlords & condominium societies to prohibit an owner from renting the units out as Airbnb rooms. Renting your apartment out without the knowledge of your landlord will have you evicted. Neighborhood ties are also a significant concern. In the area, a few inconsiderate or loud Airbnb guests will easily turn you in a pariah. If none of the challenges are insurmountable, it could be an outstanding opportunity of home-foundbusiness to become an Airbnb host.

Are You Committed to Becoming a Host

There are a variety of additional concerns to remember prior to making a definitive decision to host Airbnb:

Would you like to starta business? Then Startingan Airbnb company is like establishing any business- that you need enthusiasm, entrepreneurial spirit, &the ability to make the required effort, starting off with doing relevant background analysis and developing business plans.

Do you've energy? It could takea great amount of time to be a landlord, particularly for the short-term rents. You'll have to:

- Manage reservations and reply to interactions with prospective tenants.
- Plan to meet the guests to give out or receive keys
- ensure the property, including fresh linen, breakfast supplies, is cleaned properly and ready for the arrival of the guest (if applicable)
- Fix some property maintenance problems such as plumbing and pest control, electrical & appliance repair
- Be accessible to the visitors on a 24 into 7 basis if the property has any problems.

Demand: The deciding factor inthe popularity & price of rented accommodation is visitor demand. The highest places for rental returns are:

sought-after tourist destinations with high hotel rates (famous neighborhood ranks higher on the Airbnb searches)

situated Centrally, close to visitor attractions, shops & public transport,

Featuring panoramic views and facilities like parking, balconies, etc.

Seasonality: Demand for the property in the northern hemisphere will definitely drop drastically in winters (unless you're renting a ski chalet). In comparison, rental accommodation demand in colder southern locations (like Arizona) decreases dramatically in summers.

What are the marketing aims? Are you trying to earn a little cash or create a stable income onthe side? The financial portion ofthe business plan must show target market analysis and reasonable forecasts of your property's future rental income. The income from the Airbnb contract depends upon:

Before you start thinking about leaving your job& making a living through runningan Airbnb company, make sure that by seeingrental prices & booking regularity for comparing Airbnb listings of your area, you carefully examine the revenue potential of your property.

Extra costs: In addition to booking fees paid by Airbnb, there are extra costs involved with Airbnb hosting, including:

Insurance: Standard insurance plans for homeowners do not includethe use of the property for commercial uses, including renting on Airbnb. Airbnb has a free host compensation insurance policy in Canada, U.K., U.S., and many other nations, offering up to 1 million dollars in guarantees against personal harm or property loss. If your place is not protected by Airbnb policies, please contact your insurance provider to see if there is sufficient coverage.

Business Licenses: Airbnb hosts are being required by more & more cities to holda business license.

Repair and Cleaning: You want to keep rental properties in top condition all the time in order to keep your Airbnb host ranking at a high standard, which includes extensive cleaning during guest stays and daily repairs. The charges will contribute to your expenses if you have to sub-contract cleaning and repair duties.

Listing and Pricing Your Property on Airbnb

Accurately describe the place and make this stand out. Note that Airbnb is an online marketplace & you have to be thinking likea realtor to make listing stick out fromthe competition in order to optimize guest interest in your house. Start by looking at the same Airbnb listings insidethe region and consider the amenities/features and prices listed. If this works, makea spreadsheet. The definition of your listing must be precise, comprehensive, complete, and highlight, which makes it special. Comprehensively define the facilities and functionality of your room also as any regulations or preferences of visitors. Providing high-quality photographs of the room is incredibly necessary. Airbnb has specialist availability of photography service in certain places if you are unable to do this yourself.. You don't want visitors to be upset because the room isn't as advertised or you've exaggerated amenities. Note that the guest rankings would be partially dependent on the accuracy of your listing description.

Price Your Listing Competitively

You should also get an ideaof how to market your listing from your analysis of similar listings. It needs to be competitively priced to keep the property consistently booked (and increase profits).

Improving Your Host Ranking

Higher the property pops up in rankings, the more probable it's to be chosen by visitors, so having good rankings of Airbnb is crucial to the success of Airbnb business. Airbnb rankings are like internet search rankings.Andby building confidence and offering a fantastic experience to your visitors, you will boost your rankings.

Build Trust

Airbnb community's based on trust and guests would be searching for hosts with contact information, credentials, and favorable feedback.

Verification

For the new hosts, verification is highly essential: change your profile and include other details like the email address, phone number, Facebook profile, and etc. For giving prospective visitors some confidence that you're a reliable host.

References

You should post the references from colleagues, co-workers, relatives, business partners, etc., to build more trust. For the other Airbnb users, you may even write references.

Provide Great Customer Service

Like any entrepreneur would tell you, the cornerstone of any successful business is customer care, and becoming an Airbnb host has no difference. Positive ratings, better search scores, and more bookings reward hosts of Airbnb who havethe best experience of the guest. The hosts with the most popular are:

Responsive

The Hosts that can not be bothered for responding in a timely manner (or at some) to inquiries are a big turnoff for visitors. In reality, Airbnb keepstrack and rates your replies to guests accordingly. With higher search rankings and improved bookings, the host who hasthe highest ratings of response is awarded. At all times, Airbnb mobile application will help you to keep connected. All the time when visitors are present, be available through phone and check up with them on extended trips and see if there's something more you may do to maximize the services.

Update Their Calendars Regularly

Keeping your calendar current, also enhancing the guest experience, boosts the Airbnb rankings of search.

Fix All Problems quickly

When a guest mentions problemslike leaky taps or a burned-out lightbulb, it should be repaired promptly and render an apology to the guest. Sure ways to boost the guest rankings is to provide five-star service.

Act on Their Reviews

Fix the issue and benefit from the failures if a visitor writes a critical review. React to complaints all the time in a respectful way.

3.8The Bottom Line

In real estate, there are many ways of earning profits. The growing success in the U.S. housing sector of Airbnb and other short-term rentals has created opportunities not just for real estate developers but also for property managers. Today, there is a great demand for vacation rental managers, and industry analysts expect that over the coming years, there will be national growth. Therefore, imagine being an Airbnb property manager if you're looking for a profitable means of generating passive income.

Conclusion

In a nutshell, passive income is money that comes at regular intervals without having to invest a large amount of work into generating it. By blogging, one method of producing passive income may be achieved. If you've figured out how to produce content that attracts sufficient traffic to the host advertising, you can makea product that your customers would want to purchase. From a basic e-book toa sophisticated app that produces sales for several years after it is released, passive income could be anything. Similarly, people have a lot of things, and they still look for cheap places to store this. What might be simpler than asking people to pay you for storing their things? An investment ona large-scale in purchasing storage facilities (with the cash) or anything simple like offering the basement or the shed might entail creating passive income by offering storage. All you'll need is to make sure their goods are clean and stable. You will make money by selling them to others against such charges if you've any things that you don't use at all times, which others will love to borrow. As rental items, useful items such as a tractor, trailer, kayak,trampoline, or your own lawneven may give youpassive income. With the support of platforms like Airbnb, this also involves renting spare rooms out in your home. Upload the pictures of items, fix a date, and tellthe world they're ready for the rent on your favorite social networking site. The reason why it is necessary to have passive income is that it will help increase your financial consistency. The more passive income you make, the easier it becomes to be consistent with your financial life, from consistently saving to consistently spending to consistently donating. One of the strongest and most relevant aspects of a sound financial condition is passive income. It is beneficial for you in several ways, from enhancing your financial health to reducing your financial burden.

Bubble or Revolution? The Basics ofBitcoin and Blockchain.

The Idiot-Proof Guide toUnderstand the Crypto Market and Become a Skilled Investor and Trader Starting from Scratch.

By

Vishen Smith

Table of Contents

Chapter1. What Is Bitcoin?

Bitcoin is advanced cash that was made in January 2009. It follows the thoughts set out in a white paper by the strange and pseudonymous Satoshi Nakamoto.The personality of the individual or people who made the innovation is as yet a secret. Bitcoin offers the guarantee of lower exchange charges than conventional online installment instruments, and, not at all like officially sanctioned monetary forms, it is worked by a decentralized position.

Bitcoin is a sort of cryptographic money. There are no physical bitcoins and just adjusts on a public record that everybody has straightforward admittance to. A monstrous measure of processing power checks all bitcoin exchanges. Bitcoins are not given or supported by any banks or governments, nor are individual bitcoins significant as a product. Notwithstanding it not being legitimate delicate, Bitcoin is well known and has set off many other digital forms of money, altogether alluded to as Altcoin. Bitcoin is normally condensed as "BTC."

Understanding Bitcoin

The bitcoin framework is an assortment of PCs (additionally alluded to as "hubs" or "diggers") that all run bitcoin's code and store its blockchain. Allegorically, a blockchain can be considered as an assortment of squares. In each square is an assortment of exchanges. Since every one of the PCs running the blockchain has similar rundown of squares and exchanges and can straightforwardly see these new squares being loaded up with new bitcoin exchanges, nobody can swindle the framework.

Regardless of whether they run a bitcoin "hub" or not, anybody can see these exchanges happening live. To accomplish a scandalous demonstration, a troublemaker would have to work 51% of the registering power that makes up bitcoin. Bitcoin has around 12,000 hubs as of January 2021, and this number is developing, making such an assault very unlikely.

In any case, if an assault were to occur, the bitcoin diggers, individuals who participate in the bitcoin network with their PC, would almost certainly fork to another blockchain putting forth the attempt the agitator set forth to accomplish the assault a waste.

Equilibriums of bitcoin tokens are kept utilizing public and hidden "keys," which are long series of numbers and letters connected through the numerical encryption calculation used to make them. The public key (similar to a financial balance number) fills in as the location distributed to the world and to which others may send bitcoins.

The private key (similar to an ATM PIN) is intended to be a watched secret and simply used to approve Bitcoin transmissions. Bitcoin keys ought not to be mistaken for a bitcoin wallet, a physical or computerized gadget that works with the exchanging of bitcoin and permits clients to follow responsibility for. The expression "wallet" is somewhat deceptive, as bitcoin's decentralized nature implies that it is rarely put away "in" a wallet but instead appropriately on a blockchain.

Peer-to-Peer Technology

Bitcoin is one of the main advanced monetary standards to utilize distributed innovation to work with moment installments. The autonomous people and organizations that own the overseeing figuring control and take an interest in the bitcoin network bitcoin "excavators" are accountable for handling the exchanges on the blockchain and are roused by remunerations (the arrival of new bitcoin) and exchange charges paid in bitcoin.

These excavators can be considered as the decentralized authority upholding the validity of the bitcoin network. New bitcoin is delivered to the diggers at a fixed yet intermittently declining rate. There is just 21 million bitcoin that can be mined altogether. As of January 30, 2021, there are around 18,614,806 bitcoin in presence and 2,385,193 bitcoin left to be mined.

Along these lines, bitcoin other digital forms of money work uniquely in contrast to fiat cash; in unified financial frameworks, the cash is delivered at a rate coordinating with the development in merchandise; this framework is proposed to keep up value steadiness. A decentralized framework, as bitcoin, sets the delivery rate early and as per a calculation.

Bitcoin Mining

Bitcoin mining is the interaction by which bitcoins are delivered into dissemination. By and large, mining requires settling computationally troublesome riddles to find another square, which is added to the blockchain.

Bitcoin mining adds and confirms exchange records across the organization. Excavators are compensated with a couple bitcoins; the prize is split each 210,000 squares. The square prize was 50 new bitcoins in 2009. On May 11, 2020, the third splitting happened, bringing the prize for each square revelation down to 6.25 bitcoins.

An assortment of equipment can be utilized to mine bitcoin. Nonetheless, some yield higher prizes than others. Certain CPUs, called Application-Specific Integrated Circuits (ASIC), and further developed handling units, similar to Graphic Processing Units (GPUs), can accomplish more rewards. These intricate mining processors are known as "mining rigs."

One bitcoin is detachable to eight decimal spots (100 millionths of one bitcoin), and this littlest unit is alluded to as a Satoshiif important. On the off chance that the taking interest diggers acknowledge the change, Bitcoin could at last be distinguishable to much more decimal spots.

History of Bitcoin

August 18, 2008

The area name bitcoin.org is enrolled. Today, this space is "WhoisGuard Protected," which means the personality of the individual who enrolled it isn't public data.

October 31, 2008

An individual or gathering utilizing the name Satoshi Nakamoto makes a declaration on The Cryptography Mailing list at metzdowd.com: "I've been chipping away at another electronic money framework that is completely distributed, with no confided in outsider. This now-acclaimed whitepaper distributed on bitcoin.org, named "Bitcoin: A Peer-to-Peer Electronic Cash System," would turn into the Magna Carta for how Bitcoin works today.

January 3, 2009

The principal Bitcoin block is mined Block 0. This progression is otherwise called the "beginning square" and contains the content: "The Times 03/Jan/2009 Chancellor near the very edge of second bailout for banks," maybe as evidence that the square was mined on or after that date, and maybe likewise as significant political commentary.

Jan. 8, 2009

The principal variant of the bitcoin programming is reported on The Cryptography Mailing list.

January 9, 2009

Square 1 is mined, and bitcoin mining begins vigorously.

Who Is Satoshi Nakamoto?

No one understands who made bitcoin, or if nothing else not conclusively. Satoshi Nakamoto is the name related with the individual or social event of people who conveyed the main Bitcoin white paper in 2008 and worked on the primary Bitcoin programming conveyed in 2009. Since that time, various individuals have either declared to be or have been proposed as the certifiable people behind the nom de plume. Regardless, as of January 2021, the certified character (or characters) behind Satoshi stays blurred.

Despite the fact that it is enticing to accept the media's twist that Satoshi Nakamoto is a lone, impractical virtuoso who made Bitcoin out of nowhere, such advancements don't ordinarily occur in a vacuum. Regardless of how unique appearing, all major logical revelations were based on beforehand existing exploration.

There are forerunners to Bitcoin: Adam Back's Hashcash, imagined in 1997,8 and thusly Wei Dai's b-cash, Nick Szabo's touch gold, and Hal Finney's Reusable Proof of Work. The bitcoin whitepaper itself refers to Hashcash and b-cash and different works traversing a few examination fields. Maybe obviously, a considerable lot of the people behind different ventures named above have been estimated to have likewise had a section in making bitcoin.

There are a couple of potential inspirations for bitcoin's creators choosing to stay quiet. One is protection: As bitcoin has acquired in notoriety—turning out to be something of an overall wonder—Satoshi Nakamoto would almost certainly collect a ton of consideration from the media and governments...

Another explanation could be the potential for bitcoin to cause a significant interruption in the current banking and financial frameworks. On the off chance that bitcoin were to acquire mass selection, the framework could outperform countries' sovereign fiat monetary standards. This danger to existing cash could propel governments to need to make a lawful move against bitcoin's maker.

The other explanation is wellbeing. 32,489 squares were mined; at the award pace of 50 bitcoin per block, the absolute payout in 2009 was 1,624,500 bitcoin. One may reason that solitary Satoshi and maybe a couple of others were mining through 2009 and have a dominant part of that reserve of bitcoin.

Somebody possessing that much bitcoin could turn into an objective of crooks, particularly since bitcoins are less similar to stocks and more like money. The private keys expected to approve spending could be printed out and held under a sleeping pad. The designer of Bitcoin would avoid potential risk to make any blackmail prompted moves discernible; staying mysterious is a decent path for Satoshi to restrict openness.

Special Considerations
Bitcoin as a Form of Payment

Bitcoins can be acknowledged as methods for installment for items sold or benefits gave. Physical stores can show a sign saying "Bitcoin Accepted Here"; the exchanges can be taken care of with the imperative equipment terminal or wallet address through QR codes and contact screen applications. An online business can undoubtedly acknowledge bitcoins by adding this installment alternative to its other online installment choices: Mastercards, PayPal, and so on

Bitcoin Employment Opportunities

The individuals who are independently employed can find paid for a line of work identified with bitcoin. There are a few different ways to accomplish this, for example, making any web access and adding your bitcoin wallet address to the website as a type of installment. There are additionally a few sites and occupation sheets that are committed to computerized monetary standards:

- Cryptogrind unites work searchers and imminent managers through its site.
- Coinality highlights occupations—independent, low maintenance and full-time—that offer installment in bitcoins, just as other digital currencies like Dogecoin and Litecoin
- Jobs4Bitcoins, part of reddit.com
- BitGigs
- Bitwage offers an approach to pick a level of your work check to be changed over into bitcoin and shipped off your bitcoin address.

Putting resources into Bitcoins

Numerous Bitcoin allies accept that advanced cash is what's to come. Numerous people who underwrite bitcoin accept that it works with a lot quicker, low-expense installment framework for exchanges around the world. Albeit any administration or national bank doesn't back it, bitcoin can be traded for conventional monetary forms; truth be told, its conversion scale against the dollar draws in expected financial backers and brokers intrigued by cash plays. For sure, one of the essential purposes behind the development of computerized monetary standards like bitcoin is that they can go about as an option in contrast to public fiat cash and conventional wares like gold.

In March 2014, the IRS expressed that every virtual cash, including bitcoins, would be burdened as property instead of money. Gains or misfortunes from bitcoins held as capital will be acknowledged as capital increases or misfortunes, while bitcoins held as stock will cause normal additions or misfortunes. The offer of bitcoins that you mined or bought from another gathering, or the utilization of bitcoins to pay for merchandise or administrations, is instances of exchanges that can be burdened.

Like some other resource, the standard of purchasing low and selling high applies to bitcoins. The most famous method of storing up the money is through purchasing on a bitcoin trade, however there are numerous alternate approaches to procure and claim bitcoins.

Types of Risks Associated With Bitcoin Investing

In spite of the fact that Bitcoin was not planned as an ordinary value venture (no offers have been given), some theoretical financial backers were attracted to the computerized cash after it appreciated quickly in May 2011 and again in November 2013. Subsequently, numerous individuals buy bitcoin for its speculation esteem as opposed to its capacity to go about as a mode of trade.

Nonetheless, the absence of ensured worth and its advanced nature implies the buy and utilization of bitcoins conveys a few inalienable dangers. Numerous financial backer cautions have been given by the Securities and Exchange Commission (SEC), the Financial Industry Regulatory Authority (FINRA), the Consumer Financial Protection Bureau (CFPB), and different organizations.

The idea of virtual cash is as yet novel and, contrasted with conventional speculations; bitcoin doesn't have a very remarkable longterm history or history of validity to back it. With their expanding prominence, bitcoins are turning out to be fewer tests each day; after just 10 years, all advanced monetary forms stay in an improvement stage. "It is essentially the most noteworthy danger, best yield venture that you can make," says Barry Silbert, CEO of Digital Currency Group, which fabricates and puts resources into Bitcoin and blockchain organizations.

Administrative Risk

Putting cash into bitcoin in any of its numerous pretenses isn't for the danger loath. Bitcoins are an adversary to government cash and might be utilized for underground market exchanges, illegal tax avoidance, criminal operations, or tax avoidance. Therefore, governments may look to manage, confine, or boycott the utilization and offer of bitcoins (and some as of now have). Others are thinking of different standards.

For instance, in 2015, the New York State Department of Financial Services settled guidelines that would require organizations managing the purchase, sell, move, or capacity of bitcoins to record the personality of clients, have a consistence official, and keep up capital stores. The exchanges worth $10,000 or more should be recorded and detailed.

The absence of uniform guidelines about bitcoins (and other virtual money) brings up issues over their life span, liquidity, and all-inclusiveness.

Security Risk

Most people who own and use bitcoin have not procured their tokens through mining activities. Maybe, they purchase and sell bitcoin and other computerized monetary standards on some famous online business sectors, known as bitcoin trades.

Bitcoin trades are completely computerized and, similarly as with any virtual framework, are in danger from programmers, malware, and operational glitches. In the event that a criminal accesses a Bitcoin proprietor's PC hard drive and takes their private encryption key, they could move the taken bitcoin to another record. (Clients can forestall this just if bitcoins are put away on a

PC that isn't associated with the Internet, or, more than likely by deciding to utilize a paper wallet printing out the bitcoin private keys and addresses and not keeping them on a PC by any means.)

Programmers can likewise target Bitcoin trades, accessing a great many records and advanced wallets where bitcoins are put away. One particularly famous hacking episode occurred in 2014, when Mt. Gox, a bitcoin trade in Japan, had to shut down after large number of dollars' worth of bitcoins was taken.

This is especially hazardous, given that all Bitcoin exchanges are lasting and irreversible. It resembles managing cash: Any exchange did with bitcoins must be turned around if the individual who has gotten them discounts them. There is no outsider or an installment processor, as on account of a charge or MasterCard—thus, no wellspring of assurance or allure if there is an issue.

Protection Risk

A few ventures are safeguarded through the Securities Investor Protection Corporation. Typical financial balances are guaranteed through the Federal Deposit Insurance Corporation (FDIC) up to a specific sum contingent upon the purview.

As a rule, bitcoin trades and bitcoin accounts are not protected by any bureaucratic or government program. In 2019, the great seller and exchanging stage SFOX reported it would furnish bitcoin financial backers with FDIC protection, however just for the part of exchanges including cash.13

Extortion Risk

While bitcoin utilizes private key encryption to check proprietors and register exchanges, fraudsters and tricksters may endeavor to sell bogus bitcoins. For example, in July 2013, the SEC brought lawful activity against an administrator of a bitcoin-related Ponzi conspire. There have likewise been recorded instances of bitcoin value control, another basic type of misrepresentation.

Market Risk

Like with any speculation, Bitcoin esteems can vary. Undoubtedly, the money's worth has seen wild swings in cost over its short presence. Subject to high volume purchasing and selling on trades, it has a high affectability to any newsworthy occasions. As per the CFPB, the cost of bitcoins fell by 61% in a solitary day in 2013, while the one-day value drop record in 2014 was just about as large as 80%.

In the event that fewer individuals start to acknowledge bitcoin as money, these computerized units may lose esteem and could get useless. Without a doubt, there was theory that the "bitcoin bubble" had blasted when the cost declined from its untouched high during the cryptographic money surge in late 2017 and mid-2018.

There is as of now a lot of rivalry. In spite of the fact that Bitcoin has a colossal lead over the many other advanced monetary standards that have jumped up on account of its image acknowledgment and investment cash, a mechanical leap forward as a superior virtual coin is consistently a danger.

Splits in the Cryptocurrency Community

In the years since Bitcoin dispatched, there have been various examples in which conflicts between groups of excavators and engineers incited huge scope parts of the digital currency local area. In a portion of these cases, gatherings of Bitcoin clients and diggers have changed the bitcoin network convention itself.

This cycle is known as "forking" and it as a rule brings about making another sort of bitcoin with another name. This split can be a "hard fork," in which another coin imparts exchange history to bitcoin until a definitive split point, so, all in all another token is made. Instances of cryptographic forms of money that have been made because of hard forks incorporate bitcoin cash (made in August 2017), bitcoin gold (made in October 2017), and Bitcoin SV (made in November 2017).

A "delicate fork" is a change to the convention that is as yet viable with the past framework rules. For instance, bitcoin delicate forks have expanded the complete size of squares.

Chapter2. What is Blockchain?

Blockchain appears to be convoluted, and it unquestionably can be, yet its center idea is very basic. A blockchain is a sort of data set. Understanding blockchain assists first with understanding what an information base is.

A data set is an assortment of data that is put away electronically on a PC framework. In data sets, data or information is regularly organized in table arrangement to take into consideration simpler looking and separating of explicit data. What is the contrast between utilizing a bookkeeping page to store data instead of an information base?

Bookkeeping pages are intended for one individual, or a little gathering of individuals, to store and access restricted measures of data. Conversely, a data set is intended to house altogether bigger measures of data that can be gotten to, separated, and controlled rapidly and effectively by quite a few clients on the double.

Enormous data sets accomplish this by lodging information on workers made of amazing PCs. These workers can some of the time be constructed utilizing hundreds or thousands of PCs to have the computational force and capacity limit important for some clients to get to the information base at the same time. While a bookkeeping page or information base might be open to numerous individuals, it is regularly possessed by a business and overseen by a selected person who has unlimited oversight over how it functions and the information inside it.

Storage Structure

One key distinction between a normal data set and a blockchain is the manner by which the information is organized. A blockchain gathers data together in gatherings, otherwise called blocks that hold sets of data. Squares have certain capacity limits and, when filled, are affixed onto the recently filled square, framing a chain of information known as the "blockchain." All new data that follows that newly added block is arranged into a recently shaped square that will at that point likewise be added to the chain once filled.

A data set designs its information into tables, while a blockchain, similar to its name suggests, structures its information into pieces (blocks) affixed together. This makes it with the goal that all blockchains are data sets, however not all data sets are blockchains. This framework likewise naturally makes an irreversible timetable of information when executed in a decentralized nature. At the point when a square is filled, it is unchangeable and turns into a piece of this course of events. Each square in the chain is given a precise timestamp when added to the chain.

Decentralization

For comprehension blockchain, it is informative to see it with regards to how Bitcoin has carried out it. Like an information base, Bitcoin needs an assortment of PCs to store its blockchain. For Bitcoin, this blockchain is only a particular kind of information base that stores each Bitcoin exchange at any point made. For Bitcoin's situation, and not at all like most information bases, these PCs are not all under one rooftop. Every PC or gathering of PCs is worked by an exceptional individual or gathering of people.

Envision that an organization claims a worker included 10,000 PCs with a data set holding the entirety of its customer's record data. This organization has a stockroom containing these PCs under one rooftop and has full control of every one of these PCs and all the data contained inside them. Likewise, Bitcoin comprises of thousands of PCs. All things considered, every PC or gathering of PCs that hold its blockchain is in an alternate geographic area, and they are completely worked by independent people or gatherings of individuals. These PCs that make up Bitcoin's Network are called hubs.

In this model, Bitcoin's blockchain is utilized in a decentralized way. Nonetheless, private, concentrated blockchains, where the PCs that make up its organization are possessed and worked by a solitary substance, exist.

In a blockchain, every hub has a full record of the information that has been put away on the blockchain since its commencement. For Bitcoin, the information is the whole history of all Bitcoin exchanges. In the event that one hub has a mistake in its information, it can utilize the huge number of different hubs as a kind of perspective highlight right itself. Thusly, nobody hub inside the organization can adjust data held inside it. Along these lines, the historical backdrop of exchanges in each square that make up Bitcoin's blockchain is irreversible.

In the event that one client alters Bitcoin's record of exchanges, any remaining hubs would cross-reference one another and effectively pinpoint the hub with the mistaken data. This framework assists with setting up a definite and straightforward request of occasions. For Bitcoin, this data is a rundown of exchanges. In any case, it is likewise feasible for a blockchain to hold different data like lawful agreements, state distinguishing pieces of proof, or an organization's item stock.

To change how that framework functions or the data put away inside it, the vast majority of the decentralized organization's registering force would have to concur on said changes. This guarantees that whatever changes happen are in the greater part's wellbeing.

Transparency

On account of the decentralized idea of Bitcoin's blockchain, everything exchanges can be straightforwardly seen by either having an individual hub or by utilizing blockchain wayfarer that permits anybody to see exchanges happening live. Every hub has its duplicate of the chain that gets refreshed as new squares are affirmed and added. This implies that you could follow Bitcoin any place it goes in the event that you needed to.

For instance, trades have been hacked in the past were the individuals who held Bitcoin on the trade lost everything. While the programmer might be altogether unknown, the Bitcoins they separated are effectively detectable. On the off chance that the Bitcoins taken in a portion of these hacks were to be moved or spent some place, it would be known.

Is Blockchain Secure?

Blockchain innovation represents the issues of safety and trust severally. To start with, new squares are constantly put away directly and sequentially. They are constantly added to the "end" of the blockchain. In the event that you take a gander at Bitcoin's blockchain, you'll see that each square has a situation on the chain, called a "tallness." As of November 2020, the square's stature had arrived at 656,197 squares up until now.

After a square has been added to the furthest limit of the blockchain, it is hard to return and change the substance of the square except if the larger part arrived at an agreement to do as such. That is on the grounds that each square contains its hash, alongside the hash of the square before it, just as the recently referenced time stamp. Hash codes are made by a numerical capacity that transforms advanced data into a series of numbers and letters. On the off chance that that data is altered in any capacity, the hash code changes.

Here's the reason that is critical to security. Suppose a programmer needs to modify the blockchain and take Bitcoin from every other person. If they somehow happened to change their single duplicate, it would presently don't line up with every other person's duplicate. At the point when every other person cross-references their duplicates against one another, they would see this one duplicate stick out, and that programmer's rendition of the chain would be given away a role as ill-conceived.

Prevailing with such a hack would necessitate that the programmer at the same time control and change 51% of the duplicates of the blockchain so their new duplicate turns into the dominant part duplicate and, along these lines, the settled upon chain. Such an assault would likewise require a tremendous measure of cash and assets as they would have to re-try the entirety of the squares since they would now have distinctive timestamps and hash codes.

Because of the size of Bitcoin's Network and how quick it is developing, the expense to pull off such an accomplishment would most likely be inconceivable. In addition to the fact that this would be amazingly costly, yet it would likewise likely be vain. Doing something like this would not go undetected, as organization individuals would see such radical changes to the blockchain. The organization individuals would then fork off to another rendition of the chain that has not been influenced.

This would make the assaulted form of Bitcoin fall in esteem, making the assault at last trivial as the troublemaker controls a useless resource. The equivalent would happen if the agitator assaulted the new fork of Bitcoin. It is constructed this way so that participating in the organization is definitely more financially boosted than assaulting it.

Bitcoin vs. Blockchain

The objective of blockchain is to permit advanced data to be recorded and appropriated yet not altered. Blockchain innovation was first laid out in 1991 by Stuart Haber and W. Scott Stornetta, two analysts who needed to carry out a framework where archive timestamps couldn't be messed with. In any case, it wasn't until right around twenty years after the fact, with the dispatch of Bitcoin in January 2009, that blockchain had its first genuine application.

The Bitcoin convention is based on a blockchain. In an exploration paper presenting the computerized money, Bitcoin's pseudonymous maker, Satoshi Nakamoto, alluded to it as "another electronic money framework that is completely shared, with no confided in outsider."

The critical thing to comprehend here is that Bitcoin simply utilizes blockchain to record a record of installments straightforwardly. In any case, in principle, blockchain can be utilized to record quite a few information focuses changelessly. As talked about over, this could be as exchanges, votes in a political decision, item inventories, state IDs, deeds to homes, and considerably more.

There is a wide assortment of blockchain-based activities hoping to carry out blockchain in approaches to help society other than recording exchanges. One genuine model is that of blockchain being utilized to cast a ballot in just decisions. The idea of blockchain's changelessness implies that deceitful democratic would get undeniably harder to happen.

For instance, a democratic framework could work to such an extent that every resident of a nation would be given a solitary digital currency or token. Every competitor would then be given a particular wallet address, and the electors would send their token or crypto to whichever up-and-comer's location they wish to decide in favor of. The straightforward and recognizable nature of blockchain would take out the requirement for human vote checking and the capacity of agitators to mess with actual polling forms.

Blockchain versus Banks

Banks and decentralized blockchains are inconceivably extraordinary. To perceive how a bank contrasts from blockchain, we should contrast the financial framework with Bitcoin's blockchain execution.

How is Blockchain Used?

As we currently know, blocks on Bitcoin's blockchain store information about money related exchanges. Yet, incidentally, blockchain is a solid method of putting away information about different sorts of exchanges.

A few organizations that have effectively joined blockchain incorporate Wal-Mart, Pfizer, AIG, Siemens, Unilever, and a large group of others. For instance, IBM has made its Food Trust blockchain to follow the excursion that food items take to get to their areas.

For what reason do this? The food business has seen endless flare-ups of e Coli, salmonella, listeria, and unsafe materials being unintentionally acquainted with food varieties. It has required a long time to discover the wellspring of these episodes or the reason for infection from what individuals are eating before.

Utilizing blockchain enables brands to follow a food item's course from its root, through each stop it makes, lastly, it is conveyance. In the event that a food is discovered to be sullied, it very well may be followed back through each stop to its root. That, however these organizations can likewise now see all the other things they may have interacted with, permitting the recognizable proof of the issue to happen far sooner, conceivably saving lives. This is one illustration of blockchains practically speaking yet numerous other blockchain execution structures.

Banking and Finance

Maybe no industry stands to profit by coordinating blockchain into its business activities more than banking. Monetary foundations just work during business hours, five days every week. That implies in the event that you attempt to store a keep an eye on Friday at 6 p.m., you will probably need to stand by until Monday morning to see that cash hit your record. Regardless of whether you set aside your installment during business hours, the exchange can in any case take one to three days to check because of the sheer volume of exchanges that banks need to settle. Blockchain, then again, never dozes.

By coordinating blockchain into banks, shoppers can see their exchanges prepared in just 10 minutes. The time it takes to add a square to the blockchain, paying little heed to occasions or the hour of day or week. With blockchain, banks additionally can trade assets between establishments all the more rapidly and safely. For instance, in the stock exchanging business, the repayment and clearing cycle can require as long as three days (or more, if exchanging universally), implying that the cash and offers are frozen for that period.

Given the size of the whole in question, even the couple of days that the cash is on the way can convey significant expenses and dangers for banks. European bank Santander and its exploration accomplices put the possible investment funds at $15 billion to $20 billion per year. Cap Gemini, a French consultancy, appraises that buyers could set aside to $16 billion in banking and protection charges every year through blockchain-based applications.

Money

Blockchain structures the bedrock for digital currencies like Bitcoin. The Federal Reserve controls the US dollar. Under this focal power framework, a client's information and money are in fact at the impulse of their bank or government. In the event that a client's bank is hacked, the customer's private data is in danger. On the off chance that the customer's bank breakdowns or they live in a country with a precarious government, the worth of their money might be in danger. In 2008, a portion of the banks that ran out of cash were rescued in part utilizing citizen cash. These are the concerns out of which Bitcoin was first imagined and created.

By spreading its activities across an organization of PCs, blockchain permits Bitcoin and other digital currencies to work without the requirement for a focal power. This lessens hazard and disposes of a large number of the preparing and exchange expenses. It can likewise give those in nations with insecure monetary standards or monetary frameworks a more steady cash with more applications and a more extensive organization of people and establishments they can work with, both locally and universally.

Utilizing digital money wallets for investment accounts or as methods for installment is particularly significant for the individuals who have no state recognizable proof. A few nations might be war-torn or have governments that do not have any genuine foundation to give ID. Such nations might not approach reserve funds or money market funds and, hence, no real way to store abundance securely.

Medical care

Medical care suppliers can use blockchain to store their patients' clinical records safely. At the point when a clinical record is created and marked, it tends to be composed into the blockchain, which gives patients the evidence and certainty that the record can't be changed. These individual wellbeing records could be encoded and put away on the blockchain with a private key so they are just open by specific people, accordingly guaranteeing security.

Records of Property

On the off chance that you have at any point invested energy in your nearby Recorder's Office, you will realize that the way toward recording property rights is both difficult and wasteful. Today, an actual deed should be conveyed to an administration representative at the neighborhood recording office, where it is physically gone into the region's focal data set and general list. On account of a property debate, cases to the property should be accommodated with the overall file.

This interaction isn't simply expensive and tedious; it is additionally filled with human mistake, where every error makes following property proprietorship less productive. Blockchain can possibly kill the requirement for filtering archives and finding actual documents in a nearby account office. On the off chance that property proprietorship is put away and checked on the blockchain, proprietors can believe that their deed is precise and forever recorded.

In war-torn nations or zones with practically zero government or monetary foundation and absolutely no "Recorder's Office," it very well may be almost difficult to demonstrate responsibility for property. On the off chance that a gathering of individuals living in such a region can use blockchain, straightforward and clear timetables of land owners could be set up.

Shrewd Contract

A savvy contract is a PC code incorporated into the blockchain to work with, confirm, or arrange an agreement understanding. Savvy contracts work under a bunch of conditions that clients consent to. At the point when those conditions are met, the provisions of the understanding are naturally done.

Say, for instance, a potential occupant might want to rent a loft utilizing a keen agreement. The landowner consents to give the inhabitant the entryway code to the condo when the occupant pays the security store. Both the inhabitant and the property manager would send their particular bits of the arrangement to the savvy contract, which would clutch and naturally trade the entryway code for the security store on the date the rent starts. On the off chance that the property manager doesn't supply the entryway code by the rent date, the shrewd agreement discounts the security store. This would wipe out the expenses and cycles normally connected with utilizing a legal official, outsider arbiter, or lawyers.

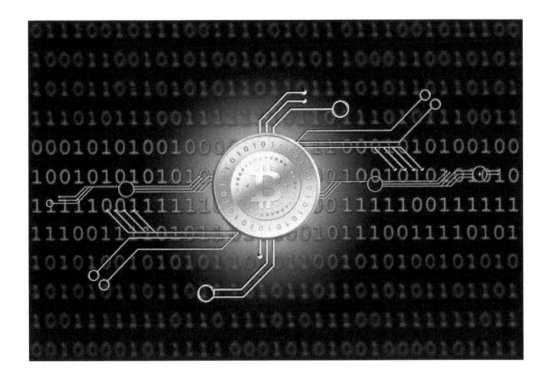

Supply Chains

As in the IBM Food Trust model, providers can utilize blockchain to record the roots of their bought materials. This would permit organizations to confirm the credibility of their items, alongside such basic marks as "Natural," "Neighborhood," and "Reasonable Trade."

As revealed by Forbes, the food business is progressively receiving blockchain to follow the way and security of food all through the homestead to-client venture.

Casting a ballot

As referenced, blockchain could be utilized to work with a cutting edge casting a ballot framework. Casting a ballot with blockchain conveys the possibility to wipe out political race misrepresentation and lift elector turnout, as was tried in the November 2018 midterm decisions in West Virginia. Utilizing blockchain in this manner would make cast a ballot almost difficult to alter. The blockchain convention would likewise keep up straightforwardness in the appointive interaction, lessening the faculty expected to lead a political decision and giving authorities almost moment results. This would dispose of the requirement for describes or any genuine worry that misrepresentation may compromise the political race.

Advantages and Disadvantages of Blockchain

For the entirety of its intricacy, blockchain's potential as a decentralized type of record-keeping is practically limitless. From more prominent client protection and increased security to bring down preparing expenses and less mistakes, blockchain innovation may well see applications past those laid out above. However, there are additionally a few burdens.

Pros

- Improved exactness by eliminating human contribution in check
- Cost decreases by disposing of outsider check
- Decentralization makes it harder to mess with
- Transactions are secure, private, and effective
- Transparent innovation
- Provides a financial other option and approach to protect individual data for residents of nations with precarious or immature governments

Cons

- Significant innovation cost related with mining bitcoin
- Low exchanges each second
- History of utilization in unlawful exercises
- Regulation

Here are the selling points of blockchain for organizations available today in more detail.

S

Benefits of Blockchain

Exactness of the Chain

An organization endorses exchanges on the blockchain organization of thousands of PCs. This eliminates practically all human inclusion in the check cycle, bringing about less human blunder and an exact record of data. Regardless of whether a PC on the organization were to commit a computational error, the blunder would just be made to one duplicate of the blockchain. For that mistake to spread to the remainder of the blockchain, at any rate 51% of the organization's PCs would should be made—a close to difficulty for an enormous and developing organization the size of Bitcoin's.

Cost Reductions

Ordinarily, buyers pay a bank to confirm an exchange, a public accountant to sign a record, or a priest to play out a marriage. Blockchain wipes out the requirement for outsider confirmation and, with it, their related expenses. Entrepreneurs cause a little expense at whatever point they acknowledge installments utilizing Visas, for instance, since banks and installment preparing organizations need to deal with those exchanges. Then again, Bitcoin doesn't have a focal position and has restricted exchange charges.

Decentralization

Blockchain doesn't store any of its data in a focal area. All things being equal, the blockchain is replicated and spread across an organization of PCs. At whatever point another square is added to the blockchain, each PC on the organization refreshes its blockchain to mirror the change. By spreading that data across an organization, blockchain turns out to be harder to mess with as opposed to putting away it in one focal data set. In the event that a duplicate of the blockchain fell under the control of a programmer, just a solitary duplicate of the data, as opposed to the whole organization, would be undermined.

Productive Transactions

Exchanges put through a focal authority can take up to a couple of days to settle. On the off chance that you endeavor to store a mind Friday evening, for instance, you may not see assets in your record until Monday morning. While monetary establishments work during business hours, five days every week, blockchain is working 24 hours per day, seven days per week, and 365 days per year. Exchanges can be finished in just ten minutes and can be viewed as secure after only a couple hours. This is especially valuable for cross-line exchanges, which generally take any longer on account of time-region issues and that all gatherings should affirm installment preparing.

Private Transactions

Numerous blockchain networks work as open information bases, implying that anybody with a web association can see an organization's exchange history list. Despite the fact that clients can get to insights regarding exchanges, they can't get to recognizing data about the clients making those exchanges. It is a typical misperception that blockchain networks like bitcoin are unknown when they are just secret.

At the point when a client unveils exchanges, their special code called a public key is recorded on the blockchain as opposed to their own data. In the event that an individual has made a Bitcoin buy on a trade that requires recognizable proof, at that point the individual's character is as yet connected to their blockchain address. In any case, in any event, when attached to an individual's name, an exchange doesn't uncover any close to home data.

Secure Transactions

When an exchange is recorded, its credibility should be checked by the blockchain network. A great many PCs on the blockchain hurry to affirm that the buy subtleties are right. After a PC has approved the exchange, it is added to the blockchain block. Each square on the blockchain contains its exceptional hash, alongside the novel hash of the square before it. At the point when the data on a square is altered in any capacity, that square's hash code changes; nonetheless, the hash code on the square after it would not. This inconsistency makes it incredibly hard for data on the blockchain to be changed without notice.

Straightforwardness

Most blockchains are altogether open-source programming. This implies that anybody and everybody can see its code. This enables inspectors to audit digital forms of money like Bitcoin for security. This additionally implies no genuine expert on who controls Bitcoin's code or how it is altered. Along these lines, anybody can recommend changes or moves up to the framework. In the event that most organization clients concur that the new form of the code with the overhaul is sound and beneficial, at that point Bitcoin can be refreshed.

Banking the Unbanked

Maybe the most significant aspect of blockchain and Bitcoin is the capacity for anybody, paying little heed to nationality, sex, or social foundation, to utilize it. As indicated by the World Bank, almost 2 billion grown-ups don't have ledgers or any methods for putting away their cash or abundance. Virtually these people live in non-industrial nations where the economy is outset and totally reliant upon cash.

These individuals frequently bring in little cash that is paid in actual money. They at that point need to store this actual money in secret areas in their homes or places of living, leaving them subject to burglary or superfluous viciousness. Keys in a bitcoin wallet can be put away on a piece of paper, a modest cell, or even remembered whether essential. For a great many people likely, these alternatives are more effortlessly covered up than a little heap of money under a sleeping pad.

Blockchains of things to come are likewise searching for answers for be a unit of record for abundance stockpiling and store clinical records, property rights, and an assortment of other legitimate agreements.

Disadvantages of Blockchain

While there are huge potential gains to the blockchain, there are additionally critical difficulties to its appropriation. The barricades to the utilization of blockchain innovation today are not simply specialized. The genuine difficulties are political and administrative, generally, to avoid mentioning the great many hours (read: cash) of custom programming plan and back-end programming needed to coordinate blockchain into current business organizations. Here are a portion of the difficulties holding up traffic of far reaching blockchain appropriation.

Innovation Cost

Despite the fact that blockchain can get a good deal on exchange charges, the innovation is a long way from free. The "evidence of work" framework that bitcoin uses to approve exchanges, for instance, burns-through huge measures of computational force. In reality, the force from the large numbers of PCs on the bitcoin network is near what Denmark burns-through yearly. Accepting power expenses of $0.03~$0.05 each kilowatt-hour, mining costs elite of equipment costs are about $5,000~$7,000 per coin.

In spite of the expenses of mining bitcoin, clients keep on driving up their power bills to approve exchanges on the blockchain. That is on the grounds that when diggers add a square to the bitcoin blockchain, they are remunerated with enough bitcoin to make their time and energy advantageous. In any case, with regards to blockchains that don't utilize cryptographic money, excavators should be paid or in any case boosted to approve exchanges.

A few answers for these issues are starting to emerge. For instance, bitcoin mining ranches have been set up to utilize sun oriented force, overabundance petroleum gas from deep oil drilling destinations, or force from wind ranches.

Speed Inefficiency

Bitcoin is an ideal contextual analysis for the potential failures of blockchain. Bitcoin's "confirmation of work" framework requires around ten minutes to add another square to the blockchain. At that rate, it's assessed that the blockchain organization can just oversee around seven exchanges each second (TPS). Albeit other digital currencies, for example, Ethereum perform better compared to bitcoin, they are as yet restricted by blockchain. Inheritance brand Visa, for setting, can deal with 24,000 TPS.

Answers for this issue have been being developed for quite a long time. There are presently blockchains that are gloating more than 30,000 exchanges each second.

Criminal behavior

While classification on the blockchain network shields clients from hacks and jelly protection, it additionally takes into account illicit exchanging and movement on the blockchain network. The most referred to illustration of blockchain being utilized for illegal exchanges is likely the Silk Road, an online "dim web" drug commercial center working from February 2011 until October 2013, when the FBI shut it down.

The site permitted clients to peruse the site without being followed utilizing the Tor program and make illicit buys in Bitcoin or other cryptographic forms of money. Current U.S. guidelines require monetary specialist co-ops to acquire data about their clients when they open a record, check the character of every client, and affirm that clients don't show up on any rundown of known or suspected psychological militant associations. This framework can be viewed as both an expert and a con. It gives anybody admittance to monetary records and permits hoodlums to execute all the more without any problem. Many have contended that the great employments of crypto, such as banking the unbanked world, exceed the awful employments of cryptographic money, particularly when most criminal behavior is as yet achieved through untraceable money.

Guideline

Numerous in the crypto space have communicated worries about unofficial law over cryptographic forms of money. While it is getting progressively troublesome and close to difficult to end something like Bitcoin as its decentralized organization develops, governments could hypothetically make it illicit to claim digital currencies or partake in their organizations.

Over the long run this worry has developed more modest as enormous organizations like PayPal start to permit the possession and utilization of cryptographic forms of money on their foundation.

What's Next for Blockchain?

First proposed as an examination project in 1991, blockchain is serenely sinking into its late twenties. Like most recent college grads its age, blockchain has seen something reasonable of public examination in the course of the most recent twenty years, with organizations overall hypothesizing about what the innovation is able to do and where it's going in the years to come.

With numerous commonsense applications for the innovation previously being carried out and investigated, blockchain at long last becomes well known at age 27, in no little part in view of bitcoin and cryptographic money. As a popular expression on the tongue of each financial backer in the country, blockchain stands to make business and government activities more precise, productive, secure, and modest with fewer delegates.

As we get ready to head into the third decade of blockchain, it's not, at this point an issue of "if" heritage organizations will get on to the innovation; it's an issue of "when."

Chapter3. Understanding the Crypto Market

There are a few things that each trying Bitcoin financial backer necessities. A digital currency trade account, individual ID reports on the off chance that you are utilizing a Know Your Customer (KYC) stage, a safe association with the Internet, and an installment strategy. It is additionally suggested that you have your wallet outside of the trade account. Legitimate techniques for installment utilizing this way incorporate ledgers, charge cards, and Mastercards. It is likewise conceivable to get Bitcoin at particular ATMs and by means of P2P trades. Notwithstanding, know that Bitcoin ATMs progressively required government provided IDs as of mid-2020.

Protection and security are significant issues for Bitcoin financial backers. Despite the fact that there are no actual Bitcoins, it is normally an impractical notion to gloat about enormous possessions. Any individual who acquires the private key to a public location on the Bitcoin blockchain can approve exchanges. Private keys ought to be kept mystery; hoodlums may endeavor to take them on the off chance that they learn huge possessions. Know that anybody can see the equilibrium of a public location you use. That makes it a smart thought to keep critical speculations at public tends to that are not straightforwardly associated with ones that are utilized for exchanges.

Anybody can see a past filled with exchanges made on the blockchain, even you. Yet, while exchanges are openly recorded on the blockchain, distinguishing client data isn't. Just a client's public key shows up close to an exchange on the Bitcoin blockchain, making exchanges secret yet not unknown. One might say, Bitcoin exchanges are more straightforward and detectable than cash; however the cryptographic money can likewise be utilized namelessly.

Following are a few stages you need to follow in the event that you need to put resources into digital currency:

1.   Choose an Exchange

Pursuing a digital money trade will permit you to purchase, sell, and hold digital money. It is by and large best practice to utilize a trade that permits clients to likewise pull out their crypto to their online wallet for more secure keeping. This element may not make any difference for those hoping to exchange Bitcoin or other digital forms of money.

There are numerous kinds of digital money trades. Since the Bitcoin ethos is about decentralization and individual sway, a few trades permit clients to stay unknown and don't expect clients to enter individual data. Such trades work self-governing and, commonly, are decentralized, which implies they don't have an essential issue of control.

While such frameworks can be utilized for odious exercises, they are additionally used to offer types of assistance for the world's unbanked populace. For specific classes of individuals – displaced people or those living in nations with practically no administration credit or banking framework – unknown trades can help carry them into the standard economy.

Be that as it may, the most mainstream trades are not decentralized and do require KYC. In the United States, these trades incorporate Coinbase, Kraken, Gemini, and Binance U.S., to give some examples. These trades have filled altogether in the quantity of highlights they offer.

Coinbase, Kraken, and Gemini offer Bitcoin and a developing number of altcoins. These three are presumably the simplest entrance to crypto in the whole business. Binance takes into account a further developed broker, offering more genuine exchanging usefulness and a superior assortment of altcoins to browse.

Something critical to note while making a digital currency trade account is to utilize safe web rehearses. This incorporates utilizing two-factor confirmation and utilizing an extraordinary and long secret phrase, including an assortment of lower-case letters, uppercase letters, exceptional characters, and numbers.

2.   Connect Your Exchange to a Payment Option

Whenever you have picked a trade, you presently need to accumulate your reports. Contingent upon the trade, these may incorporate photos of a driver's permit, government managed retirement number, just as data about your boss and wellspring of assets. The data you may need can rely upon the area you live in and its laws. The cycle is to a great extent equivalent to setting up an average investment fund.

After the trade has guaranteed your character and authenticity, you may now interface an installment alternative. At most trades, you can associate your ledger straightforwardly, or you can interface with a charge or Mastercard. While you can utilize a Visa to buy cryptographic money, it is by and large something that ought to be kept away from because of the instability that digital currencies can insight.

While Bitcoin is legitimate in the United States, a few banks don't take excessively benevolent to the thought and may address or even stop stores to crypto-related locales or trades. It is a smart thought to check to guarantee that your bank permits stores at your picked trade.

There are differing expenses for stores by means of a financial balance, charge, or Visa. Coinbase is a strong trade for fledglings and has a 1.49% expense for ledgers, with a 3.99% charge for charge and Mastercards. It is critical to investigate the charges related with every installment choice to help pick a trade or pick which installment alternative works best.

Trades additionally charge expenses per exchange. This charge can either be a level expense (if the exchanging sum is low) or a level of the exchanging sum. Visas cause a handling charge notwithstanding the exchange expenses.

3.   Place an Order

Whenever you have picked trade and associated an installment alternative, you would now be able to purchase Bitcoin and other digital forms of money. Lately, cryptographic money trades have gradually become standard. They have filled altogether regarding liquidity and their broadness of highlights. The operational changes at cryptographic money trades equal the adjustment of impression of digital currencies. An industry that was once considered as a trick or one with problematic practices is gradually transforming into a genuine one that has attracted interest from every one of the enormous players the monetary administrations industry.

Presently, cryptographic money trades have arrived at a point where they have almost similar degree of highlights as their stock financier partners. Whenever you have discovered a trade and associated an installment strategy, you are all set.

Crypto trades today offer a few request types and approaches to contribute. Practically all crypto trades offer both market and breaking point requests, and some likewise offer stop-misfortune orders. Of the trades referenced above, Kraken offers the most request types. Kraken takes into account, as far as possible, stop-misfortune, stop-limit, take-benefit, and take-benefit limit orders.

Beside different request types, trades likewise offer approaches to set up repeating speculations permitting customers to dollar cost normal into their ventures of decision. Coinbase, for instance, allows clients to set repeating buys for consistently, week, or month.

4.   Safe Storage

Bitcoin and cryptographic money wallets are a spot to store computerized resources all the more safely. Having your crypto outside of the trade and in your wallet guarantees that lone you have authority over the private key to your assets. It additionally enables you to store finances from a trade and keep away from the danger of your trade getting hacked and losing your assets.

A few wallets have a larger number of highlights than others. Some are Bitcoin just, and some offer the capacity to store various altcoins. A few wallets likewise offer the capacity to trade one token for another.

With regards to picking a Bitcoin wallet, you have a few choices. The main thing you should comprehend about crypto wallets is hot wallets (online wallets) and cold wallets (paper or equipment wallets).

5.   Hot Wallets

Online wallets are otherwise called "hot" wallets. Hot wallets will be wallets that sudden spike in demand for web associated gadgets like PCs, telephones, or tablets. This can make weakness in light of the fact that these wallets produce the private keys to your coins on these web associated gadgets. While a hot wallet can be advantageous in the manner you can access and make exchanges with your resources rapidly, putting away your private key on a web associated gadget makes it more helpless to a hack.

This may sound unrealistic;however individuals who are not utilizing sufficient security when utilizing these hot wallets can have their assets taken. This is certainly not an inconsistent event, and it can happen by one way or another. For instance, gloating on a public discussion like Reddit about the amount Bitcoin you hold while you are utilizing almost no security and putting away it in a hot wallet would not be savvy. All things considered, these wallets can be made to be secure insofar as insurances are taken. Solid passwords, two-factor verification, and safe web perusing ought to be viewed as least prerequisites.

These wallets are best utilized for modest quantities of digital currency or cryptographic money that you are effectively exchanging on a trade. You could compare a hot wallet to a financial records. Ordinary monetary shrewdness would say to hold just going through cash in a financial records while the heft of your cash is in bank accounts or other speculation accounts. The equivalent could be said for hot wallets. Hot wallets incorporate versatile, work area, web, and trade account guardianship wallets.

As referenced beforehand, trade wallets are custodial records given by the trade. The client of this wallet type isn't the private key holder to the digital currency held in this wallet. On the off chance that an occasion was to happen where the trade is hacked, or your record becomes bargained, your assets would be lost. The expression "not your key, not your coin" is intensely rehashed inside digital money gatherings and networks.

6.   Cold Wallets

The easiest portrayal of a cool wallet is a wallet that isn't associated with the Internet and stands at a far lesser danger of being undermined. These wallets can likewise be alluded to as disconnected wallets or equipment wallets.

These wallets store a client's private key on something that isn't associated with the Internet and can accompany programming that works in equal so the client can see their portfolio without putting their private key in danger.

Maybe the most secure approach to store cryptographic money disconnected is by means of a paper wallet. A paper wallet is a wallet that you can create off specific sites. It at that point produces both public and private keys that you print out on a piece of paper. Getting to digital money in these locations is just conceivable in the event that you have that piece of paper with the private key. Numerous individuals cover these paper wallets and store them in wellbeing store boxes at their bank or even protected in their homes. These wallets are intended for high security and long haulventures since you can't rapidly sell or exchange Bitcoin put away thusly.

An all the more generally utilized kind of chilly wallet is an equipment wallet. An equipment wallet is normally a USB drive gadget that stores a client's private keys safely disconnected. Such wallets have genuine benefits over hot wallets as they are unaffected by infections on one's PC. Private keys never interact with your organization associated PC or possibly weak programming with equipment wallets. These gadgets are likewise normally open-source, permitting the local area to decide its wellbeing through code reviews as opposed to an organization announcing that it is protected to utilize.

Cold wallets are the most secure approach to store your Bitcoin or other cryptographic forms of money. Generally, be that as it may, they require somewhat more information to set up.

Chapter4. Investing in Crypto Market

Putting resources into cryptographic money has advanced a ton since the pinnacle of 2017, when anybody could rapidly bounce in, get some Bitcoin on their nearby trade, and make a benefit. What the market has instructed us is actually similar to the financial exchange, a more key and thoroughly examined approach should be taken. This eBook contains the nuts and bolts of beginning in this market for the individuals who have no past experience putting resources into cryptographic forms of money. The part that follows, "The One Strategy," that anybody can apply to take their crypto contributing to the following level.

1. Safety First

Before you jump online to begin constructing your pinnacle of crypto power, we should ensure your establishment is strong. This implies that before you start exchanging, your PC, apparatuses, and association should all be just about as free from any and all harm as could really be expected. In the crypto world, there is no bank to run crying to in the event that somebody takes your charge card and purchases 1000 dollars of treats. On the off chance that you get hacked, and your coins are taken, they are GONE. So offer yourself a tremendous kindness and find the accompanying ways to get your venture cash.

Secure Device

A simple spot to begin is to ensure you are utilizing a PC that is tidy and has forward-thinking security programming introduced. Preferably, it's likewise acceptable to exchange from a gadget exclusively utilized for crypto and not one that you additionally use to ride every one of the dull corners of the Internet. Secure organization As hip as it very well may be to purchase Ethereum from your smooth PC in your nearby coffeehouse with an almond milk latte in your grasp, don't exchange utilizing a public organization. No libraries, no eateries, and no malevolent companions' homes. Utilize your organization that is set up to be scrambled and secure.

Great Password Habits

An apparatus we firmly suggest is a secret key supervisor. You've likely caught wind of how significant a solid secret phrase is for limiting your danger of getting hacked (at least fifteen characters, including upper and lower-case letters, numbers, distinctive accentuation marks, and so forth) however, you actually use "timmy123" for the entirety of your records. We get it- - how are you going to recall each one of those diverse convoluted passwords? A secret key director is a piece of programming you can download that allows you to deal with every one of your passwords effectively and successfully, and you can get a beautiful darn great one free of charge

2.   Fiat to Crypto

You've currently done, at any rate, what we've requested that you do to put resources into crypto with some degree of safety (perhaps somewhat more since you're that committed to the wellbeing of your future resources.) Now you're prepared to get rolling...

Register at an Exchange

To begin transforming your money into Bitcoin or some other coin (otherwise known as Altcoin), you need to set up a record on a trade. CoinBase is presumably the most notable, yet there are a couple of others, all of which offer fluctuated charge designs and coin contributions. Joining incorporates making a record with various layers of safety and interfacing an installment strategy, which are all clarified bit by bit in the trade's arrangement cycle. Whenever you are done, you are allowed to buy Bitcoin and a few other "fundamental" altcoins, including Ethereum, Bitcoin Cash, and Litecoin.

3. Buying Different Coins

In the event that you will probably go farther than purchase and hold a portion of the principle coins, you'll need to get familiar with purchasing altcoins. Albeit new coins and organizations are promising incredible computerized arrangements springing up consistently, most won't ever proceed to become wildly successful. However, in case you're one of the first to contribute, easily, in another coin that succeeds, you could wind up winning the big stake. To purchase altcoins, you first need to discover which trades offer the Altcoin you might want to put resources into.

Enlisting at one of these trades will be basically the same as the enrollment cycle for your underlying trade. On the off chance that you did it the first occasion when, I have confidence that you can do it a second.

When set up, you should move crypto from your first trade to your new trade. This can be perhaps the most difficult advances in the event that you have never done anything identified with crypto. Basically, this is finished by reordering a location or code for the area you will send your assets to. For a nitty gritty model, we will utilize the guidelines for moving cash out of CoinBase.

Web

- Navigate to the "accounts" interface on the fundamental route bar.

- Select the "send" button for the computerized cash wallet that you'd prefer to send from.
- In the send discourse, select "wallet address" in case you're shipping off a computerized cash wallet outside to CoinBase or "email address" in case you're sending through email.
- Enter the measure of advanced money you'd prefer to send in the "sum" field.
- Alternatively, you can determine the sum you might want to send in your nearby money. Note that the finances will consistently be sent as advanced money, not your nearby cash.
- Click "proceed".
- Confirm the subtleties of the exchange and complete the send.

iOS (For CoinBase portable application)

- Tap the menu symbol close to the upper left of the screen to open the Navbar.
- Select the wallet you wish to send from, situated in the Navbar.
- Tap the paper plane symbol in the upper right hand of the screen.
- Enter the sum you wish to send
- Tap the up/down bolts to switch between monetary forms. • Press "send."
- Enter the email or wallet address and any notes you wish to incorporate.

- Review the subtleties of your exchange and select "send" in the upper right corner of the screen.
-

On the off chance that you have been given a QR code

- Tap the QR symbol in the upper right.
- Take an image of the QR code
- Enter the ideal sum and press "proceed."
- Review the subtleties of your exchange and select "send" in the upper right corner of the screen. Android (For the CoinBase versatile application)
- Tap the menu symbol close to the upper left of the screen to open the Navbar.
- Select the wallet you wish to send from, situated in the Navbar.
- Tap the "+" symbol close to the lower right hand of the screen.
- Select "send."
- Enter the sum you wish to send.
- Use the up/down bolts to switch between kinds of money.
- Enter the email or wallet address and any notes you wish to incorporate.
- Review the subtleties of your exchange and tap the "forward" bolt in the upper right corner of the screen.

Android (For the CoinBase portable application)

- Tap the menu symbol close to the upper left of the screen to open the Navbar
- Select the wallet you wish to send from, situated in the Navbar.

- Tap the "+" symbol close to the lower right hand of the screen
- Select "send."
- Enter the sum you wish to send.
- Use the up/down bolts to switch between sorts of money.
- Enter the email or wallet address and any notes you wish to incorporate.
- Review the subtleties of your exchange and tap the "forward" bolt in the upper right corner

Or then again in the event that you have been given a QR code

- Tap the QR symbol in the upper right.
- Take an image of the QR code
- Enter the ideal sum and press "proceed."
- Review the subtleties of your exchange and tap the "forward" bolt in the upper right corner of the screen. Since you've become a crypto reorder star, you are prepared to purchase altcoins and prepared to proceed onward to figuring out how to utilize a wallet for care.

4.   Using a Crypto Wallet

A crypto wallet isn't exactly similar to the ordinary wallet, which you push into your jeans pocket for putting away your fiat cash. Without getting a lot into the hidden innovation (in light of the fact that those of you who need to comprehend everything about everything can Google it for more data), a wallet is a product program that stores public and private "keys" so that individuals can send and get crypto and screen their equilibrium, which is recorded and scrambled on the blockchain.

At the point when somebody sends you cryptographic money, it's simply a trade of responsibility for cash to your wallet's location. To get this going, the private "key" put away in your wallet should relate to the public location the money is appointed to. In the event that people in general and private keys match, the exchange is finished, and you can give a major moan of alleviation that you didn't unintentionally glue in the URL of a dumb feline video on YouTube that you shipped off a companion an hour sooner. There are a few various types of wallets.

Portable

Wallet applications for your cell phone are helpful to get to and can even be utilized in certain stores however are generally not as refined and can't store as much information like different sorts because of a telephone's restricted stockpiling limit.

On the web

These wallets run on the cloud and are available from any gadget, anyplace. This makes it simple for you to get to your crypto. Lamentably, it additionally makes it simple for anybody hacking the outsider organization dealing with your wallet to take your crypto. Pick your wallet organization carefully in the event that you go this course.

Work area

These wallets are downloaded onto a solitary PC or PC and are just open from that point and no other gadget. This makes it less open, and somehow or another more secure, than an online wallet. In any case, if your gadget is hacked, gets an infection, or unintentionally drops off a bluff into the sea, you could wind up without something other than an unrepairable PC.

Paper

This is a technique for printing your public and private keys onto actual duplicate, which would then be able to be (and ought to be) securely put away. This is protected in light of the fact that it is put away disconnected however can at times be troublesome to get to.

Equipment

Regularly as a thumb-drive-type gadget, an equipment wallet gives an incredible harmony between disconnected wellbeing and simple access. With a speedy addition into a USB port, you can approach, send, and get digital currency.

Whichever structure you pick, it is critical to ensure that you duplicate your resources into a wallet when you are finished exchanging on a trade. On the off chance that your crypto is sitting in a trade and the site gets hacked, your coins are effectively available for the taking, and you'll most likely never get them back.

5.   Basic Strategies

It's absolutely impossible we can make somebody with next to zero insight into a specialist crypto financial backer by perusing a couple of pages of text, however we can attempt to point you the correct way with the accompanying essential standards.

To be predictable with the general effortlessness of this guide, we'll give you three:

Purchase Low, Sell High

"Much obliged, Captain Obvious," you may be thinking, however in the event that this were so self-evident, for what reason do such countless individuals lose cash in contributing? It is the key law of contributing, yet to do this successfully, you should be straightforward with yourself about what sort of broker you are, just as what amount of cash, what amount hazard, and how long you can stand to contribute? The less you know your capacities, the less you will realize whose counsel to follow, which can eventually lead you to exchange a counterproductive way.

Examination, Research, Research

Simply doing what every other person is doing is a profoundly powerful method of getting messy seconds. Don't simply find out about market patterns. Become familiar with the organizations behind both new and existing coins. Who is an individual from their administration and specialized groups, and what is their central goal for what's to come? These basic advances can frequently remove a large number of the coins bound to come up short from the beginning.

Keep it Simple

From the start, simply contribute a limited quantity to get the hang of the "how to." Don't get extravagant. Get a portion of the top coins and sit on them. In the event that there is one thing that is steady about the unbelievably conflicting crypto market, genuine development requires years, not days. This way to sit and hold and don't get excessively combative and be a wild crypto pirate except if you realize that you understand what you're doing.

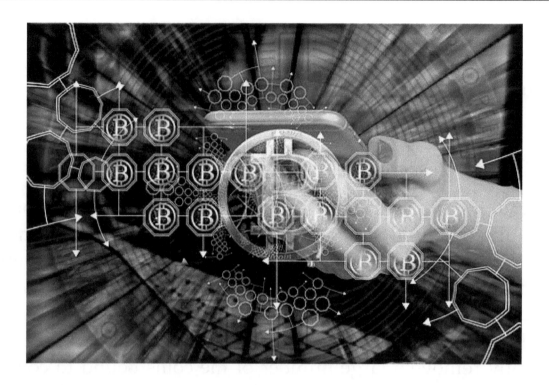

The One Strategy

Since you comprehend the fundamentals of putting resources into digital currency, it's an ideal opportunity to examine procedure. While a few specialists may trust it's beneficial to show many years' worth of contributing and exchanging mastery, we comprehend that this isn't commonsense for the vast majority. What number of us has the opportunity to learn everything about the unpredictable innovation of the blockchain world and how it means the organizations and tokens available? What numbers of us need to focus on turning into a specialist in the complexities of resource exchanging? What number of us can sit throughout the day before the PC watching the ongoing patterns on the lookout?

The appropriate response is, a great many people don't. Therefore, we need to discuss approaches to reasonably contribute, expand, and follow proficient techniques without taking up a great deal of your everyday life or turning into a full-time master dealer yourself.

Before most financial backers move into another market, there's a warm-up period that includes understanding a specific resource class and how it may find a way into your monetary picture. With digital forms of money and blockchain instruments, there are extra layers of intricacy, including the thought of cryptography, diggers, blockchains, tokens, hashing, and verifications. There's an extraordinary level of newness and intricacy related with digital forms of money for the unenlightened. However, the ordinary financial backer is relied upon to bounce onto a trade and begin exchanging, particularly in the event that exchanged nothing as long as they can remember.

Expansion is Key

Hand-picking digital currency ventures is a test. Cryptographic money markets are profoundly unpredictable, and surprisingly the most established are still truly in their outset stage. The choice cycle for token postings changes broadly among trades and is as of now not very much managed. Choosing champs from washouts or attempting to time the market has demonstrated to be amazingly troublesome. An investigation by Bitwise highlighted the worth of expansion on account of the limit changeability in the profits of even the best ten coins.

List Style Investing

In 2007, world-well known financial backer, Warren Buffett, bet 1,000,000 dollars that a record asset would outflank an assortment of multifaceted investments more than ten years. He won that bet and pointed out the viability of deliberately enhanced and sporadically rebalanced portfolios. There are numerous crypto portfolios available, however approaching one curated by a real expert, not a self-announced master on YouTube, is another story. These records are simply open to licensed financial backers (those with a total assets of in any event $1,000,000, barring the worth of one's main living place, or have a pay off at any rate $200,000 every year throughout the previous two years) however what numerous individuals don't know is that they all put their portfolio allotment online for people in general! Just by following the allotment rates of every token, you can take your venture and expand it very much like these selective and expertly oversaw reserves do.

Despite the fact that it will require some investment to do the exploration and choose which list reserve you might want to reflect, just as to figure and buy every token independently, fortunately these portfolios commonly just rebalance about once per month, so you will not need to do this regularly. Thus, the writing is on the wall, a manner by which, even with simply the most essential information, you can put resources into crypto with enhancement, adequacy, and expert ability.

Chapter5. The Beginner's Guide

Exchanging cryptographic money can make a tremendous benefit. Notwithstanding, it's likewise profoundly hazardous. You can win and lose a lot of cash rapidly. This implies crypto exchanging is energizing, and it tends to be hard to hold significant serenity under hefty tension. There are numerous approaches to bring in cash in the digital currency markets, however not the entirety of the ways are viable and safe. I will investigate some demonstrated methods of putting resources into cryptographic money. Here are the main 10.

1.   Trade digital money CFDs

Any item with value vacillations can be exchanged a Contract For Difference. CFD is a T+0 edge exchanging device, which permits you to exchange a bigger situation with a couple of capitals. For instance, you can exchange just 0.1 parcel bitcoin with a little store as an underlying edge.

The benefit of utilizing CFD is you can go long or go short regardless of the market moves; you will have the chances for dangerous gets back from business sectors fluctuating. Additionally, exchanging Bitcoin CFD is more adaptable, and you can exchange 24 hours and seven days.

It's likewise famous to utilize CFDs to support actual portfolios for financial backers, particularly in unstable business sectors.

As an ASIC-directed (AFSL398528) forex agent, Mitra de offers 100+ mainstream worldwide instruments, including forex, products, records, US stocks, and digital currencies. Mitra de offers you the chance to BUY (go long) or Sell (go short) on all Bitcoin exchanges, so you can utilize your favored methodology paying little mind to what direction the money is moving.

Pros:

- Speculate on crypto cost without possessing the crypto
- No compelling reason to manage crypto trades or open a crypto stockpiling wallet
- Low store, Higher influence
- The capacity to open long/short positions
- T+0 exchanging is more adaptable

Cons:

- The principle hazard related with CFD exchanging implies influence.
- Not reasonable for standing firm on a foothold in long haul

Presently, Mitrade gives advancements to new clients; You can apply for a 50USD free Trail Bonus to exchange any monetary resources with no dangers, which is useful for novices and amateurs.

2. Day Trading

Assume you are keen on bringing in cash with digital money in a quicker way. Around there, you can attempt crypto day exchanging, which is an exchanging methodology where financial backers purchase and sell orders on different occasions in a single day.

The high instability of Bitcoin and digital forms of money makes the crypto market like a thrill ride, which is ideal for day exchanging, as during the day, you will have enough good and bad times to get a decent benefit.

Preferably, you'll search for a low-evaluated freedom to purchase in and afterward sell it at a more exorbitant cost. In spite of the fact that this might be a little pay, this can acquire extensive benefits to financial backers the since a long time ago run.

Day exchanging is an expertise, very much like whatever else. On the off chance that you set aside more effort to see how it functions, it very well might be a full-time experience. Obviously, nobody will win in each exchanging, yet the objective of day exchanging is just to win more occasions.

So day exchanging requires financial backers more information and abilities. You can attempt to rehearse with a demo account on Mitrade, which gives a 50000 USD practice account. When you have a lot exchanging experience, you can choose to exchange a genuine record.

Pros:

- Relatively minimal effort
- Trading bitcoin on value changes

Cons:

- Need more abilities
- Much time and energy

3.   Bitcoin Mining

Mining digital forms of money is not quite the same as the over two different ways of exchanging. Mining might be more troublesome than different ways, yet it very well might be more productive when you mine effectively. Albeit the mining cycle should be possible from a PC, you actually need essential programming, explicit equipment, crypto wallets, and much power. For the vast majority, mining is an exceptionally specific industry that isn't reasonable for singular financial backers. Most Bitcoin mining is done in an enormous distribution center with modest power.

In some cases, the equipment is additionally costly. For instance, during the positively trending market in 2017, the cost of GPU raised steeply, while as the market breakdowns, you can purchase great mining hardware with less expense.

In the early years, bitcoin excavators could acquire coins moderately rapidly. However, by 2019, cryptographic money mining is more convoluted. Numerous expert diggers have fabricated enormous exhibits to mine, making it harder for more modest excavators. Obviously, you can join a bitcoin mining pool to be more successful, however that accompanies a charge. I likewise discover some crypto excavator application in the crypto business professing to help you mine crypto coins. It's more similar to diversion mining. Try not to depend on the application to bring in extraordinary cash for you.

Pros:

- Earning possibilities is higher

Cons:

- High cost to begin

- relatively troublesome

4. Long Term Investing

This is the simplest method to bring in cash with digital currency. Numerous individuals choose not to exchange cryptographic forms of money but rather purchase a specific number of coins and afterward put them in their wallets until the value ascends to make benefits. The reason of long haul contributing is that you have investigated and accept the digital currencies you put resources into will get more piece of the pie after some time.

In spite of the fact that there are a wide range of advanced coins, we suggest that you pick safe and profoundly fluid monetary forms, like BTC, LTC, and XRP. These coins have been famous available. In the event that you put resources into another crypto coin, it very well might be modest, however the coin is probably going to vanish after the market preliminary. Presently, numerous individuals acquire a major benefit from Bitcoin on the grounds that they purchased Bitcoin in the year 2011 or 2012, and they hold these computerized coins for quite a while regardless of whether the cost of bitcoin had ascended to 18,000 USD.

Pros:

- Easy to begin
- Beginner-accommodating

Cons:

- Take quite a while

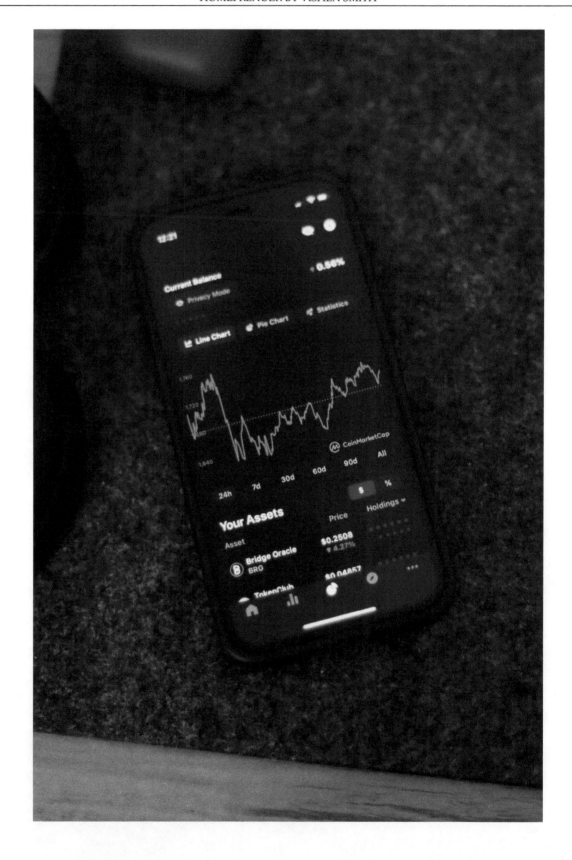

5.   Arbitrage

A few financial backers additionally utilize the method of exchange to bring in cash with digital forms of money. This implies when you purchase a computerized coin in crypto trade and afterward sell it on another crypto trade. Yet, truly, crypto exchange is uncommon that likely will not cause you to get rich rapidly.

Pros:

- Instant benefit
- Low prerequisites for section

Cons:

- Good openings are uncommon
- High hazard of losing benefits because of the great unpredictability in the digital currency markets

6.   Cryptocurrency spigot

In the event that you are tracking down a compelling method to benefit from modest quantities of digital forms of money, at that point a Crypto fixture might be one decision. A Crypto spigot resembles a trickling fixture. It is a site delivering very limited quantities of digital currencies, like Bitcoin, like clockwork. You need to do a few assignments as per the site necessities.

The crypto spigot site will bring in cash with publicizing and traffic. At the point when you're looking out for the page, there will be promotion arrangements.

Pros:

- Easy to utilize
- Easy to procure coins

Cons:

- Quite a limited quantity of coins
- Need to invest a lot of energy
- It can't cause you to get rich

7.   ICO

ICO implies Initial Coin Offerings, which are like crowd funding. ICO permits business visionaries to raise assets by making and selling their virtual money without hazard capital. It can make an enormous profit from your venture, however it likewise brings tremendous instability and dangers. ICO has a ton of traps. You must be cautious about picking the privilege ICO. In the event that the ICO coin isn't entirely significant, you may hazard losing cash. In this way, you would do well to contribute when you think the undertaking is sufficient and just put resources into what misfortunes you can bear.

Pros:

- Opportunity to put resources into point of view ventures at a beginning phase
- Low section limit

Cons:
- Many tricks
- Hacker assaults
- High chances

8.   Crypto gaming

This is additionally a genuinely regular approach to acquire Bitcoin, messing around to get BTC; it is like joining the Bitcoin taps above. There will be new titles delivered, and they need to have more individuals download and mess around to make the game better known. These games will grant BTC prizes to clients. Your work is basically to have a telephone, download these games, and afterward sit and play. Subsequent to finishing the game, you will get a specific measure of BTC.

Pros:
- Easy to acquire Bitcoin

Cons:

- Have to invest a lot of energy
- Quite a modest quantity

9. Be a blockchain engineer.

Blockchain improvement isn't very different from normal web advancement. Numerous designers have built up their own dispersed applications (DAPP) on certain stages, like Ethureum and NEO. At that point, you can bring in cash by showing advertisements, buys, memberships, and so forth, inside the application. Nonetheless, making and keeping a typical blockchain isn't simple. Above all else, the code is public and apparent to everybody. Anybody can see the code and check for blunders and weaknesses. This permits any software engineer to attack.

Pros:
- High pay
- Safe approach to acquire coins

Cons:

- You should think about coding

10. By advertising crypto with affiliate marketing

In the event that you own a site or blog for crypto, this might be a decent method to acquire an optional pay. The cryptographic money industry, particularly Bitcoin, is developing, however the substance around Bitcoin on the Internet is still "scant." You can accept this open door to make a site work in posting news, tips, and directions for Bitcoin exchanging.

Pros:

- Low speculation costs
- Passive pay
- Flexible working timetable

Cons:

- You should have a site
- You don't control partner promoting programs
- Freelance occupations are not for everybody

What's preventing fledglings from making a steady pay from exchanging cryptographic money?

- **Make cash with digital currency will take a great deal of time and steady exertion**.

In contrast to proficient financial backers, most fledgling brokers figuring out how to exchange aren't full-time dealers to drench themselves in the business sectors.
That implies they need more an ideal opportunity to get themselves to the level where they can exchange like a star.

- **You have no unmistakable exchanging methodology.**

Ask yourself an inquiry: "What is my exchanging procedure?" If you replied: "System? Indeed, I just purchased and held up in trust, so was that viewed as a system? ". Presently we need to talk. On the off chance that you don't have a reasonable exchanging methodology, regardless of whether it depends on specialized pointers or essential information on crypto resources, or dependent on innovation (algorithmic exchanging), at that point surely there is very There are numerous potential issues that you may experience.

Notwithstanding, first, you need to get yourself and your exchanging style better. Advanced resources are quite possibly the most unpredictable resources nowadays, and yet, fundamental blockchain innovation sets out a freedom to get more extravagant later on.

- **You indiscriminately desire to recuperate.**

The visually impaired any expectation of a bounce back or Bull Run is something each broker has encountered in any event once. That is the reason you will see rehashed updates in speculation archives that, "What occurred in the past isn't a pointer of future value developments." Indeed, there is a contrast between specialized examination and gazing at the screen and reciting "Bitcoin will arrive at 21,000" until that occurs.

- **You are averaging your situation during the downtrend.**

Another difficult you may discover in the bear market is the normal of the downtrend, or all in all, to inundate you on the lookout. Some altcoins are viewed as promising or genuine prospects, however pause and wonder why you continue to stay nearby this coin and can't get out. Purchasing when the market is falling is a decent method to purchase low, however you likewise need to sell when it feels right, or perhaps you should see the cash's decrease significantly more profound before it shows any benefit.

You likely realize that a few group can purchase A for 100, the value tumbles to 80 and still doesn't cut misfortunes as recently suspected, and afterward to 60 individuals who trust that the market will return, go through cash, purchase in to trust you're not kidding "normal" position and diminish misfortunes. At that point it goes down once more, and you become terrified.

- ## You totally disregarded danger the board.

Without addressing why an altcoin (or even Bitcoin) is so unpredictable will lead us to the following justification responding to the inquiry, "for what reason are you losing cash in the bear market?" If you don't focus on hazard the board, you are putting yourself at a misfortune. Ask yourself your present normal danger level by resources and trades? Will I get an opportunity to recuperate on the off chance that one of the coins is delisted or the trade is hacked? In the event that you don't have clear responses to these inquiries - you might be strolling in a minefield.

- ## You don't gain from your own mix-ups.

The last explanation is presumably the most significant. Nearly everybody has begun a couple of times at the screen and asked for an expansion in venture. Or then again a few groups keep on purchasing a sinking crypto resource that is probably not going to recuperate. Yet, they have taken in a couple of things. In case you're committing an error from this bear market, focus on them. It is the expense of instruction, albeit the misfortune isn't fun; in the event that you don't make the most of that chance and gain from botches, particularly because of unnecessary expectation or restricted information, you will lose more expectation.

How to become a professional crypto trader?

The principal thing we will begin with is a clarification of who is a "proficient cryptographic money dealer" and what is "exchanging": In basic words, exchanging implies trading or selling activities between two market members, where exchanging resources change hands.

Digital currency exchanging is a trade exchange between crypto-to-crypto or digital currencies to-fiat cash. Purchasing digital money like Bitcoin for US dollars is a trade activity, which implies you trade your money for crypto.

Being a merchant is something other than a diversion. It is a genuine energy or calling, which requires a ton of time and no less specialized information just; for this situation, exchanging will bring standard benefit.

A digital money merchant is a client of a cryptographic money stage or trade following up on its drive by exchanging advanced resources (cryptographic forms of money and fiat cash) to benefit from the exchanging interaction itself (purchasing and selling reserves). The motivation behind exchanging is to get cash for proficiently performed tasks (shut with benefit).

Cryptographic money exchanging is getting increasingly mainstream. Consistently an ever increasing number of individuals might want to attempt themselves as dealers. There are numerous fantasies around this calling, and most accept that to turn into a broker, you need higher monetary schooling or have an over-created instinct, over-reason, be an expert from God, and so forth Indeed, this would be a huge reward, yet in no way, shape or form an essential. What's more, today, we will demonstrate it!

Would i be able to see myself as a broker after a few effective exchanges?

The notable principle of "novice's karma" applies here too. You can benefit once or even a few times from opening exchanging positions indiscriminately, at the same time, tragically, it works in an unexpected way. For fruitful and successful digital money exchanging, you need to comprehend a few perspectives:

- Current market circumstance.
- How exchanging instruments work (what sorts of requests are accessible, and so forth);
- Understand how to understand graphs. For instance, you need to realize how to check the ethereum cost in pounds on the off chance that you are keen on exchanging this cash pair.
- Most critically, examine exchanging examples and developments on the outline to fabricate the correct exchanging procedure.

A broker's demonstrable skill lies he would say on the lookout, how he responds in upsetting circumstances, the amount he thinks out his exchanging steps, and "fallback alternatives."

Despite the exchanging system sought after, the primary exchanging objective remaining parts unaltered. To be specific, "Purchase less expensive – sell more costly" – the lone justification any exchanging activity is to benefit.

What information do I have to improve my exchanging abilities?

Market examination is the establishment of a fruitful exchanging methodology and makes a benefit. Not a solitary exchanging system, even Buy&HODL, is effective without seeing how market developments work and the primary exchanging candle designs.

Try not to BE SCARED

You don't need to be an expert to begin exchanging! Indeed, even a novice can bring in cash by purchasing/selling digital currencies with the privilege and insightful advances. Experience characterizes an expert, and experience is the thing that you need to procure. Hence, go through this way of turning out to be from an odd one out to a swan! For our situation, from amateur to proficient ;).

From the very beginning, it is critical to comprehend the kinds of orders gave on the stage utilized and what "pictures on the diagram" mean, how to put orders and what instruments are accessible on the stage. Interestingly, this will be all that anyone could need!

We can draw a similarity with power – to turn on a TV, forced air system, or night light – you don't really have to know how they work in the engine. It's sufficient to figure out how to work them. A similar rationale applies here!

Is there a simple success exchanging strategy to bring in cash on cryptographic forms of money?

Slight an interesting inquiry in light of the fact that the appropriate response is both "yes" and "no" all the while.

The truth of the matter is that the cryptographic money market is unstable; hence, it generally gives a chance to bring in cash for the individuals who follow the market "at the current second" and ability to utilize exchanging devices effectively.

"Purchase less expensive sell more costly" that is the proverb of any exchanging methodology.

The Buy&HODL system can be viewed as winning under specific conditions. Its substance is to purchase a resource and stand by till it develops. The primary concern isn't to miss the second and sell on schedule. Subsequently, when purchasing a specific exchanging resource for hold it, you need to make a primer investigation and get a few signs that the resources cost being referred to will probably flood. Something else, there is a danger of misfortunes.

How to pick a stage for crypto exchanging on the off chance that I am a novice?

Check the state's public assessment and notoriety. Security is critical! The stage should agree with the most elevated security norms to ensure your information and assets. Discover the rundown of the upheld nations: not all administrations cover clients' entrance all throughout the planet. Check if occupants of your nation can be the stage's clients. It is additionally critical to have client assistance nonstop. You need to ensure you can find support from the client care whenever you need it.

Benefits of the cryptographic money market:

Market instability no monetary market can contrast with the changes in digital money rates. Today, it is the most adaptable approach to bring in cash on exchanging; the cost of certain resources can make x100 in a real sense in a day. Despite the fact that note, they can likewise drop as quickly as they develop.

Cryptographic money accessibility advanced monetary forms are accessible whenever. The digital currency market works day in and day out, and you can exchange, store, or your crypto resources when you need. Namelessness regardless of whether the exchange can be followed – you'll see the wallet address, not the ID information of the proprietor. Unwavering quality cryptographic forms of money are protected. Be that as it may! Just on the off chance that you utilize a demonstrated and secure assistance. Slender discharge is useful for cryptographic money tokens. The less coins were given, the more interest for them.

Cryptographic money is decentralized cash; no single element or middle person controls the exchanges. Low exchange expenses the commission for moving assets is a lot of lower than the bank moves, for instance.

Why stopping? Go, pick the stage, make a record, and begin exchanging. Simply remember one principle consistently do your exploration first!

Deducting | The Right Way

Untangling Small Business Accounting and Taxes Based on Online Activities

By

Vishen Smith

Table of Contents

Introduction

You'll definitely have to do a lot of day-to-day daily duties, including accounting, when you first launch your small online business. Knowing how to track and forecast your business's income and expenses is a valuable skill for growth, so familiarise yourself with the basics of accounting.

And if you're willing to outsource your accounting and bookkeeping right now, learning the fundamentals can help you appreciate your finance professional's findings and correctly evaluate your company's financial wellbeing.

We've broken down all you need to understand about small online business accounting, including how to monitor and evaluate your business's main financial indicators, in the parts below.

Chapter: 1 Online Business and its importance?

There has never been a better or easier time in history to start your own business than now. Everyone is connected now, regardless of their income status or geographic location, thanks to the development and growth of easy-to-use website creation tools and social media.

Whether you are rich and powerful or impoverished, you can now freely share your abilities and connect with people around the world.It can also be very inexpensive and simple to get started for those looking to start an online business.

Many people have started online businesses for less than 200 dollars. (the cost purchasing a domain name, hosting service and professional theme).

You can start a business if you can connect with others and fill a need.

In fact, there are numerous advantages to starting and owning your own online business, ranging from increased income and freedom to assisting others in achieving their own personal goals;

however, in order to keep things simple and to the point, I will only go over seven of the many advantages to starting and owning your own online business.

1.1 The importance of eCommerce

1. eCommerce Helps You Reduce Your Costs

To make your online store, it isn't essential that you have every one of your items introduced in an actual space. There're various organizations that work online where they just demonstrate all their stock through their electronic business.

This suggests not just saving by not requiring a purchase or rental of premises, yet besides all that includes electric power, the internet, and so forth or then again in the event that you need to have one, so clients have an actual space, it doesn't need to be just about as extensive as all that you offer. Regardless, you'll reduce your expenses.

2. eCommerce Helps Businesses Go Global

Straightforwardly identified with the previous point, this reality permits you to put your items available to be purchased anywhere on the planet. They won't have the express need to venture out to where you're to perceive what you've to bring to the table.

If you're running an actual store, it'll be restricted by the geological zone that you can support, yet possessing an eCommerce site will offer you the chance to expand your effort. It will offer your items and administrations to clients around the entire world, paying little heed to the time zone and distance.

Besides, this wipes out a wide range of topographical and etymological tango hindrances. Your online business converted into various dialects will permit them to purchase from various nations.

With eCommerce & mobile business also, the whole world is your jungle gym. Your services and products are accessible for many clients sitting on another edge of the world.

In this way, if you need to develop your online business worldwide, it is a good thought to begin making your online store & localize it in various dialects.

3. eCommerce Can Also Be Done through Fewer Overheads and Fewer Risk

Beginning an online store might mean essentially bring down expenses of a start-up contrasted with a physical retailer. The retailer or the online entrepreneur does not need to think about the shop rent high costs, employing a sales associate to facilitate the client, efforts, service charges, safety, and so forth. This, can empower you to sell them at good costs. Moreover, an online shop allows you to grasp expanded productivity with less danger.

4. eCommerce Can Broaden Your Brand & Expand the Business

Having some eCommerce store can be used to widen the scope of items or administrations available to be purchased, extending your business, bringing you a huge number of customers, and broadening your deals. It is the ideal method to take a personal brand from a conventional block & mortar store to a novice, all-around adored one.

With eCommerce, there's no compelling reason to have more than one branch, only one particular online store permitting you to completely arrive at clients without agonizing over moving areas; you can deal with your online business from home.

It's imperative to specify that eCommerce will be useful for Both B2B & B2C businesses to help personal brand mindfulness in the online market.

5. eCommerce Offers Better Marketing Opportunities

Your eCommerce website is the best advertising device that you could at any point have. On a web account, anybody can advertise via online apparatuses such as web-based media advertising, email promoting, web search tool advertising, pay per click advertisements, and SEO assists you in constructing valuable connections & contacts.

For instance, with great SEO, your online store will show up in the top searches of SERPs. Likewise, online media organizations will give you a stage to draw in and construct trust with your clients through audits and appraisals, just as keeping them acknowledged with normal posts about your items and offers.

6. Your Online Store Will Stay Open 24*7/365:

Additionally, one of the incredible significances of eCommerce that eCommerce merchants can appreciate is store timings are currently all day, every day/365 as the eCommerce stores are working 24 hours per day, 7 days per week, contrasted with the customary stores.

Along these lines, merchants can expand their deals by boosting the number of requests. Nonetheless, it's additionally useful for clients when they can buy items and administrations at whatever point they need, whether it's early morning/midnight.

7. eCommerce Is Easier & More Convenient

Individuals' lives are rushed; getting to an actual store implies taking a ton of time and exertion. In this way, beginning an online store implies you can find a way into your client's bustling lives, making the items they need available when they need them.

The agreeable thing about eCommerce is purchasing those choices that are fast, simple, helpful, and simple in understanding with the capability to move supports on the web.

"In web-based shopping, your product is consistently a single tick away instead of actual shopping where you might be compelled to hang tight for quite a long time or months before a product you requested is accessible," says Heritage House, who sell kid suits on the web.

On account of eCommerce's accommodation, shoppers can save heaps of time, endeavors just as cash via looking for their items effectively and making buying on the web.

8. Personalize Your Shopping Experience

In the event that there is one of the unmistakable favorable circumstances of having an online store, you will have the option to know what your buyer does. Genuinely, it would be entirely awkward for a likely purchaser to enter your store, and you were constantly behind him, inquiring what he needs or for what valid reason he doesn't accept your item.

Web-based business permits you, for instance, to know when in the process you left the buy midway and even recall that you left it in the center by sending an email. This, also, can assist you with improving your shopping experience for other events: shortening the means to finish the request or offering those purchaser items with comparable attributes.

9. Improve the Image of Your Business

Among the benefits of having some online store, there's no uncertainty that it likewise incorporates improving the picture of your organization. Offering a decent online deals stage to clients will give your organization an extraordinary corporate appearance.

Not exclusively will it end up being state-of-the-art; however, it will likewise show interest in encouraging buyer buys. For instance, it keeps you from making a trip to the actual spot of offer and permits you to analyze costs from home. Likewise, because of what we have referenced as devotion or input, you can even actualize upgrades in your items that clients will esteem emphatically

10. Easily Receive Feedback on Products

Have you generally needed to understand consumers' opinions about what you are selling to offer more or make it greater?

Indeed, the online store will permit you to get that input to actualize enhancements in the business, through star appraisals, with the chance of leaving remarks.

Also, the client will feel heard after their buy. There could be no greater method to thank you for your trust in buying your organization's items. Besides, in the event that you offer the quality, you'll have nothing to stress over. Empowering an immediate channel where others notice what they can anticipate from the given resource is an extraordinary public illustration of trust in online business.

11. Maximum Security of Transactions

Today, working on the internet is practically more secure and dependable than doing this in an actual store. From home, without anybody watching on your mysterious number or Mastercard. The eCommerce site should have an SSL endorsement.

This testament not just permits safe perusing on the website. What's more, it keeps the information scrambled to be protected to add keys & passwords. This won't just be important for the client's business account yet to utilize much more touchy information, for example, Mastercard data with complete, true serenity.

It merits referencing that 33% of eCommerce specialists distinguished security, versatile installments, and portable applications as the main interests in 2019. Security will keep on being one of the best spotlights on eCommerce.

With changes in innovation, client practices, and shopping designs, dealers should give arrangements guaranteeing the trust and security of shopping measures.

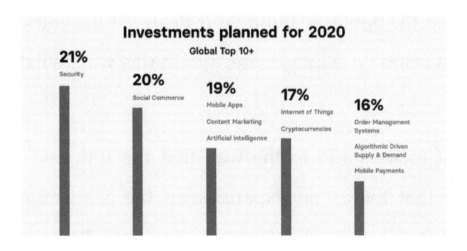

12 Ready for the Trade of the Future

It's another significant detail considering the long haul of the business. Search customer spending and patterns, the headway of innovation, and the most recent insights gauge that by 2040, 95 percent of buys will be executed through the web.

Along these lines, it's not just discussing a pattern of the present yet additionally about what the business relations of things to come will be. Furthermore, similarly, as though you are not on the internet, you don't exist; if your business doesn't sell on the web, it is monstrously restricting its deals.

13. Increase in Sales

Everything mentioned previously is centered around a certain thing: having the option to build your deals. At the end of the day, the business relies on selling more, and in this way, what it will be based on.

All the past focuses add to the way that the 10th and last bit of leeway are that there's an expansion in the acquisition of your items. Arriving at more clients, improving your items on account of remarks, or being accessible 24 hours daily will without a doubt add to the entirety of this.

As a rule, it's normally beautifully simple, with minimal risk and cost to begin an eCommerce business. As you choose your benefits/items incisively, have a suitable plan, got the right partner to help you construct your store, there is very much potential for automated revenue & high ROI.

Chapter: 2 Accounting and Its Purpose

Accounting is the structured method of defining, tracking, assessing, classifying, checking, and transmitting financial records. It shows a company's profit or loss over a specified time, as well as the value and quality of its assets and liabilities, as well as its shareholders' equity.

2.1 Why is Accounting Important?

Accounting is very important and necessary for small business owners because it requires owners, administrators, investors, and other stakeholders to determine the company's financial results. Accounting provides key facts regarding profit & loss, costs & earnings, assets & liabilities for decision-making, scheduling, and risk management within an organization.

Accounting's main goal is to document financial transactions in books of records in order to recognize, calculate, and transmit economic results. Furthermore, tax reporting authorities mandate you to maintain simple books that track profits and expenditures.

2.2 What Is the Purpose of Accounting?

Accounting is regarded as the "Language of Business." It is a system of communicating financial information to multiple uses for decision-making purposes. The major objects of accounting are:

1. Recording transactions

Accounting's primary purpose is to control a systematic, accurate, and full record of a company's financial activities. The accounting system's backbone is made up of these reports. When appropriate, company owners should be able to review and evaluate transactions.

2. Budgeting and planning

Business owners must prepare how they can distribute their limited resources, such as workers, cash, machinery and equipment to meet the company's goals.

Budgeting and planning, an integral aspect of business management, enable companies to prepare accordingly by forecasting requirements and resources. This assists in the coordination of multiple corporate segments.

3. Decision making

Accounting assists in a variety of decision-making processes and facilitates business owners in developing policies to improve business process efficiency. The price to be charged for products and services, the resources required to produce these products and services, as well as financing and business opportunities are all examples of decisions based on accounting information.

4. Business performance

Business owners may use financial records to assess how good their organization is doing. Financial reports provide a credible tool to evaluate important performance indicators, encouraging business owners to compare their output to that of their rivals as well as their past performance.

5. Financial position

The financial statements issued at the end of the accounting period represent a company's financial position at the time. It displays the amount of capital invested, the number of funds utilized by the company, the profit and loss, as well as the number of assets and liabilities.

6. Liquidity

Mismanagement of funds is a common cause of small business failure. Accounting assists in assessing a company's liquidity, which is characterized as the cash and other liquid capital available to pay off debts. Via the identification of bottlenecks, the information lowers the risk of bankruptcy.

7. Financing

Accounting assists business owners in the preparation of historical financial records and also financial forecasts that may be utilized while preparing for a loan or securing investment.

8. Control

Accounting assists in avoiding losses attributable to stealing, fraud, mistakes, injury, obsolescence, and mismanagement by enforcing different checks within the company. Internal monitoring secures the company's finances to eliminate long-term risks.

9. Legal requirements

Businesses must retain correct financial statements of their activities and disclose those records with shareholders, tax officials, and regulators, according to the statute. The financial statements and details are often needed for the filing of indirect and direct taxes.

Chapter: 3 Why Is Accounting Useful for Small Business Owners?

One of the most common causes of small business failure, especially in the first year, is poor financial management. Accounting plays a critical role in providing information that assists small companies in their growth and advancement when they have a restricted budget and other resources.

Accounting is important for small business owners for the following reasons:

➢ Maintain a careful watch on the cash balance. You should enforce strategies for effective record-keeping and a solid financial strategy to prevent the company cash flow from running dry.

➢ Cost management may help small business owners grasp the principles of fixed expenses, variable costs, and how to correctly cost a project. This way, you won't waste funds on a project you felt would be profitable.

➢ Accounting helps you to have a clearer view of the company's health. Learn to interpret a balance sheet, financial statement, and cash flow statement to do this.

➢ It helps you in identifying and avoiding consumer, employee, and supplier bribery and stealing.

➢ You'll be more able to tackle investigations if you grasp corporate accounts and transactions.

➢ When working with corporate leaders who have a strong grip on the company's finances and are mindful of the financial consequences, bankers are more comfortable.

If you're a sole proprietor or have workers, the trick to expanding your small company is to monitor your financial records on a routine basis and build a comprehensive budget that helps you to recognize operating inefficiencies. Saving a little money on a few things will add up to a lot of money in the long run.

Chapter: 4 Accounting basics How to Run a Successful Online Business

A painful task is accounting. It is the dull side of the business. But you can't ignore it if you want your business to grow. You could try to dump all your receipts into a drawer and hand them over to a stranger. Yet you are going to give them financial power. That means losing your business's future. You will hand them a sweet slice of change to do it all for you, too. I guarantee it isn't as hard as you may be afraid of, though. And, for day-to-day operations, you shouldn't require an accountant. You should still know the fundamentals yourself, even though you are paying for guidance. You may acknowledge and challenge what someone is talking to you in this context. It's your business at stake, after all.

The following accounting fundamentals help you need to know to grasp your money.

1. Get Accounting Software

Don't bother using excel or a calculator to piece it all together. Do yourself a favor and get software for accounting. FreshBooks are sold to clients that operate e-commerce businesses. Or there are a variety of accounting software apps you should get right in their app store if you use Shopify. Your business and interests would rely on the right choice. Make sure you choose a bookkeeping system while you're shopping in the app store. Look for software to monitor revenue, expenditures, and inventory. Keep away from programs that generate invoices only or include reports only. You want a tool that's able to do everything for you. Select one that can sync directly to your e-commerce store, whether you want apps like Shopify or go for something different. It would make things even better.

2. Monitor Cash Flow

Get one if you don't have a separate bank account with your business yet. You need to realize that making money is your job. And watching the cash balance is the best way to see this. When you've got more coming in than heading out, you actually do well, don't you? The timing of money going out and coming back can also be monitored. After all, what if, tomorrow, all your bills are due? When you have one million rolling's in next month, it won't mean a whole lot if you can't pay the workers by then. Bear in mind any investments on your accounts that you have. What ways of payment do you give your clients? Are some of them putting a grip on the money? From the moment a consumer spends to the time the money is in your accounts, is there a five-day delay? When you're finding out when you have resources to spare, you ought to remember this. For monitoring currency, Shopify offers a free template. With Excel, you can quickly build your own.

Per week, monitor what you plan to spend. Track the money that you plan per week to come in. You realize you're going to have a challenge if what you need to pay is more than the new bank balance and what's coming in. To improve to boost your cash flow, adopt these tips:

- Do not spend anything sooner than you have got to. If it is due within thirty days, compensate it within thirty days.

- To ensure revenue stays through, suggest selling recurring payment contracts or subscriptions to consumers.

- Hold a reserve 'just in case' in your company bank account.

- Do not overcomplicate yourself. You do not require massive statements of cash balance.

3. Determine how inventory should be counted

Ignore this step if you're selling a service. Inventory is the product that you sell or all the materials that you use to make that item. Do not forget to include any costs for your product being wrapped or packaged. Decide what minimum inventory volume you want to have on hand, and make sure you are tracking inventory before you pass this point so you can reorder. The last thing you want is for inventory to run out and lose sales.

Why does inventory form part of the basics of accounting?

Money equals inventory.

It is the money you spent buying that stuff. You will not make any money back until you sell your product. And while it is sitting in your warehouse, the money tied to your inventory can change (or store, or apartment).

If I purchase 50 items for 100 dollars each, and the price rises up to 150 dollars tomorrow, then immediately, my inventory is worth more.

So, if tomorrow's price falls to 50 dollars, the worth of my inventory is less.

And beware of 'shrinkage'!

That's why, unexpectedly, you have fewer inventory than you should have.

You know you've purchased 50 items. You understand that you sold and delivered 40. You should be left 10 items, right? What if you have only 8 left? This is shrinkage. Perhaps an item was misplaced, or robbed, or destroyed and had to be discarded away. There are plenty of explanations for why this happens. When you don't have a physical department location, the positive thing is the shrinkage is smaller. Currently, factory shrinkage is pretty poor. Less than 1% of the overall product is a normal shrinkage. It's also less probable that you will have shrinkage if you're running a business out of your house. After all, if you're the only person around it, you are less likely to see anyone rob the inventory. Compared with a large warehouse, it's also a lot tougher to lose stock in an apartment. Having said that, shrinkage will happen to everyone. This is why it's necessary to routinely physically count inventory. If you have missed 100 dollars worth of goods and factor it into your accounting, you ought to know.

CGS, which means cost of goods sold, is an expense directly linked to the goods sold by you. This is inventory sold, and also how much it costs to produce that inventory. Suppose say there is one widget you sell. The cost of goods sold for that widget should be whatever it costs you for the parts and also whatever it costs to build it. If the widget parts cost 60 dollars, the packaging cost is 15 dollars, and you paid someone 15 to put it together, that the total cost of the widget will 90 dollars.

MATERIAL COST	60$
PACKAGING COST	15$

LABOUR COST	<u>15$</u>
TOTAL COST OF GOODS SOLD	90 $

4. Calculate all Expenses

You already understand that the costs are directly tied to the volume of sales. Next, you need to know how much it costs you for anything else. Any costs that do not grow as you sell more or drop when you sell fewer are known as 'fixed costs.' Let's say If you pay a monthly rent, for instance, the price is set. If you sell one widget or a million, it won't shift. Such costs are not part of the cost of the goods sold, and the profit margin is not compensated for. However, they do control your earnings and your cash flow.

Some Common fixed expenses are

➢ Utilities

➢ Rent

➤ Interest on loan payments

➤ Property Tax

➤ Wages

These expenses are considered a fixed expense because even though you sell nothing next month, you have to reimburse them. Do not confuse this with an expense where every month is the very same amount. An expense such as electricity may be more than one month longer than the next. Or maybe there's more to it in winter than in summer. In accounting standards, it is always a fixed expense. You will use an average for budgeting if expenses change month to month.

5. Find out Break-Even Sales

Budgeting and planning are essential aspects of operating a business. Next, you are not only going to want to know if last month you made a profit, you are going to want to know if this month and next you want to earn more.

Your break-even sales amount is the amount of sales dollars you need to earn to cover all your costs.

Let's assume, for instance, all the fixed costs add up to 5,000 dollars a month. This ensures that you have to sell enough of the product to meet the cost of producing it (including labor cost) and also an additional 5,000 dollars only to break-even (no profit, no loss).

Break-Even Sale = $\underline{\text{Fixed Cost}}$

  Revenue per unit-Variable cost per unit

$$= \underline{\text{Fixed Cost}}$$

        Unit Margin

If your break-even number of units are 5,000 and you sell only 3000, then you are in problem. And if break-even 5000 and you sell 7000, then you are in a good position.

6. Schedule your right tax rates for customers

Here is the aspect for which most citizens groan: taxation. Taxes are necessary, and they may become very complex. At this point, you may want to contact a tax consultant specialist, if you sell a number of various goods & services to a lot of people around the world. Thankfully, systems these days are fairly smart. For you, the software can take control of much of this.

7. Prepare your Tax Payments

Now, if you are properly set up to collect tax, you also need to make sure you are ready to pay it. Your tax laws will rely on where you are located, actually. At a minimum, believe that as much tax as you have earned must be submitted. This suggests that it is necessary to consider that money of tax is set aside. If not, then when you submit tax return, you face some hurdles. Many online shopping platforms allow you to pay tax on your purchase price, such as Shopify.

For example, if you buy a product that price is 100 dollars and the tax rate is 20%, then you will pay the amount included tax.

Product Cost	100 $
Tax Rate (15%)	15 $
Total amount included Tax	**115 $**

8. Balance Sheet

At the end, you must understand your balance sheet. We have already addressed all as well as cash balance on the income statement. The balance sheet is the final thing to cover. This is what helps you watch the long-term performance of your business and see how your business is performing in general. An income statement is a timely overview. The broader image is a balance sheet. Assets, liabilities, and equity make up the balance sheet.

BUSINESS CONSULTING COMPANY BALANCE SHEET As at December 31, 2015				
Assets		**$**	**Liabilities & Stockholders' equity**	**$**
Current assets:			Liabilities:	
Cash		85,550	Notes payable	5,000
Accounts receivable		4,700	Accounts payable	1,600
Prepaid building rent		1,500	Salaries payable	2,000
Unexpired insurance		3,600	Income tax payable	3,000
Supplies		250	Unearned service revenue	4,400
Total current assets		95,600	Total liabilities	16,000
Non-current assets:			Stockholders' equity:	
Equipment	9,000		Capital stock	50,000
Acc. dep. - Equipment	3,600	5,400	Retained earnings	35,000	85,000
Total assets		101,000	Total liabilities & stockholders' equity	101,000

I have finally discussed all the accounting basics you should be practicing day to day and month to month. Start with simple accounting software. It can make your life a lot easier.

Then, note that cash is king, and keep a grip on your cash flow. You should be doing this on a frequent basis unless you have a large cash reserve built.

Next, you ought to consider the revenue, expenditures, and earnings. This is your income statement, which lets you know whether you are earning money per week, month or year.

Do not neglect to schedule for taxation. Set up the e-commerce platform to receive them if you need to. Place the money together to reimburse them should you need to.

Finally, construct the balance sheet. Or let the accounting software do it for you. This will help you exactly how 'healthy' the business is long term. It's a simple way to know if you have so much debt.

There are plenty of other accounting rules and methods that will help you save money at tax time.

There will also be reporting options that can be addressed whether you're seeking to get investors or a loan for growth.

But for running your company, don't get pulled into the complicated laws. It will only distract you from your crucial day job of operating your business.

An accountant will assist you with something beyond and above the fundamentals if you require to.

Chapter: 5 Common Accounting Mistakes and How to Avoid Them

Numerous new business visionaries handle their bookkeeping and accounting when they are beginning. Here are how to stay away from some normal DIY bookkeeping ruins.

When numerous business visionaries first begin, they attempt to deal with their bookkeeping to set aside cash. Notwithstanding, following each penny of pay, costs, charges, and seller installments are messy and tedious. Errors can happen effectively & they can charge your huge business loads of cash.

To help you forestall these monetary blunders, the absolute most regular bookkeeping ruins are below that entrepreneurs make and — all the more significantly — how to keep away from them.

1. Lack of organization

Accounting requires extraordinary association abilities. You'll need to record each exchange, digitize or store receipts for future reference, figure duties, and the sky is the limit from there. In case you're not appropriately following or putting away data, you'll probably miss a significant exchange or lose a receipt, which could get you into difficulty come season of tax.

2. Not following a regular accounting schedule

With the wide range of various duties, you have as an entrepreneur, refreshing your books may tumble to the lower part of your plan for the day. Notwithstanding, it's imperative to set a normal timetable for including late payments and costs. While every day refreshes are ideal, you ought to, in any event, enter your exchanges consistently.

3. Failing to reconcile accounts

While you are recording monetary information and income in your books, you need to routinely return and guarantee your ledger mirrors that equivalent equilibrium. In the event that there's a difference between the two, there's likely a mistake that requires quick thoughtfulness regarding keep the issue from deteriorating. Consistently exploring your business financial balances against your books can likewise help you get any fake exchanges that may have happened.

4. Ignoring small transactions

It's not difficult to disregard that little thank you blessing you sent to a customer or the ream of printer paper you got on your way back to the workplace. Regardless of how immaterial the exchange is, it's critical to record it & get some receipt. In case of an assessment review, you should have the option to give the IRS records of all your costs of doing business, even the little ones.

5. Not backing up your data

Envision if the gadget on which you put away your business' monetary data was lost, hacked, or taken — and you did not have it upheld up anyplace. These problems can emerge whenever, and you should be set up to reestablish your books. Luckily, there are numerous reinforcement alternatives accessible that will empower you to keep an extra, state-of-the-art duplicate of the business financials.

6. Not using an accounting software

In case you're monitoring your business funds in an Excel bookkeeping page or a paper record, you might need to consider moving up to programming. Putting resources into the correct bookkeeping programming can assist you with maintaining a strategic distance from botches and, at last, make it simpler to deal with your accounts.

Most bookkeeping programmings incorporate the financial balance, meaning less manual work. These projects likewise make it simple to back up your information if there should be an occurrence of a crisis. Also, if you wind up expecting to recruit a bookkeeping administration for your business, having unified programming will guarantee the bookkeeper has all the recorded information they require to deal with your books, finance, and assessments.

Regardless of whether you're taking care of your bookkeeping or moving to an expert, accounting mix-ups can cause significant issues for your business. It is ideal to forestall & face these problems.

Chapter: 6 Business Challenges & Solutions

Small enterprises experience a number of obstacles throughout their first few years of operation. Others are more challenging to resolve than others, and according to the U.S. Bureau of Labour Statistics, about 20% of small companies collapse during their first year. Fifty percent go under by the close of their fifth year, and that figure increases to 80 percent by the tenth year.

With so poor survival rates, it's clear to see why people are worried for their first few years of the company. In fact, though, many common market issues and problems are actually fixable. You can notice several moments when you need to take a step back, make an effort to understand the pressure points that you experience and re-think your plan.

Each small business faces some problems here, including some tactical tips about how to solve them.

   1. Find the Customers

2. Increasing Brand Awareness

3. Designing Email List

4. Lead Generation

5. Delighting the Customers

6. Hiring Talented People

7. Managing Workflow

8. Financial Strategy

9. Scaling

1. Find Customers

This first one is not just an issue for small enterprises. Marketers of well-known firms such as Toyota, Apple, KFC, and McDonald's are not yet waiting for the leads to come in: Also, the largest, most popular firms have employees working tirelessly to attract new customers every single day.

Finding consumers may be especially challenging for small companies that are not well-known. It seems, for instance, like there are too many platforms you may choose to concentrate on. How do you decide what to prioritize and where money can be allocated?

How to solve it:

Seeking consumers begins by deciding who the target consumer is. It does not work for everyone to spray and pray — you need to ensure you distribute the message to the correct people.

By designing buyer personas, you will get a feel of what your potential buyers are like, what they are doing, and where they spend some time online.

It will significantly boost the market outcomes by producing very particular ones. When you have developed your buyer personas, you can start developing content and reaching out to your potential buyers in areas where they invest time online and with ads that appeal to them.

2. Brand Awareness

Customers can not purchase from you if they don't know who you are. Often it may seem like the largest brands of today seem to have sprung up from nowhere. When did it turn into a household name? Why did they continue to spread so quickly? Is it feasible for your organization to expand in the same way?

Of note, the hard work, mistakes, and rejections of each of these businesses existed behind the scenes. But there are tactics how you can begin right away to spread the word about your company and create a strong reputation.

How to solve it:

There are several approaches to increase brand awareness, but concentrate on three in this book about public relations, blogging & co-marketing.

- **Public Relations**

Public relations are less about competing for a place on a news site and more about concentrating your message on the consumer and discovering your location. I suggest reading First Round Capital's excellent research about what entrepreneurs and small companies often get wrong regarding public relations, which also provides some useful guidance about how to find out who reports the industry, develop relationships, and communicate with reporters.

- **Blogging**

Running a high-quality blog on a daily basis can also help you create brand recognition. A blog not only helps push traffic to your website and turn the traffic into leads, but that also helps you to build authority and confidence among your prospects in your industry. It will also assist you in the creation of an email list, which takes us to our next step.

- **C0-marketing**

Collaborating with another brand allows you to inherit some of their name and credibility while still producing brand evangelists outside of your immediate radius. It's an ideal opportunity to complement the organic marketing activities by acquiring a wide range of potential connections. More details about how to get acquainted with co-marketing can be found in ourebook.

3. Designing Email List

You must create confidence by being top-of-mind and continually delivering value to drive prospects down their buyer's path to finally becoming your client.

The first move is to link prospects to your email list.

As if creating an email list is not complicated enough, the typical marketing account degraded by 22.5 percent last year. That means you'll need to expand your email list by nearly a quarter just to hold it up to date, let alone develop it. Seeking opportunities to continuously introduce fresh, different email addresses to the lists is the task of the marketing staff.

Yet what many people term "making an email list" is simply purchasing an email list, and it is never a smart idea to purchase an email list. I repeat not a good idea. It is not only a waste of resources, but it'll also damage your email deliverability and I.P. credibility. If purchasing or renting email lists is your new plan, then it's time to rebuild and find appropriate ways to position certain tools.

How to solve it:

Develop opt-in email lists instead of purchasing or renting lists. Subscribers who willingly give you their email address so that you can send them updates make up an opt-in email list.

The process of opting in needs the accessibility of the website that catches their email address. This can be accomplished with a shape builder or other method to transform (more on that later).

Creating a market is the other part of the puzzle. Through making excellent blog posts, you will do this and make it convenient for people to subscribe, which can help you improve your web visibility, build up search credibility, and develop evangelists from your content at the same time.

Create an informative opt-in message and email it to your old list, inviting contacts to re-opt-in and pledging to delete any contacts that don't reply.

Rising your email list does not often mean growing your sales-qualified lead list, which leads me to my next stage.

4. Lead Generation

Lead generation is another concern most small companies share, namely, creating sufficient leads to maintain the sales staff satisfied.

However, the most critical goal of a marketing team is to produce high-quality leads in vast amounts. A decent lead generation engine transforms website users into future buyers and maintains a constant stream of sales leads flowing in as you sleep.

How to solve it:

To make the lead generation method function for your business, you must first increase the conversion rate of your current website. The most critical asset you have for converting opportunities into clients is your website. Look and question yourself from your website:

Do visitors specifically direct each of the webpages to take some action, or do they leave them uncertain what to do next?

Can you use a program, like HubSpot's free lead generation tool, that instantly pulls the inputs from your forms and brings them into your communication database?

For any single campaign that you manage, can you build custom landing pages?

Do you have CTAs for any of your blog posts for lead generation? (Have you got a blog at all?)

First, prioritize the most major blogs on your website. The homepage, "About" page, "Contact Us" page, and probably one or two of the most famous blog posts are usually the sites that pull in the bulk of visitors for most companies. Learn how to decide which sites to prioritize and how to customize them in this topic.

Then, utilizing conversion applications such as:

- Hello bars, hello

- Pop-up windows

- Diaposit-ins

Finally, free lead generation tools and applications for startups can be used. It is a huge obstacle in and of itself to afford ads in general, but it can be a game-changer to identify and incorporate the most effective free marketing methods.

5. Delighting the Customers

A perfect target is consumer loyalty, but much greater is customer delight. After all, the ones who purchase from you again, write expert opinions and accept case studies, and recommend you to others they trust, are delighted consumers.

You have to transcend standards and offer an unmatched service in order to gain true consumer delight such that your consumers become promoters of your brand.

How to solve it:

For your customer, it takes effort to begin solving in a fashion that converts them into crazed fans. Here are few moves that will bring you into the proper mindset:

> Realize why you were picked by your customers and what they want and need

> At the beginning of the commitment, set clear goals

> Deliver on certain requirements (and serve the wishes of your customers)

> Dream of innovative approaches to include unique extras that go beyond and above the call of duty.

> Continue to monitor consumer loyalty and allow changes.

6. Hiring talented workers

Without a great team who knows your mission and encourages your actions, none of the above will happen at large.

Hiring is one of the most challenging tasks for small companies, particularly when small corporate leaders are often under-resourced to start with. Hiring new hires is a huge deal and a difficult operation, and most businesses invest about 4,000 dollars per new hire on onboarding. Employee attrition can be very costly if you do not recruit properly.

Still, as Howard Bernstein, CEO of 2020 On-site Optometry, says, it is hard to recognize anything on your own. That's why it is crucial to identify and recruit the best people and others who are genuinely passionate about what you are doing.

How to solve it:

For a short-term recruiting approach, it is simple to send out a work description, screen candidates, and make a decision. However, owing to the high expenses of recruiting the incorrect employee, it's essential to dedicate a considerable amount of time to the hiring phase. When you may locate excellent workers, do not settle for decent staff, even though it takes more time. Good workers are what can drive the business to the next stage.

And when you build customer personas for your employers, for your career seekers, create nominee personas. For each new job you recruit for, the personas must be different, but they may share certain basic characteristics across the culture of the business.

Next, take care in drawing applicants to the name of your company and making them involved in knowing more. This would assist you in creating a recruitment pipeline that will have the same certainty in hiring as it does in revenue. Then translate certain opportunities into applicants.

7. Managing the Workflow

When you have the staff in position to make the magic possible, handling operations as you scale is the next obstacle. You want to make sure the staff has the procedures and resources they need to perform successful work fast.

Around the same moment, as a corporate owner, you will not be everywhere at once. So, how can you remain centered on the market but still ensuring that everybody in the organization gets everything they require?

How to solve it:

By providing opportunities for them to get suggestions, the only approach to diagnose the barriers the team encounters and improve productivity is to build ways to identify them. It is possible to do this via:

> Surveys on employee satisfaction

> Frequent discussions of immediate reports one-on-one

> Assuring the success of your direct reports Hold one-on-one conferences for their direct reports

➢ Occasionally, skip-level meetings are conducted.

➢ Asking regarding group risks and the things that cause them the most "pain" in their positions

➢ Seeking the similarities & the bottlenecks in the reviews you get

8. Financial Strategy

More capital (whether staff, resources or time) can ideally improve productivity and output. Providing all of the support you can to the staff is the first move in maintaining smooth operations.

In principle, it seems easy, but have you realized the caveat, everything. Can you? Unfortunately, corporate owners have revenue-based and margin-based spending constraints.

It becomes a struggle then to maximise productivity when operating under such limits, investing in the company without going overboard. By making sound choices focused on strong financial planning, this is solved.

How to solve it:

Each business is going to be different, so by remaining in front of invoices and bookkeeping, you'll need to use business credit carefully, reduce expenses where possible, and control cash flow. You will be assisted by corporate accountants and investment planners who evaluate the financial condition and help you to make sound choices.

9. Scaling

According to NickRellas,Drizly's co-founder and CEO, "There's this balance of creating power efficiency early, versus doing just what you have to do to get it all completed."

This is a complicated one, especially because every scenario is different. This topic can be seen in any aspect of the industry, including product growth, promotion, and content design, recruiting, and so on.

Most business leaders, for instance, would drive production at all costs. However, if you develop your business too fast, you'll find yourself trying to recruit staff quickly. Since preparation requires time, this can overwhelm the more seasoned team members. And if you wouldn't adequately prepare your staff, it might backfire.

How to solve it:

There's no right solution here, sadly. "The scale can tip one way or the other based on where you are in your business' lifecycle,"Rellas says, "although I do agree you need both at various times."

Not obsessing about every aspect, but obsessing about the correct specifics, is what it comes right down to. For example, obsessing over product excellence may be less relevant than obsessing over customer care. It is easier to set away your worries and introduce a product that is not flawless so it can be changed and enhanced at all times. After all, you will understand a lot more easily what's effective and what isn't until the goods are in possession of your consumers.

Chapter: 7 Key Accounting Terms

The following are some standard accounting terminology that any small business owner should be acquainted with:

1. GAAP (Generally Agreed Accounting Standards)

2. Cash basis accounting

3. Accrual basis accounting

4. Accounts payable

5. Accounts receivable

1. Generally Agreed Accounting Standards (GAAP)

GAAP is a series of standard accounting principles that most American corporations are expected to follow. These guidelines detail how to keep track of, calculate, and report on the company's assets to third parties.

2. Cash basis accounting

Cash basis accounting is one of the two most popular accounting techniques, as it involves recording revenue and expenditures where they are earned and charged. Small companies like this approach because it is easy, despite the fact that it can offer a false impression of your cash flow (e.g., if you receive payment for a bill the month after you issued it).

3. Accrual basis accounting

Accrual basis accounting is needed for companies with a turnover of more than $25 million. You must log revenue as you charge it, rather than when it is paid, which implies you might be paying taxes on the money you haven't even received. However, opposed to cash basis accounting, it offers a more reliable long-term perspective of the finances.

4. Accounts payable

Accounts payable contains all unpaid payments for goods and services that you owe to suppliers. To accurately forecast cash flow, these liabilities must be considered against the company's assets and income.

5. Accounts receivable

Any of the money owing to the company by its consumers or clients is paid for in the accounts receivable. These accounts are normally monitored by invoices, which specify payment conditions (e.g., within a specified number of days of receipt) so you know when to expect incoming funds.

Chapter: 8 Common Accounting Reports

As part of their financial accounting procedures, every business must learn how to prepare a few main financial reports. Outside participants, such as owners, suppliers, and creditors, can use these documents to record the business's profits and expenses.

8.1 Profit & Loss Statement

When it is time to file your company returns with the IRS, accountants and tax preparers would most certainly ask for a (P&L) statement, but you will still need to share it with lenders if you apply for financing. Your profit and loss statement (P&L) outlines profitability of your company by listing gross margin, profit, sales, cost of goods sold and other primary indicators over a specific time period (monthly, quarterly and annually).

Profit and Loss Statement Template

[Company Name]

[Street Address], [City, ST ZIP Code]
[Phone: 555-555-55555] [Fax: 123-123-123456]
[abc@example.com]

Profit & Loss Statement
For the Period Ended _____

Income	$	$
Sales	0000000	
Services	00000000	
Other Income	00000	
Total Income		**0000000**
Expenses		
Accounting	0000000	
Advertising	000000	
Assets Small	000000	
Bank Charges	000000	
Cost of Goods Sold	00000	
Total Expenses		**00000000**
Profit/Loss		**00000000**

8.2 Balance Sheet

Balance sheet is a "snapshot" of the company's financial condition at any specific point in time. It includes a summary of the company's capital, assets & liabilities, both of which may be used to assess the valuation of your company.

ACCOUNT FORMAT

BUSINESS CONSULTING COMPANY
BALANCE SHEET
As at Date_____

Assets	$	Liabilities & Stockholders' equity	$
Current assets:		Liabilities:	
Cash	88,560	Notes payable	5,000
Accounts receivable		Accounts payable	
Prepaid building rent		Salaries payable	
Unexpired insurance		Income tax payable	
Supplies		Unearned service revenue	
Total current assets		Total liabilities	
Non-current assets:		Stockholders' quity:	
Equipment	6,000	Capital stock	
Acc. Deal - Equipment	3,000	Retained earnings	36,000
Total assets	101,000	Total Liabilities & Stockholders' equity	101,000

8.2 Cash Flow Statement

A cash flow statement is a financial statement that records and categorises each actual cost and revenue line by line, helping you to maintain track of the company's financial operation. About any line item in the cash flow statement would be identified as an operation, investment, or financing task.

You will also be liable for making a stockholders' equity statement whether the business includes shareholders or partners with equity in the company. This declaration, which is part of your balance sheet, outlines all adjustments in the valuation of the stockholders' equity rights over time, normally from the beginning of the end of the year.

Example Corporation Statement of Cash Flows	All numbers in thousands	
Operating Activities	$	**10,100**
Net Income from Operations	$	10,000
Add: Depreciation Expense	$	100
Investing Activities	$	**(500)**
Purchase of Equipment	$	(1,000)
Sale of used equipment	$	500
Financing Activities	$	**4,500**
Increase in Long Term Debt	$	2,500
Issuance of Stock	$	5,000
Dividends Paid	$	(3,000)
Net Change in Cash Flow	$	**14,100**

Chapter: 9 Taxation

Taxation is the method of enforcing or levying a tax on individuals and corporate companies through a government or the taxing authority. Taxation applies at all levels, from corporate tax (GST) to goods and services tax.

9.1 What is Taxation

The federal and state governments have a major influence on how taxes are set around the country. The state and federal governments have enacted numerous policy changes in recent years to streamline the taxation mechanism and maintain accountability in the region. The Goods and Services Tax (GST) was one such reform that eased the tax system relating to the selling and distribution of goods and services in the world.

9.2 Purposes of Taxation

In the nineteenth century, the common assumption was that taxation could be used solely to support the nation. Governments have used taxes for more than just fiscal reasons in the past, and they do so again today. The differentiation between wealth sharing, income inequality, and economic prosperity is a valuable

HOMEPRENUER BY VISHEN SMITH

way to look at the function of taxes, according to American economist Richard A. Musgrave. (Sometimes global growth or progress and foreign competition are identified as distinct priorities, but they can be absorbed under the other three in general.) The first target, resource distribution, is reinforced if tax policy does not intervene with economic allocations in the absence of a legitimate justification for intervention, such as the need to minimize emissions. The second aim, wage redistribution, is intended to reduce income and wealth inequality disparities. The aim of stabilization is to sustain high jobs and market stability, which is achieved by tax reform, monetary policy, government budget policy & debt management.

9.2 Classes of Taxes

Taxes have been categorized in different forms in the theory of public finance, based on who pays for them, who carries the ultimate responsibility of them, the degree to which the burden may be transferred, and other considerations. Taxes are more generally categorized as either direct or indirect, such as the income tax of the former category and the sales tax of the latter. The requirements for discriminating between direct and indirect taxes are contested by economists, and it is uncertain which group such taxes, such as property tax or corporate income tax, should fall under. A direct tax is generally said to be one that cannot be transferred from the individual to anyone else, although it can be an indirect tax.

1. Direct Taxes

2. Indirect Taxes

Now we learn about direct and Indirect Taxes

1. Direct Taxes

Direct taxes are mainly imposed on individual citizens and are generally dependent on the taxpayer's capacity to compensate as determined by revenue, spending, or net worth. The following is a list of the most popular forms of direct taxes.

Individual income taxes are usually based on the taxpayer's gross personal net income (that might be an individual, couple, or family) that reaches a specified level. The conditions surrounding the capacity to pay, such as marital status, amount and age of the child, and financial pressures arising from sickness, are more widely tailored to take into consideration. Taxes are often charged at phased scales, which ensures that rates rise as income increases. A taxpayer's and family's personal exemptions can produce a range of income that is entitled to a zero-tax rate.

Net worth taxes are imposed on a person's overall net worth, which is proportional to value of assets less his liabilities. As in income tax, the taxpayer's specific situation should be taken into account.

Personal or direct consumption taxes (also referred to as taxes on spending or taxes on expenditure) are essentially imposed on all receipts that are not channeled into savings. In comparison to indirect spending taxes like the sales tax, a direct consumption tax may be customized to a person's financial circumstance by taking into account considerations like age, marital status, family status, and so on. This tax method has been implemented in only two nations, India & Sri Lanka, although it has long been appealing to theorists; both cases were short and ineffective. The "flat tax," which produces economic results close to those of the direct consumption tax by exempting many capital gains, came to be regarded favorably by tax analysts at the end of the 20th century. No nation has introduced a flat-rate tax base, while many have just one rate of income tax.

Inheritance taxation, in which the taxable object is the bequest earned by the individual inheriting, and estate taxes, of which the taxable object is the cumulative estate inherited by the deceased, are the two kinds of taxes imposed upon death. Inheritance taxes also take into account the taxpayer's specific conditions, such as the connection of the taxpayer to the beneficiary and his net wealth when the bequest is received. Estate payments, on the other hand, are normally phased depending on the value of the estate, although in certain nations, they include tax-free transfers to the partner and account for the number of heirs. Tax regimes which include a tax on gifts in excess of a certain threshold rendered by living individuals in order to avoid death duty from being circumvented by an exchange of property prior to death (see gift tax). Transfer taxes usually do not raise any money, if only because substantial tax collections can be prevented conveniently by estate planning.

2. Indirect Taxes

Indirect taxes, including imports and exports, are imposed on the output or sale of products and services or on transactions. Examples include general and limited excise taxes, VAT, taxes on some aspect of production or manufacturing, taxes on lawful purchases, and customs or import duties.

General sales taxes are levies that cover a large amount of consumer spending. The same tax rate may be extended to all taxable items, or separate rates can be applied to different products (such as food or clothing). Single-stage taxation may be levied at the retail level, like some states in the United States do, or at a pre-retail level (such as production or wholesale), as some developed countries do. At each point in the production-distribution process, multistage taxes are introduced. VAT, which grew in prominence during the second half of the 20th century, is usually collected by enabling the taxpayer to exclude from the sales debt the tax credit charged on transactions. At each point of the manufacturing and delivery process, the VAT has effectively substituted the turnover levy-a tax, with no tax relief charged at previous levels. Tax cascading, or the combined impact of the turnover tax, distorts economic decisions.

While they are usually applicable on a wide variety of items, sales taxes often exclude low-income families from the obligation to lower their tax burden. Excises, by contrast, are imposed only on individual products or facilities. Although almost all, including basics such as beef, flour, and salt, to non-essentials such as food, beer, cigarettes, coffee, and tea, to luxuries such as jewels and furs, taxes on a small category of goods, tobacco items, motor fuel, and alcoholic drinks, place excises and customs duties on most nations. Taxes on customer durables were extended on luxury items such as carriages, saddle horses, pianos, and billiard tables in earlier centuries. The car is currently a primary luxury tax item, primarily because registration regulations promote tax administration. Any nations also tax gaming & state-run jackpots have similar consequences as excises, with "take" of the government being, in essence, a gambling tax. Taxes on raw products, intermediate commodities (e.g., natural oil, alcohol), and equipment are imposed by certain nations.

Some excise duties and customs duties are particular, i.e., they are assessed on the grounds of the quantity, weight, duration, volume, or other particular features of the taxable product or service. Such excerpts, such as income taxes, are ad valorem, as determined by the price, depending on the valuation of the item. Legal transaction taxes are charged on the issue of bonds, on the selling (or transfer) of houses and land, and on sales on the stock market. They sometimes take the form of stamp duties for administrative reasons; that is, the legal or commercial paper is stamped to signify payment of the fee. Stamp taxes are regarded as an annoyance tax by many tax analysts; they are more often seen in less-developed countries & slow down the transactions on which they are applicable.

Chapter: 10 Small Business Tax Return

Most people are dreaming of holiday shopping, celebrations, and holidays as the year draws to an end. You're already worried about your 2017 tax return as a small business owner. Filing taxes, mostly as a small company, can be perplexing, daunting, and even cause you want to rip your hair out. It won't be too terrible if you take your time to make sure you have everything you need. Here's a short guide to filing a small business tax return in five easy measures.

1. Determine how to file

2. Collect all the documents

3. Find what forms you need

4. Make sure you are getting the deductions you deserve

5. Recheck your work with the help of a CPA

1. Determine how to file

The first step in planning for tax season as a small business owner is to know what sort of business you have. It would have an effect on the way you prepare your taxes. Are you a single proprietorship, an LLC, an S company, a general partnership, or a C corporation? When setting up your company, this should have already been known, but now it comes into play again. Different company forms have various criteria for tax returns, so it is necessary to consider what sort of business you are in order to understand what would be needed.

2. Collect all the documents

You've already learned that filing taxes needs a bunch of documentation, and this is true. Your documentation can be made up of real documents, or the documents might be digital. In any scenario, be-ensure you have them.

"The IRS says, "The company with which you are affects the kind of documents you need to maintain for federal tax purposes when it comes to what sort of documentation you can obtain. A list of your company activities should be included in your recordkeeping method.

Payroll, sales slips, bank slips, bounced checks, invoices, certificates, and cash register recordings are also exampling documents. Don't forget to keep track of travel costs, any sales, and records of items you buy and are using in your company, such as furniture or machinery. Last but not least, job documents are needed. Do the utmost to maintain track of these items during the year, instead of struggling throughout the tax season, to make it easy on yourself.

3. Find what forms you need

It's an unfair fact that while filing the taxes, there would be some filling-out of paperwork. The kind of small company you have may influence the forms to fill out, as described earlier. Every state may have its own types and specifications, so here's a short rundown on some of the federal income tax measures:

Form 1120 U.S. Business Income Tax Return-Form 1120 is for tax reports submitted by C companies. C businesses are organizations where the shareholders do not incur taxes on individual reports themselves.

Form 1120 S U.S. Income Tax Return – For S Companies, this is the form to use. S Company owners, unlike C Companies, pay income tax on their corporate income tax reports. As a consequence, each shareholder is expected to complete a Schedule K-1 Method.

Form 1065 U.S. Relationship Benefit Tax- You would need to plan one of these types if your small corporation is set up as a collaboration. Since partnerships do not incur income tax, this type is just for information purposes. Every participant may also need to fill out a Schedule K-1 Form if you are part of a relationship, which goes into specifics regarding the profits, dividends, and losses of each particular partner.

*Form 1099 MISC-*This is a form that is processed and issued as part of the tax return to any independent contractors you might have employed, and it is often submitted to the IRS.

You may still need to complete separate documents for the boss, such as Form W-2 Pay and Tax Declaration.

4. Make sure you are getting the deductions you deserve

Deductions are the one aspect of paying the taxes that may be deemed pleasant.

Taxes are not all about the government having its due, Drew Hendricks of Forbes points out. Some tax laws are loopholes that provide for deductions – which are simply opportunities for the government to get you and your company to use money the way it wants."

You have put in a lot of time this year because operating a small company is an expensive activity. Making the best of the tax deductions, but be mindful of what is and is not an appropriate deduction. The Internal Revenue Service (IRS) offers certain basic guidance in this regard. The deductible business cost must be "usual and essential." Supplies, car costs, corporate transport, contract labor, staff compensation, pensions, employee benefits, and employee investment systems are some of the most typical ones on a small business tax return. Be vigilant not to combine personal expenditures with work expenses and be mindful of what company costs are 100% deductible versus a lower percentage.

5. Recheck your work with the help of a CPA

It may be confusing to submit a tax return as a private citizen, and filing as a small businessman is much, much harder. It's important to consider the measures involved in processing a small business tax return, as well as the criteria. It is advised, however, that you enlist the assistance of a licensed CPA to ensure that everything is properly and accurately filled out, particularly if this is your first filing as a small business. A CPA will help you manage all the forms, locate deductions, and advise you what reports and documentation to gather are required.

Chapter: 11 How to Audit Your E-commerce Business

E-commerce is one of the fastest-growing business markets nowadays, so make sure you are prepared with an online business audit to help you develop the site. To boost traffic, make profits, and create a long-term consumer community, e-commerce companies need great material.

> ➤ How is the content performing?

> ➤ Is there anything that you should be doing?

> ➤ What was the last period you performed a comprehensive e-commerce audit?

Itis important to take a step back and audit the material on a daily basis and ensure that it is fulfilling your company objectives. Continue reading to learn how to audit (and improve) your e-commerce material.

11.1 Review your current vision

Before you start your e-commerce business audit, you can do some deep thinking. This involves having a good, hard look at the new plan and finding some places that you might be falling short.

Do you really have any editorial calendar for the company's site and social network, for example? An editorial calendar is an important and basic function that many e-commerce company owners ignore.

> ➢ Take into consideration if the material is advertised. Are you making the best out of your email & social network accounts?

> ➢ Do the landing pages have well-defined objectives?

Prior to implementing some modifications or improving your approach after an e-commerce market analysis, you must first recognize existing issue areas that need to be resolved. You are already mindful of where (and why) you've been deficient in strategic guidance. Tackle certain places with passion, and bid farewell to your strategy-poor past.

11.2 Be critical

Now it's time to get back to work for the content auditing.

Create a list of every website on the e-commerce platform, beginning with the home & landing pages and making your way down to specific blog posts and product pages. Now go to each page and ask yourself the following questions:

- ➢ Is the website producing as it promises? Are your headings in line with your text? Do the call-to-actions execute on their promises?

- ➢ Is anything current? Since search engines don't value old material as much, it's crucial that the connections, items, and material are accurate and up-to-date.

- ➢ Is there a conceptual framework for each piece? Examine the organization on the website. It should sound normal and not haphazardly placed together.

- ➢ Is it easy to find? Internal links should be plentiful in your material, linking it all together. It's not just SEO-friendly, but it's still user-friendly.

- ➢ Is it efficient? Using the site analytics to see if any specific piece of material gets a tonne of traffic or converts. Don't forget these metrics if you want to expand your e-commerce business.

When undertaking an e-commerce company audit, don't be delicate with yourself: a stern eye on each material feature can sound harsh, but it will deliver the best outcomes.

11.3 Use tools to source the accurate data you need

Since an e-commerce company audit involves effort and time, it's a smart idea to use one of the numerous free or low-cost tools available to assist you to organize and quantify data easily. You have access to a wide variety of content resources, each of which is customized to a particular target.

➢ **Google Analytics:**

Google Analytics is helpful for finding issue areas and assessing the success of content by indicators.

➢ **Screaming Frog:**

Screaming Frog is an SEO tool that crawls your site and returns valuable (and actionable) details.

➢ **Site Analyzer:**

Site Analyzer offers a thorough review of the site, as well as an overall rating dependent on criteria such as speed, style, and copy.

> **Yoast:**

Yoast, a wonderful WordPress SEO plugin that offers a fast rundown of keyword targeting for blog posts and websites.

But be careful: with so many auditing tools at your hands, it's possible to get too dependent on them. To get the best out of the e-commerce quality audit, invest just in a handful and use them wisely. Don't get paralyzed by research paralysis. There are many resources that will assist you.

11.4 Get into auditing to maximize the value of your business

Finally, don't feel too cozy. Auditing is a constant phase that necessitates daily focus. Your content isn't a stand-alone entity; it's up against a slew of other products in a saturated sector, and standing away requires effort.

A content audit is a valuable practice that will help you keep on top of things. It's also a particularly rewarding talent to practice.

Flipping websites is a popular route for aspiring entrepreneurs, and a content audit will make it simple for you to acquire an online company, transform it around, and then market it for a profit — it's a talent that can pay off again and again. It all comes down to providing outstanding web content in terms of profitability, performance, and market resale value.

Chapter: 12 The impact of Covid-19 on eCommerce

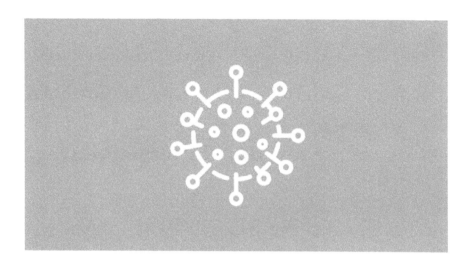

2020 was a difficult year for almost all individuals. Simultaneously, the online business developed more than ever. What would we be able to anticipate from 2021? SearchNode distributed another report on the most recent web-based business patterns and the effect of Covid-19.

A year ago, SearchNode distributed a report on online business patterns in 2020. Obviously, in those days, there was mostly secret about the Covid that would spread all over the globe. In the overview, there were loads of discussions with Magento, an improved spotlight on personalization and natural manageability.

2020 was, of course, all about Covid-19.

What has changed in a year? You should discover, as the Lithuanian tech organization distributed another report on online business patterns. In October 2020, the organization interrogated 100 internet business leaders from Europe and North America.

12.1 Six% eCommerce revenue decreased during the lockdown

There were inquiries concerning Covid-19. It appears to be that most web-based business organizations saw their online income increment during the worldwide lockdown in the spring of 2020. As per the study, 90% of organizations saw their online deals increment at any rate a piece, with 50% of respondents asserting it developed by more than 100%. Yet, 6% say their online business income diminished during Covid lockdown.

After the lockdown was finished, numerous purchasers began shopping at physical retailers once more. 86% of respondents say that their online incomes expanded, and just 4% say it diminished.

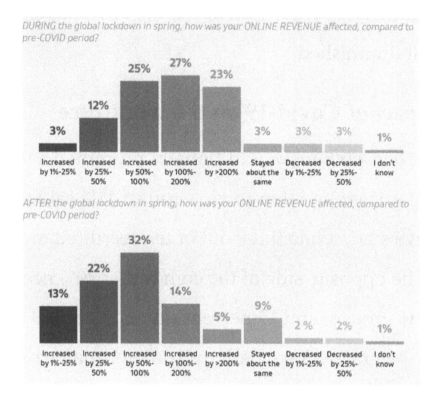

12.2 Online profit margin increased by 38%

Producing on the web deals is a certain something; the entire Covid-19 circumstance has additionally prompted things like disturbed inventory chains, inadequately staffed client assistance, and the sky is the limit from there. This straightforwardly influences the online net revenue. It appears to be that for 38% of internet business leaders, their online net revenue developed during the worldwide lockdown, while for a comparative rate

(40%), the circumstance expressed about the equivalent. Just 15% asserted that it diminished.

12.3 The impact of Covid-19 on the workforce

The pandemic has, obviously, additionally prompted a few changes in organizations' labor force. Around 44% said they needed to move staff, while three out of ten recruited more individuals. The opposite side of the coin is that 26% needed to terminate a few groups, and 15 percent say they needed to lessen their workers' pay rates. Also, perhaps somewhat amazing for a few, yet 5 percent figured out how to expand compensations. What's more, much astonishing: 21% of organizations didn't change their labor force by any means.

21% of organizations didn't change their labor force.

23% of omnichannel players observed disconnected deals increment

Another intriguing finding from the investigation is that for retailers on the offline and online stores, 23% say their disconnected deals expanded, and 16 percent figured out how to keep it comparative. Lamentably, for 43%, their disconnected deals endured a shot.

12.4 Measurements for physical retailers

Numerous physical retailers needed to change their business on the off chance that they needed to maintain a strategic distance from to leave the business. In this way, numerous new practices were presented a year ago. Among the members, 31% presented in-store pickup, while 26% decided to present home conveyance. Sadly, around one of every five needed to close down some actual stores for great.

[For those with physical stores] What new practices you introduced because of COVID-19?

	%	Practice
1	31%	In-store pickup
2	26%	Home delivery
3	21%	Shut down some physical stores for good
4	19%	Whole eCommerce infrastructure
5	16%	Touchless payments
6	9%	Mobile App
7	7%	Pickup lockers
8	3%	Safety measures
9	3%	All the above were already being done
10	3%	Phone sales
11	1%	Video calls for customers
	32%	Doesn't apply

Covid has vigorously affected online retailers on various levels. Among the fundamental difficulties for internet business organizations, upset stockpile chains and satisfying interest for items were the, for the most part, referenced ones. Yet, restricted tasks because of the lockdown, overseeing stock, and the general absence of representatives were likewise vital difficulties for online retailers. What's more, 17% said it was testing since they need to shut down their actual stores.

An upset store network was the primary test for some online retailers in Europe.

12.5 Shifted strategies

A year ago, numerous respondents said they would generally execute, improve or change personalization, site-search and omnichannel. This year, the essential vision has moved because of Covid-19. The majority of the organizations (45%) will presently have more spotlight on the advanced piece of their business by changing the combination, putting resources into new online business programming or emphasizing additionally on internet advertising channels.

One of every five said they would increase activities, which means they need to execute their methodologies and act quicker. One out of ten says they are currently centered around actual store changes, and 8 percent went for inventory network changes, from minor ones to new store networks or coordination's.

12.6 Financial consequences

Notwithstanding all the terrible things occurring because of the flare-up of the Covid, monetarily 2020 wasn't so awful for some web-based business organizations. The greater part of them (63%) say the year (up to October) was effective. Furthermore, 28% case their web-based business was progressing nicely, while their actual stores didn't. What's more, an astounding 2% said the inverse!

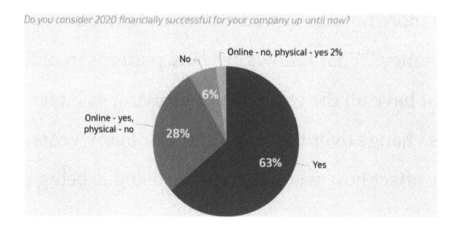

Chapter: 13 What is the Future for Online Business?

With the online world changing apparently from one day to another and an expanding number of sites (today, there are just about 2 billion sites out there), the future for organizations working on the web consistently appears to be unsure. From the finish of unhindered internet to the limitations on YouTube adaptation to progressing computerized innovation and that's just the beginning, the inquiry is the thing that patterns will be generally noticeable for online organizations within a reasonable time-frame.

Right now, with the US economy extending, it appears to be that the not-so-distant future for online organizations is splendid gratitude to more noteworthy customer certainty and ways of managing money. What follows are new patterns in online business that have all the earmarks of growing as buyer propensities change over the following, not many years, which will significantly affect how web-based advertising is being performed.

Expansion of Cryptocurrency

While there has been impressive information about the inconveniences related to bitcoin, digital money itself has all the earmarks of being extending quickly and turning out to be standard. With more organizations and governments going to cryptographic money as an alternative, the exchanges will turn out to be solidly advanced. This implies an adjustment in the manner purchasers purchase across all business sectors, which implies that online organizations should be set up to acknowledge this type of cash soon.

The advent of Machine Learning

This type of innovation is ready to venture into deals and client service, implying that how organizations work with clients will be improved. AI will be through utilizing discourse examination, which better aids client assistance divisions in how to react to every one of their clients. This improves connection which means assembling a more grounded brand and enduring fewer misfortunes because of mistaken assumptions.

Increased Security Spending

In light of ongoing hacks and break-ins that have uncovered the individual data of millions of clients, more organizations are venturing up their security conventions to keep it from happening to them. This has implied a move in accentuation from avoidance towards recognizing interruptions and reacting in like manner. Better security implies more costs, which may tremendously affect the monetary situation of little and medium-sized online organizations.

Personalized Marketing

With such countless online organizations attempting to arrive at similar clients, it can get hard to get over the clamor. This is why individual promoting patterns have been developing and will keep on extending as more organizations spring up around the planet. Effective online organizations will zero in on brilliant showcasing that arrives at the individual, not simply the ideal buyer gathering. On account of new advanced innovation, specific Artificial Intelligence (AI) (web-based business organizations are now confronting this test), the progressions are now occurring and will keep on developing.

Rise of the Sharing Economy

The blend of the sharing economy, which is most broadly addressed by ride-sharing administrations like Uber. It has additionally dug into retail with monsters, for example, Google and Amazon getting into this pattern. For online organizations, the sharing economy addresses an incredible pattern ready to attack medical care and monetary administrations, which may change how numerous online organizations work.

For online entrepreneurs, the extension of the web to world business sectors implies a new wilderness of clients just as contenders. The individuals who succeed will be adaptable to the inescapable change that happens and finds a way to remain one stride ahead to guarantee their future.

Conclusion

Accounting is described as "the processing, review, and systematic documentation of numerical business transactions, the preparation of financial reports, and the examination and evaluation of these reports for management's knowledge and guidance."

Accounting is an accounting mechanism that observes, tracks, and communicates an economic entity's monetary activities.

It is the method of defining, evaluating, and communicating economic data in order for consumers of the data to make educated choices and decisions. Human life is evolving in this ever-changing environment.

Accounting has taken on a different form as a consequence of technical advances, such as holding records mechanically.

With the widespread usage of electronic accounting tasks, a modern arena has arisen. As a consequence, it is obvious that the concept of accounting will evolve in the coming years.